THE
QUAKERLY GRIDIRON BROTHERS

GEORGE SCHOOL FOOTBALL
1923-2015

JOHN GLEESON

Print ISBN: 978-1-66785-708-4
eBook ISBN: 978-1-66785-709-1

To Dylan and Connie who lived this experience with me.

Table of Contents

Preface 1

1. The Quakerly Debate 3

2. Let the Games Begin 7

3. Minders of the Light.. 12

4. Lessons, Values, and Memories 18

5. The Forties--A Time of Change... 26

6. As Sure as God Made Little Green Apples 41

7. The Sixties- a Time of Questioning, Turmoil, and the Arrival of Dusty 60

8. The Seventies- a Time of Rapid Adjustment...................... 81

9. The Nation Strives for Upward Mobility............................... 95

10. Time to show up, suit up, and keep 'em choppin'. 113

11. The Twenty-first Century Starts with a Bang...................... 146

12. A New Decade of Hopes and Promises............................. 199

13. A Final Reflection 221

Appendix.. 223

About the Author.. 243

Preface

The following manuscript aims to capture the spirit of George School football as told through the voices of the athletes and coaches who make up the George School football family. It is a compilation of phone interviews, mailed questionnaires, the school newspaper (The George School News), and the local newspapers (The Bucks County Courier Times, The Trenton Times, The Philadelphia Inquirer). Many of the former players reflected back on how their GS gridiron experiences affected their thinking both personally and professionally.

As a former player and head coach I got to share this spirit with so many wonderful people. I only regret not having the space to include them all. The story is an ongoing one and hopefully will continue for many years.

John Gleeson
Co-captain of the 1964 team
Head Coach 1986-2015

The Quakerly Debate

Theories about the origins of modern football are as varied as they are inventive. One legend traces the roots to eleventh century England where several peasants out hunting came upon the skull of a Danish warrior. Undoubtedly spurred on by a hatred for the detested invaders, the Brits began kicking the skull about, an exercise that soon became a popular pastime among fellow countrymen. Eventually, deterioration or lack of replacement skulls, forced the substitution of an inflated cow's bladder for the disheveled Dane, and the game of 'futballe' was born.

Another romantic version, adhered to by the followers of Notre Dame football, professed that a divine presence clad in green robes and surrounded by a golden aura visited South Bend, Indiana. There the celestial being laid out the first gridiron and, seeing that the creation was good, entrusted its care to godlike creatures bearing such distinct monikers as Knute and The Gipper. Though seemingly improbable, this version undoubtedly gained support in many a Hibernian pub.

Where one could argue for hours about the seeds of modern foot-ball, its arrival on the George School campus is readily traced. In 1922 Stan Sutton, having taught five years at Germantown Academy and two at Virginia Polytechnic Institute, hired on as athletic director. Where documentation fails to pinpoint Stan's motives for coming to a Quaker boarding school, evidence for his love of football abounds. The words of Jack Dutton, class of 24 and captain of George School's first football team, capture both Mr. Sutton's passion for the game and his persuasive manner. "The one person most responsible for playing football at George School would be Stanley B. Sutton. What Stan did his first year I am not sure. He must have looked over the student body and decided that there were enough large bodies and talent to make a football team. Stan must have brought the matter of a football team at George School up at a faculty meeting and was told by George Walton that there was no reason George School couldn't have a football team, if the faculty and the students were in favor of one. That was all Stan needed!!!!!! He organized students for football, held meetings of students and faculty. Anything and anybody who could help him get football, he went to work on. He literally worked day and night on it. The school had set a date for the school and faculty to determine whether George School would play football or not.."

The date was February 28,1923 but, in true Quaker fashion, much discussion and debate needed to take place prior to the unleashing of any gridiron heroics. As reported in the George School News, on December 11, 1922 a straw vote was taken among the students. The December 15, 1922 edition of the George School News reported that of the 235 ballots cast, 137 supported football and soccer for boys with football being the major sport; 65 endorsed football alone; and 33 preferred soccer as the sole fall sport.

More telling perhaps than the statistics were the accompanying comments by several student leaders. Gardiner DeCou, captain of the soccer team offered support. "Yes, I am in favor of football if the boys who are coming back next year want it. Football should be the major sport with soccer for those who want it. I think football is a better game and will develop more spirit."

Alfred Fegely, Secretary of Forum, concurred, stressing the school spirit aspect. "Yes, we want football here at George School. Football would include a larger number of boys and would make G.S. a leading school. It would also help to keep the students here over the weekends to see the games." Robert Borden, cheerleader, took a more patriotic view, "Of course, I am in favor of football. Football is a better all-American game and would give us better relations with other schools."

Garret Kirk, President of the Student Council, showed interest in the school's reputation. "I am in favor of football for a major sport and soccer for a minor sport. Football tends toward better school spirit. I think that a successful football team will be a great factor in making G. S. one of the best known prep schools of the East. Fellows who leave G. S. and represent her in college athletics would be far more prominent if they were well-trained football men rather than members of the soccer team."

Of course, any debate without an opposing voice would prove inconclusive. Wilson H. Wilcox, President of Forum, offered such a dissenting viewpoint. Among his reasons, he claimed, "Football is a game that requires a more physically developed set of fellows than George School now has. Football develops one leader, soccer develops eleven. With football comes a different type of fellows than we now have. The students who are already here will lose at least two or three years of sport while a team that has any winning ability will be developed."

Apparently more concerned with the physical well-being of the players than their record, Christine Cox, President of Archa, stated, "I think soccer should be the autumn sport. Are the boys heavy enough to play football?"

Opinion among the faculty followed an equally varied pattern. Jack Dutton recalled one woman whose thinking paralleled the logic of Wilson Wilcox. "How well I remember one faculty member who was vehemently opposed to football. Her two sons had attended George School and played soccer. After dinner, one evening, a group of us cornered her in the Main hall by the bulletin boards and questioned her as to why she was so opposed to football. Her answer and her reasons were...(I can close my eyes and still see her telling us this---) She said that soccer developed eleven leaders whereas football developed only one. When pressed to tell us who that one leader was, she told us that, 'He was the player who passed the ball back between his legs.' That was the end of Mrs. DeCou and her objections."

Where Mrs. DeCou, house mother of Orton Dormitory, might have been momentarily assuaged, the faculty deliberation continued. In a letter printed in the George School News, Headmaster George Walton offered a balanced account of the major issues. Defining the reasoning behind adopting the sport, Mr. Walton stated that, "Some boys find in football a training of character superior to other games. These boys instinctively hunger to try their strength in actual physical contact with other boys. Football disciplines the boy's temper and exercises his physical skill under the shock of contact, thus making the rough instinct a foundation for developing character. Soccer does not afford the same bodily contact."

Mr. Walton further stressed the cooperation required for success on the gridiron. "Football is also superior for boys who instinctively enjoy working in unison with others in carrying out definite preconceived plans, against obstacles. Football gives constant exercise to this instinct and develops a type of team play or social cooperation which fits exactly in spirit with the efficient organization of modern industry."

Mr. Walton's opposing arguments, in some ways, reflected the thinking of Theodore Roosevelt who in 1906 threatened to ban the playing of football in America because it had become dangerously violent. According to the Headmaster, two arguments ran against the adoption of football, especially the variety that stressed winning at all costs. "Football injuries are more serious than soccer, more conspicuous on the field, and are played up by the press as essential details of the game. On account of great popular interest in football, and consequent publicity, undue importance is attached to developing a championship eleven. The tendency is to consider teams as failures or of little importance, except champions."

The ensuing years would show that in many ways George Walton's wisdom serves as the philosophical basis for football at George School. The emphasis is education and development of character, not the domination of every opponent. A boy's growing and gaining self-confidence becomes the biggest victory. The "Committee on Management" saw this potential and on February 28, 1923 granted their approval.

Let the Games Begin

Quaker consensus reached, Stan Sutton next addressed the minutiae, the necessary details of recruiting players from within the student body, finding an appropriate field, providing proper equipment, and determining a team mascot. Though seemingly less awesome than facing the "Committee on Management", the task was not without difficulty.

At the time, the school's athletic facilities consisted of six tennis courts, a gymnasium and two earthen-floored "playrooms" in the basement of Main. A quarter-mile track surrounding what was named Sharon Field provided the only outdoor arena. Designated as the playing area for soccer, intramural football and baseball, Sharon Field suffered not only from excessive usage but poor drainage. Water ran from the track onto the playing field, thus creating a surface more suitable for hog wrestling and bog trotting than football.

To alleviate the situation, Stan the Man, as he would affectionately be called by his players, set his sights on the neighboring fields. With the board's approval, a portion of the farmland across Route 413 (the Pike) was rented and converted into a gridiron. According to Captain Jack Dutton, "I remember that we played in a cow pasture field that was directly across the Newtown-Langhorne road from the entrance to George School. The spectators stood along the sideline." Though not offering the lavish concession stands and plush stadium seats featured in many a modern arena, Sidcott Field proved a suitable location for the fledgling footballers to test their mettle.

Not wanting to tax the athletic budget, Stan stuck to the basics when equipping his charges. As recorded in his team and financial report, he purchased 12 head guards, 12 shoulder pads, 20 pairs of socks, 20 jerseys, 20 numbers, 7 pairs of knee guards, field stakes, 7 balls, bandage material and rub down oil. Adding in official's fees, transportation, and other miscellaneous expenses such as shoe laces, the total cost ran somewhere in the neighborhood of four hundred dollars.

Properly attired, the team now needed a mascot. Some beast as awe inspiring as the Yale Bulldog or the Princeton Tiger would undoubtedly help arouse the intensity and tenacity of the players. As indicated in the school newspaper, the possibilities were many. One offering dubbed the George School team the "Suttonmen" in honor of their determined founder. Another labeled them the "Men in Brown", a reference to the basic brown colored jerseys they sported. Yet another called them the "Buffians", a term highlighting the two buff stripes that adorned the sleeves of their jerseys. Still another voice rallied around the title "The Fighting Quakers", perhaps an allusion to Melville's reference in Moby Dick.

The players, meanwhile, opted to leave the intricate mascot search for the writers and get to work prepping for the opening game. First, they needed to learn the basics and then apply them to Mr. Sutton's balanced single wing attack. In this formation, the quarterback and left halfback did most of the running and all the passing except the reverse pass. The strategy preached sticking to the fundamentals. Jack Dutton manned the all- important quarterback position. He recalls that, "there were four of us in the backfield. The center passed the ball directly to a player. There was none of this tricky stuff."

Inherent in the idea of gridiron 'simplicity' is the emphasis on "working in unison" alluded to by George Walton. If the blockers do not do their job even the trickiest runner will fail. Stan Sutton embedded this concept in his players' thinking from the first day of practice. It became a driving force in Jack Dutton's love of the game, "The best part is that you play with your other fellows. You must cooperate. If this guy doesn't take the other fellow out and give you a hole to go through you don't go anywhere. So much depends upon your working together."

By Friday, October 12, 1923, the Suttonmen were ready to see just how well they had meshed their individual talents. Opening at home against Germantown Academy, the Men in Brown would perform in front of a spirited crowd which included four men "instrumental" in bringing football to George School. Dr. Curtis Eves, W. Russel Green('10), Henry B. Coles, and Irvin R. Cleaver ('98) all wanted to see their vision turn into reality.

From the start, the Buffians dispelled any doubt that they could play a quality brand of football. Germantown received the kickoff but fumbled the ball at their own 25 yardline. Walton Coles alertly pounced on the loose pigskin. It took GS just two runs off tackle to net the first touchdown in school history with Captain Dutton scampering the final seven yards to paydirt.

The elusive and talented Dutton would score two more touchdowns and kick four more Points After Touchdown, known then as Goals From Touchdown, as George School won its inaugural contest by a convincing 40-6 score. Rich Fletcher and Bob Rogers also tallied for the home team. The Suttonmen showed complete domination, allowing Germantown inside its thirty-yard line only once in the first half. By halftime they had built up a 20-0 lead.

Captain Dutton's success came as little surprise to the GS faithful. A track star with previous football experience, Jack knew how to run. As he good-naturedly recalls, " Sports was my life. I was lucky I was created fast because I wasn't big. My mother always said, 'Thee never walked anywhere, Jack. Thee always ran.' I like to run around people. That was my forte."

The Buff and Brown warriors proved equally successful in their next outing, beating Peddie's 'B" team 19-0 and setting up their first away game with perennial power Bordentown Military Institute. Coach Sutton anxiously antici-pated this game, feeling it a true test of his players' readiness. He wrote in the October 26 issue of the George School News that, "the outcome of tomorrow's game is the test by which we decide whether the season is successful or not. If the team comes through with the goods, we have a fighting chance to win."

The outcome of the game, a 0-9 loss, did not settle well with Stan Sutton. He decided his charges needed a more rigorous approach to practice. According to the school newspaper (November 2) "Monday a stiff workout was held, with line bucking and practice on taking out men featuring the line's work. The ends and backfield were drilled on catching punts and blocking them besides doing a good deal of tackling. The hard scrimmages left Coach Sutton saying, 'the eleven men who show the most fight and work the hardest this week will start the Trenton game'."

The fighting eleven obviously got the message as the newly aroused Suttonmen trounced the Trenton High School Reserves 39-0. The lopsided victory proved a suitable warm-up for the GS gridders season finale, a home contest with what would become its archrival, Bryn Athyn Academy. Unfortunately, prior to the game an illness sidelined Coach Sutton, in essence denying him a first hand view of his team's growth and proficiency. The Suttonmen, who presented their fallen leader with a bouquet of flowers in his hospital room prior to the game, totally dominated the Bryn Athyn invaders.

As he had all season, Captain Dutton provided the scoring punch tallying four touchdowns and leading GS to a 51-3 victory. The school newspaper again sang praise for the mercurial running back. "Captain Dutton was the star of the game, his generalship and long spectacular running, bringing the crowd to their toes many times. This was Jackie's last game of football at George School and he will long be remembered as one of the best players ever produced here."

Thinking back at the one-sided affair, Jack could only ponder, "They must not have had a line."

Though not recalling the specifics of his scoring heroics, Jack vividly remembers one play. "I ran the ball and tried to get out of bounds. I ran into our infirmary nurse and broke one of her legs. That evening I went over to the infirmary to tell her how badly I felt. She said to me, 'Jack, don't feel badly. That was a very good run thee made'."

The school paper offered a more detailed account of the misfortune. "Nurse Miss C Meyers received a double fracture of the left leg and had her right arm broken when she was struck by one of the players in the football game with Bryn Athyn. Miss Meyers was standing on the North sideline during the first half when the accident happened. A George School man running up that side of the field on a kickoff collided with a Bryn Athyn player and was thrown against Miss Meyers who was unable to step back because of the crowd behind her."

Obviously, where the spectator section of Sidcot Field needed attention, the determination and ability of the Suttonmen did not. They had proven Wilson Wilcox's fear that they could not develop a "winning ability" ill-founded. In playing what the school paper called a "collegiate brand of football", the George School gridders posted an impressive 4-1 record. Boasting only three players with previous experience, the Men in Brown scored 149 points while surrendering only 19. They gained 867 yards to the opposition's 293. They made 43 first downs while allowing only 9.

The December 7, 1923 edition of the George School News added one final laudatory comment about Jack Dutton's contribution to the team. "Captain Dutton will long be remembered as the shining light of a brilliant team. He was the high scorer, tallying 12 touchdowns and 11 points with his trusty toe for 83 points."

Jack and his teammates had definitely laid the foundation for what would prove a rich football tradition at George School.

Minders of the Light

Entering the 1924 campaign, Coach Sutton recognized that new challenges faced his team. In a year when Knute Rockne was bidding farewell to his legendary Four Horsemen, Stan tried to figure out gridiron life without such talents as Dutton and Fletcher. GS boasted only three returning lettermen on its roster, Don Amelia, Walt Coles and Bob Rogers. The learning process would have to begin anew. Also, opponents remembering the success of the inaugural season would no longer consider the Georgians neophytes and potential pushovers.

As the start of the season indicated, Stan Sutton had obviously revamped his troops. The Men in Brown opened with a hard-fought 6-0 win over Central High School. Improving with every game, they handled the Peddie reserves 38-0. Gaining momentum, they trounced the Germantown Boys Club by a 53-0 score. The gridders were well on their way to a historic season.

Then disaster struck. The culprit came not in the form of an opposing team but in a force even Stan Sutton could not defend against. A scarlet fever epidemic caused several games to be postponed and eventually forced the athletic director to concede and cancel the remainder of the schedule.

Undoubtedly disheartened that his youthful program was dealt such a setback, Coach Sutton refused to allow the football spirit to atrophy. He divided his healthy players into two squads and carried out a Princeton-Yale intramural series. This move helped sharpen the players skills and maintain their focus.

As the 1925 season showed, the wisdom of Sutton proved flawless. The gridders, led by three year letterman Don Amelia, took on the challenge of a rugged nine game schedule. Playing their home games on Sharon Field, GS opened by losing a close 6-7 decision to a tough Northeast High School team. They then traveled to Central High School where they lost another squeaker by a 6-9 margin. Not allowing the close losses to dampen their spirits, the Suttonmen went on a tear winning or tying all but one of their next seven games against such worthy foes as Temple Prep, Swarthmore Prep, BMI, and, of course, Bryn Athyn Academy.

An article written by John Wilson appeared in the December 9, 1925 edition of the school paper and summed up the 5-3-1 season. "Nine hard games played is a record. Three lost. All of the big games, won or tied. A fine season and an excellent record for a team which will go down in football history at George School. Too much credit cannot be given to Captain Amelia for his fight, spirit, and his splendid leadership."

Coach Sutton's skill at molding a respectable and successful football team had become most manifest. More importantly, however, Stan shaped the character and values of all the young men who played for him. A story by one of the players on the '25 team was featured in Jack Talbot's tribute to Mr. Sutton in the 1962 Georgian. It exemplifies the deeper lessons Stan Sutton taught.

George School, after losing two close contests, won its third game of the season, a "mean game in which two or three of their boys were hurt. We all boarded our bus and you never saw a happier group of boys as we celebrated our victory. We discussed what a dirty bunch the other boys were and how we had taught them a lesson and put several of them on the sideline. The greatest lesson to be taught that day was still to come. Just before our bus pulled out, Mr. Sutton boarded it, stood at the front and told us that this was the first time in his life he was ashamed that he was a George School coach. Never before had he ever been so disappointed in any group of boys because of the way they played the game. That was all he said. Not one other word was spoken the rest of the way back to GS. I have attended many a meeting at George School and elsewhere, but never was the silence more complete, the message more meaningful."

Where Stan could understand youthful enthusiasm, he would not tolerate foul play. A victory gained at the expense of sportsmanship was not a victory. Reveling over fallen foes rather than celebrating your own accomplishments was unacceptable. Obviously, the bus ride home brought the more lasting lesson.

Coach Sutton continued to challenge his players, adding Trenton High School, Haverford School, and the Swarthmore College freshmen to the 1926 schedule. Not surprisingly, the Buffians, posting a modest 2-6-1 record, were buffeted about by such a notable assemblage of opponents. The season was made, however, when the Suttonmen beat rival Bryn Athyn 7-0. In what has developed into the oldest rivalry in Eastern Pennsylvania, often the success of a GS team is measured by how well they played against Bryn Athyn. This year, a cross field pass from Howard Sipler to A. B. Lockhart brought the bragging rights to George School.

Though not equal in number to the 110,000 fans who attended the Army-Navy game in Soldiers Field, George School 'crowds' continued to be spirited if somewhat befuddled. The George School News described the home opener saying, "The game was played before the mothers of the school, as this was the date set for the meeting of the Mothers-in-Council. They seemed to enjoy the game although most of them were not able to distinguish their sons from the other players."

In 1927, the Suttonmen returned to their winning ways, finishing with a 5-2-1 record. Again, a thrilling 6-0 victory over Bryn Athyn highlighted the campaign. Captain Morris Hires led the charge against the Swedenborgians when he raced sixty yards only to be pushed out of bounds on the Bryn Athyn one yard line. Howard Sipler plunged into the endzone for the deciding tally. Hires' play earned him plaudits in the GS News, "This season during which 'Pop' captained the Buff and Brown eleven marked his second year of varsity play. Hires became the regular quarterback in 1925 when his ability to circle the ends, pass or kick made him a dependable back. During all three seasons he has also been a star on defense, a hard tackler for a man weighing only 130 pounds."

As the 1928 season proved, speedy backs who could outrun defenders were not the only headline grabbers. In what has come to characterize George School teams, the linemen, though not massive in size, played with self-less determination. Exemplifying the effort of these trench warriors, Jack Wilson gained the attention of the newspaper's sports staff. Describing the opening 12-6 win over Central High School in the October 10, 1928 edition of the school paper, one crack reporter wrote, "Young Jack Wilson, displacing all of one hundred and thirty five pounds, avoirdupois in the rain, was worth his weight in tackles. The kid played the game of his life."

Where "avoirdupois" sounds more like a delicate French pastry, Jack's style of play was anything but soft. One of many two way performers, Jack played the equivalent of today's defensive linebacker and offensive center. Looking back over his gridiron career, he assumes a rather modest view, "I was a member of the class of 1930 and for some reason never clear to me, was named captain in my senior year. My tackling technique was so poor, primarily grab-and-drag-down, that I ruined my knees while dragging. I've been a hacker all my life and I guess there was no better hacker. My opinion of my play wasn't that great. I was a small fish in a very small pond. It was fun at the time."

Part of the fun in the 1928 season was playing in the first and only Alumni game. Recent legends, such as Jack Dutton, returned for one more glorious romp across Sharon Field. There they met a determined varsity eleven who walked off with a close 7-0 victory. The school reporter, (probably the French scholar) wrote that, "the George School alumni wilted under the slithering fire of the Alma Mater shrapnel."

Undoubtedly, Jack Wilson provided a good deal of the "slithering fire". His tenacious play won him the vote for captain his senior year, 1929. The season started inauspiciously enough with the Georgians being shutout in the first three games. In game four Jack's efforts assumed heroic proportions when he broke through the line and blocked an extra point kick to preserve a 7-6 win over Williamson Trade School. The Georgians went on to win four of their next five games including big victories over LaSalle and Temple High School.

The one loss however, did partially sour the sweet taste of the four wins. The Suttonmen lost for the first time to archrival Bryn Athyn, 6-7, in a game the paper said was "characterized by spasms of fight and aggressiveness on the part of both teams."

Though only the sixth meeting in this growing rivalry, The Game already bore great meaning. As Jack recalls, "I remember that game. They were our principal opponents in those days. They were the ones we pointed for. We were pretty even with them. They were good, one of the best teams we played."

Loss to Bryn Athyn aside, the Georgians, rallying around their spirited captain Wilson, finished with a respectable 5-4 record. The school newspaper did not miss the opportunity to praise Jack one last time. "Jack, the scrappy captain of the Georgians, played superb football throughout the year. As a letterman last year, he became the nucleus of this year's team and he played every minute. His defensive play at center was one of the season's most outstanding developments, and as a snapperback was unexcelled." (GS News December 6, 1929)

By 1930 Stan's vision of a football program had become a very definitive part of George School athletics. As he noted in a school newspaper article, boys competed in the sport on several levels. "Cub team, Dub team, Scrub team and what nots have been grinding out every possible opportunity for play, competition and development for several years now." (GS News December 5, 1930)

Joe Thomas, one of the players who worked his way through the ranks, started as a neophyte and grew into one of the stalwarts of the Georgian offensive and defensive lines. Joe values the total experience. "I had two brothers who played soccer at George School and I guess I decided to play football. Al Carter was the coach of the 130 pound team and he was most encouraging and taught us the fundamentals. Football was very demanding and I learned from the very beginning to give my very best and to support my teammates. Stan Sutton and Al Carter both shaped my outlook and physical well-being which I still enjoy."

The first task of the coaches was to teach the aspiring gridder the game's fundamentals. As Joe good-naturedly recalls, "My most lasting memory of George School football was while I was on the 130-pound team I picked up a live ball and started to run--the wrong direction."

Joe learned his lessons well. By his senior year he had made Stan Sutton's all-George School football team. "I was selected for the guard position. This recognition was particularly meaningful as I played the entire nine games except for the last quarter of the last game. In those days there were no offensive and defensive teams. The 1930 team won all but one game of the nine game season."

The team's final record of 6-1-2 was the most wins recorded by a GS team. Included in the victories were impressive conquests of Lawrenceville, Bordentown, and the Haverford College freshman. Most satisfying for Joe and his teammates, however, was the 14-6 win over Bryn Athyn. "That was considered the big game of the season, and it was always an intense and exciting highlight."

Understandably, Coach Sutton felt a great deal of pride in his team's successful campaign. His praise reflects his emphasis on team play. "The spirit of the men has been the most outstanding example of team; never a star, not a weak spot, everyone working for the fellow alongside him. How could such men be anything but successful?" (GS News December 5, 1930)

Lessons, Values, and Memories

The first seven seasons proved that football, George School style, meant more than final scores and impressive records. Obviously, Stan Sutton's vision went beyond occupying the students and providing an outlet for their youthful energy. He had created a true learning environment, an immediate testing ground where the individual could begin defining his true self and, in so doing, find his place among the others who shared moments of victory and defeat.

During the next eleven years under Coach Sutton's leadership, the GS gridders would meet with varied success in terms of won-loss records. One constant, however, remained. Almost every player who wore the Buff and Brown uniform finished their scholastic gridiron career with a greater self-awareness and an appreciation for the real lessons Mr. Sutton taught, lessons going beyond requisite skills and team strategy. He was not just a coach. He was an educator, one devoted to the growth and development of the total individual.

Mr. Sutton's efforts did not go unnoticed by his devoted charges. Tom Paxton Sherwood, class of 1933, welcomed the chance to laud his former coach. "I think he was one of the most impressive men I ever met. All along I learned so many lessons from Stan Sutton. I'm so happy to tell about him."

The laudatory comments carry an even greater impact considering Tom's post-George School commitments. "I flew with Colonel, later four star general, Curtis Lemajo. We were the first bombers to fly out of England over Germany. I was shot down and kept as a prisoner of war for thirteen months."

To be considered among such elites indicates the respect Coach Sutton gained from his players. For Tom, the reverence started before he even got to George School. His father, a 1904 GS graduate, had participated on the Sutton led track team that won the prep school division at the Penn Relays. Little wonder Tom's first steps on campus headed him in the direction of Coach Sutton's apartment. "When I got to GS in the fall of 32 I wondered where I could find Mr. Sutton and I went to his house. I said I was interested in playing football and asked when I could get a suit."

Breaking into the Buff and Brown lineup as a senior presented a challenge for the eager newcomer. Such experienced veterans as Ben Lackey and Charles McKillips manned the backfield positions, the spots the 125 pound 'rookie' hoped to play. Tom's opportunity came when every gridder's arch enemy, injury, struck Lackey. "I was a right halfback and a substitute under Ben Lackey. He was much larger and heavier than I was. He dislocated his shoulder in the first half and Mr. Sutton called on me and I played the whole season after that."

The learning process had begun for Tom. On one level, he quickly discovered his physical potential. "We went up against Princeton Prep and the boys said they're all ringers over there. They're on scholarship. I remember they had a left tackle, Matt Stoerr, who later became an All American at Princeton. When I was going around right end he would grab my helmet and our right ends and just push us out of the way, walk through and grab the quarterback. They only beat us by three or four touchdowns. Later I figured if you are going to get hit you might as well get hit by the best."

The final score of the Princeton Prep game was a 'respectable' 33-0 in favor of the future Tigers. Tom and his teammates did not lament the loss. Unlike many other prep schools, George School did not recruit college prospects and 'redshirt' them, in essence allowing them to play a post-graduate year to prep them for a specific college team. Coach Sutton took any 'wannabe' who came his way and then helped him grow. As Tom Sherwood exemplifies, GS players gained a good sense of perspective. They were not brought in to get George School headlines in the newspaper. Though many players did go on to participate in college, that was not their sole focus. Sherwood's teammate Tom Clements, who went on to work for the DuPont company helping with nuclear research during World War II, feels that playing at GS, "prepared me physically for playing four years of college football at Swarthmore."

Part of the sound perspective each player developed emanated from the Coach's philosophy. Tom Sherwood recalls going up against Church Farm School. "They had a good old fashioned field and they played a whale of a ball game. The important part was that we had a very fast and good quarterback, Charles McKillips. He went to Mr. Sutton, unbeknownst to me, and said, 'We have a sophomore boy who is very fast. Why don't you play him instead of Sherwood.' Chuck was right. This boy was very fast. Sutton told Chuck that he couldn't put the boy in because his ligaments weren't set and he'd have a fellow hit him and maybe ruin his whole future. I later saw the same boy help win the Pennsylvania State quarter mile relay. Stanley Sutton saved that boy's career. Sutton saw the future. That man was a wonderful instructor. He was willing to lose a football game to save a boy's future. I just admired him with a total belief."

Tom also valued the beauty of the George School's campus and especially Sharon Field. Though having drainage problems it beat rolling around on stones and ashes. "It was such a great thing to be playing on mowed grass. I previously went to school in Western Pennsylvania. The homes were heated by coal and the ashes were all over the field. When we played we got ashes all over us. At George School people would sit on the bank. No band; no fuss; just get out there and play your game. That's the way I loved it."

Despite its rugged schedule, the '32 team finished with a 3-4 record. The school yearbook summarized the season saying the Buffians were "handicapped by the late opening of school which necessitated canceling the opening game with Chestnut Hill. The fighting team beat Haverford College's Junior varsity 20-0 in the first game."

The lessons learned under fire during the '32 campaign definitely carried over to the next season. The Suttonmen melded into a cohesive unit possessing both talent and experience. The season opener featured the running of Joe Hancock, Harry Walters and Charles Huey, who combined to score five times giving the home team a 31-0 win. As printed in the GS News, "Hancock bucked the line for three TDs". The Georgians followed suit in their next outings beating Rutgers Prep 20-0 and then trouncing Church Farm 45-0 before encountering the Princeton Tigers Prep team. Coach Sutton felt confident his boys would make a better show against their potent foe. "They have a more impressive record this year than we have through their beating of Lawrenceville and Blair. We will play creditable football and whether we win or lose, our followers will be proud of the team." Stan proved prophetic as GS succumbed but by a narrow 0-13 score.

Winning two of their final three games, the Men in Brown posted an impressive 5-2 record. They outscored their opponents by a 159-43 margin. A closing 6-24 loss to Bryn Athyn proved the only blemish in an otherwise great season.

Stan Sutton understandably took great pride in his team's effort, a feeling he expressed in the school yearbook. "Though we lost our last game in true upset style, I feel that, as individual players, and as a collected team, we have produced the qualities and the playing ability that has characterized outstanding teams everywhere."

Ben Lackey, captain of the team, echoed his mentor's sentiments, placing special emphasis on the team camaraderie displayed by the '33 squad. "Much of the success of the team this year was due to the friendliness of the players."

Stan Sutton worded the concept in a slightly different fashion when analyzing the team's success in the school paper, " Our backfield proved fast and capable with Eric Clark directing play in splendid style from quarterback. Cox, Huey, Hancock, and Cadwallader worked with precision and power."

Coach Sutton's unyielding demand for team unity and selfless play greatly impressed Roger Farquhar, the Georgian's left end, who even today recalls that, "Stan Sutton was a fine man, a fine coach. I was a devoted player.

He didn't teach winning is everything, a la Vince Lombardi, just play the best you can. Play for the team."

The emphasis paid off in more than convincing wins. The fraternal feeling accompanying any meaningful and challenging shared experience certainly marked the George School football team. Many lasting friendships began on the gridiron. Ray Acuff, lineman on the '33 squad, greatly valued these connections, "I enjoyed the physical workout. More importantly, one of my friends Jacob Esser also played. I met Jake at George School. I was the left tackle and he was the left end. Jake came to a birthday party my mother threw for me at the house. We played golf together on Sunday afternoons with George Walton who was the principal of the school at that time. George Walton had a funny golf swing, but he liked to play."

Though obviously not an Arnold Palmer, Mr. Walton certainly appeared a visionary in recognizing the "social co-operation" inherent in the sport of football. What even the venerable headmaster could not foresee was the seeds of what would grow into a football family tradition. In later years, off-spring of the very players battling on Sharon Field in the 1930s would display their own prowess before supportive George School crowds. Ray Acuff's two sons Marc and Frank would perform admirably for the old Buff and Brown. Joe Hancock would thrill to the GS gridiron exploits of his three sons Joe Jr., Dan, and Steve. The list goes on with such names as Baldwin, Cadwallader, Seabrook, Ambler, Hardy, among many others joining the ranks of father-son GS gridders. Obviously, that special brand of football started by Stan Sutton held a good deal of sustaining power.

One ironic twist to the extended family concept manifested itself in the 1934 season. Continuing to do battle with such teams as the Swarthmore and Haverford junior varsity, often the Buffians found themselves pitted against former teammates. The yearbook reported that in their Alumni Day encounter with the Haverford JV, "A friendly jealousy existed between Himes of Haverford and his friends on the opposing team." Fortunately, GS got the better of the spat, taking a 21-7 win. It was one of three wins for the Suttonmen that year.

Victories were equally tough to come by in 1935 with the team posting a 3-5 record. Tellingly, three of the losses were by less than a touchdown.

Given any luck, the Georgians might well have wound up with a 6-2 mark. The yearbook allowed for the fortunes of war experienced by the Suttonmen. "Discounting several losses which were dubious, the gridders had a very fine season, showed teamwork and fight, and upset the dope a couple of times. Despite the fact that they won only three games over a schedule of eight, the varsity green machine which represented the system of Stanley B. Sutton on the gridiron for George School last fall showed power."

It's not clearly stated who the "dope" was but it probably included all those doubters who believed a Friends School could not field a competitive football team. Certainly not lacking in spirit or talent, the Georgians' most notable weakness was size. Finding themselves outmanned by their bigger opponents, the Buff and Brown warriors learned to play a shrewder brand of football. The " light and inexperienced" 1936 team led by Captain Curtis Eves garnered only two victories. The nature of their 19-13 win over the Haverford JV impressed the yearbook staff, "Using trick plays and deception to great advantage the Buff and Browners showed the most promise of the year against the Haverford College Freshmen."

This new 'heady' brand of football continued into 1937 with GS once again pitted against stronger foes. 'Learning' in their first five losses, the Suttonmen never quit and finished the 'successful' campaign by beating Bryn Athyn 19-6. The yearbook praised their steady growth. "For the first five successive games, the Suttonmen met defeat in the hands of heavier opponents. Through these crushing defeats by stronger and more experienced teams, the Buff and Browners learned to play hard and intelligent football."

The magic of the final win over Bryn Athyn unfortunately did not carry over to the 38 season. Despite the presence of several talented players, including Stan's son Don, the Georgians could garnish only one touchdown giving them their sole victory, a 7-0 conquest of the Haverford JV. The losses, however, did little to dampen the sense of satisfaction felt by the players. Lewis Walton, who played both guard and tackle, still holds his fellow players in deepest regard. The biggest reward he gained from his GS football career was, "The camaraderie with my teammates. We each knew that all our teammates were doing their best even though we won only one out of seven games played in the fall of '38."

The wisdom of George Walton once again echoed across Sharon Field. Where many in the media equated success with victories, George School football emphasized growth and character building. You did not need to score the winning touchdown to feel a sense of satisfaction. Honest effort leading to self-improvement was rewarding in itself. Lewis Walton rates his team's loss to Bryn Athyn as the biggest game he played in. Sixty two years later he still cherishes the fact that, "In that game I had the best open field tackle I ever made."

Unlike many high pressure programs accepting nothing less than a championship performance, George School spectators backed the efforts of their young battlers. Lewis felt, "We got good support both on and off the field but happily it was free of the 'hero' stuff."

The '39 team broke the scoring jinx of the previous year, tallying at least one touchdown in every game. Most notable in their 3-5 record were lop-sided wins over Chestnut Hill Academy (32-0) and Rutgers Prep (26-0). In clobbering Chestnut Hill, the Buffians employed a 'stage play', a "check play" and a "tricky guard pass from Johnny Campbell to Bill Ashton" (GS news). The yearbook showered specific praise on the leaders of the Georgians. "The inspiring leadership and brilliant play of Captain Cadwallader and Ex-Captain Waddington was particularly inspiring."

While deserving every laudatory comment, Captain Gus Cadwallader followed an increasing list of GS players who honored the intangibles growing from their gridiron career, qualities not measured by scores alone. A three year starter and letter winner, Gus feels the greatest rewards were the, "Sportsmanship, hard work and physical conditioning. It was a sport that was good for physical development and gave the school a team spirit that pulled the students together."

No amount of spirit, however, could fight off the opponents that shortened the 1940 season. After only four contests, the Suttonmen found themselves victimized by what the yearbook called "an epidemic in the neighborhood". 48 George School students ended up in the infirmary with a digestive ailment similar to one experienced throughout Newtown, Pa. The school was quarantined.

The football team struggled in their initial outings, losing to Episcopal, Penn Charter, and Lawrenceville. In order to stem the losing tide, Mr. Sutton called for bi-weekly briefing sessions. The football team's board of strategy met in Coach Sutton's office at 9:15. Included in the meetings were Captain Stan Green, star runner Frank Dudley and Bill Marble. The aim was, "to acquaint the boys with difficult situations likely to occur on the gridiron. Two fellows would play a game on the blackboard. They had to use judgement to determine the plays. Mr. Sutton supervised and pointed out mistakes." (GS News, Nov. 8,1940)

The plan worked as the gridders rallied to record a 19-0 win over Chestnut Hill, a game that would prove to be the season finale. At the end of the shortened season, two players gained the particular attention of the GS fans. Still playing Coach Sutton's version of the single wing offense, "Stan Green, a star blocker and line bucker, led this year's outfit from the quarterback spot. Frank Dudley was the climax runner of the squad." (1941 yearbook)

Employing the same reasoning he used when the 1924 season ended due to scarlet fever, Coach Sutton divided his troops into two teams and played an intramural game. Brad Snipes, wingback on the team, remembers the impact that decision had on him. "In my senior year sports were quarantined so we divided the squad in half. In defending the team I was on I rose up to catch a pass and collided with Stanley Green. I fell to the ground and in about five minutes came to."

Brad's collision proved a fitting capper to the ill-fated season.

The Forties--A Time of Change

Change became the key word of the new decade. On December 2, 1941 the Japanese attacked Pearl Harbor, ending any attempt on the part of the United States to maintain its isolationist policy. With our entry into World War II, Americans needed to adjust and refocus. No longer could previously held luxuries be taken for granted. Gas rationing, food stamps, and patriotic service took the place of our lavish and leisurely lifestyles.

The war's effect was felt in every phase of American life. The need for sacrifice and adjustment took precedence over playing games. Many professional athletes opted for patriotic duty. In baseball, such immortals as Ted Williams and Bob Feller, interrupted the peak of their careers to willingly serve the greater cause. In pro football, due to a shortage of players, the Philadelphia Eagles and Pittsburgh Steelers merged for the '43 season.

College gridiron wars were equally affected. In 1942, the Army-Navy game, usually drawing 100,00 spectators, drew only 12,000 as the government restricted wartime ticket sales to residents within 10 miles of the stadium. The enlistment of many college age kids in the armed forces led to the birth of several outstanding service teams such as the Army All-Stars, The Great Lakes Naval Training and the Iowa Seahawks. Back home the manpower shortage brought about a change in the eligibility rules with freshmen now allowed to participate on the varsity level. Wartime travel restrictions forced many schools to alter their schedules and attendance dropped appreciably.

The first change witnessed in the George School football program seemed relatively small. The Georgians entered the '41 campaign clad in brand new uniforms purchased by the Boys Athletic Association. The garb included brown jerseys with eight buff stripes on the sleeves. Each stripe represented one of the eight varsity sports played at the school. The warriors also donned Buff headwear and short brown socks with a buff stripe.

The snappy new attire unfortunately did not guarantee victories as the Suttonmen posted a 2-6 record with wins over Haverford College JV and Rutgers Prep. Coach Sutton did see progress in his devoted charges. "This team, although light and inexperienced, showed keen interest and fighting spirit which indicate a continual progress throughout the year."

More important than the summation was Mr. Sutton announcing that 1941 would be his last year as head coach. Having been at the helm for nineteen seasons and guiding his charges through 141 games, Stan decided to focus his attention on his athletic directorship, a position he held until retiring in 1962. True to his commitment to education, Stan did not ease into retirement. In 1943, students could experience the rigors of combat training in the form of the Sutton "Commando" course. This grueling challenge included climbing, running, and jumping while Stan calculated your performance with his stopwatch.

Though no longer head coach, Stan's love of the game kept him close to the football program as an in-house recruiter, avid fan, and inspirational mentor. Dave Eldredge, guard on the 1947 team, remembers Stan's influence in bringing him into the football fold. "In elementary school I was captain of the soccer team having chosen against playing football and I planned to continue soccer at George School. However, at the ninth grade physical in the GS gym the last stop was weighing in before Stan Sutton (whose legend, physique and authority cowered us), and then selecting your sport. I weighed in at a reasonably fit 170 pounds. Before I could say 'soccer' Stan had observed me and announced, 'Son, you're a football player!'".

Stan went beyond the role of Quaker persuader. He accompanied the team on away games, offering sage advice and tension breaking anecdotes. Charles 'Dusty' Scudder, blocking back on the '48 and '49 team, sat close to Stan on one of those outings, "I remember two things about riding on the bus with Stan "The Man" Sutton. I hope GS didn't pay too much for these buses because some of them were borderline junk. The big challenge came very early in the trip-the Langhorne Hill. Stan would be very quiet as we went under the RR bridge half way up. After making it over the top, however, he would smile slightly on one side of his face and tell the same old story about the time that the whole team had to get out and push the bus up the last few yards. He also had a favorite comment as the bus came down off of the bridge into Burlington, NJ. 'This is where the mainland ends and the sandbars begin.'"

Obviously, finding a successor who would be both coach and educator would be difficult at best. Rees Frescoln got the nod. An English teacher at GS, Rees was also a member of the Newtown Fire Company. Believing whole-heartedly in Stan Sutton's system, coach Frescoln stayed with the single wing attack rather than switch to the T formation which Missouri coach Don Faurot introduced to the college ranks in 1941.

The season started on a rather ominous note. On the opening kickoff against Langhorne High, captain Dave Wilson made a smashing head-on tackle. He injured his neck and was carried off the field on a stretcher. Transferred to Abington Hospital, he remained a few days while doctors treated his bruised vertebrae. He would return to action several games later. Though undoubtedly stunned, the Buffians refused to surrender, battling the local high schoolers to a 7-7 tie, a game in which the quick kick became the main offensive weapon for both teams.

The tie seemed to help unify the troops as the Georgians went on a tear, defeating Lambertville 2-0, Peddie 27-6, and Haverford College JV 27-6. The streak was broken by a 0-20 loss to Swarthmore, a defeat the school Newspaper attributed to nerves. "A school team is at a psychological disadvantage when playing a college squad. They expect the college team to be far superior to their prep school combination." (Oct. 14, 1942)

The Frescolnmen calmed their psyches in time to beat Bryn Athyn 13-0 and Bensalem 33-6 to finish with a 5-1-1 record. The GS News lauded the efforts of the team's leading rusher David "Dixie" Boring while claiming he, "Wasn't born. He was assembled at Lockheed." They also recognized the Buffian braintrust, including head coach, Rees "Wimpy" Frescoln and his two assistants, "Sleepy Jim " Carson, and "General" Grant Frazer. The real kudos, however, were reserved for the trench warriors. "There is little doubt that the reason for the Buffs' successful season was its line of granite. The forward wall containing men like Wilson, Sinclair, Hunter, Haines, Baker and Johns, held like Rock."

By 1943, World War II's influence could be felt in every phase of George School life. Cut backs and sacrifice became the call of the day. Whether collecting Christmas presents for young Japanese children held in internment camps or doing physical labor on farms, everyone pitched in.

Ted Wright, center on the '43 and '44 team, remembers the times well. "During the war we were sort of unable to do what we'd like to have done because of the limitations of the war. You couldn't get this or that, such as gas for travel."

With gas being rationed getting to and from games became a drudgery only the truly devoted would attempt. As Ted recalls, "I remember getting to Episcopal Academy by public transportation and that was murder. We had a bus to Langhorne Station. We then went from Langhorne to Thirtieth Street Station, took another train out to Episcopal and then walked to get to the field. It took all day."

Just toting shoulder pads, pants, cleats, helmets and uniforms all over creation in itself provided a definite workout, though Ted readily admits that there was not as much gear back then. "I wore a pair of khaki color pants with pads sewn into them. I played in those things everyday, rain or shine. We looked like the raggedy ass cadets. The only real uniform was a long sleeve shirt and a yellow leather helmet without any face mask."

The yellow helmeted warriors also faced a very tough schedule. Again, travel costs proved prohibitive. Also, a manpower shortage left several regular opponents either short of coaches or lacking in sufficient numbers of players. As a result, GS found itself matched against such local teams as Bristol, Langhorne and Cheltenham High School. The stiff competition did not allow for a very impressive won-lost record as the '43 team went 1-7, with the only victory being a 13-6 win over Langhorne. For the only time in its long rivalry, the Georgians played Bryn Athyn twice, losing both times to their arch enemy.

The first encounter with Bryn Athyn saw the Buffians suffer a sound 0-33 thumping. The GS News took a kind approach in writing the game up. "The Bryn Athyn game was played in driving rain. Due mostly to the greasy pigskin, the Frescolnmen were prevented from using their trick plays."

A locker room vantage point offers a different story. Ted Wright will never forget "Wimpy" Frescoln's halftime speech. "After a tough first half, Coach Frescoln chewed us out because we hadn't done better. 'You're playing against their second team,' he exclaimed."

In some ways the drubbing was not that surprising for Ted and his teammates. They knew the going would be tough. "Some of those teams such as Bristol and Langhorne had some tough buggers on their squads and they maltreated George School. We also played Haverford and Swarthmore. They also pummeled us. I don't think we won more than one or two games during those two years."

Lack of practice time undoubtedly reduced the effectiveness of the Buff and Brown men. As part of their contribution to the war effort, GS sent many students out to help local farmers with their crops. As reported in the May 27, 1943 edition of the GS News, 4,200 work hours were put in by both boys and girls. A total of 556 students worked at Kings Farm and 229 at Starkey's Farm.

For Ted and his teammates, the personal satisfaction gained from the volunteer work outweighed the practice time deficit. "We had to go serve on the farms. The trucks would pull up everyday and we'd climb on and go out and cut rutabagas or asparagus during the football season. That cut into our practice time greatly. That was significant. But it was great because it meant everyone had to work because the farmers needed help. That experience was a great leveler in the student body."

The self-discovery and learning done off the field served to complement the lessons of the gridiron. Ted valued the total experience so much he returned to GS as an assistant line coach in 1953. "Playing football at George School took me from a 'clueless rookie' to someone who appreciated the finer points of the game, the necessary organization, the required skills, distinctions, and terminology so that arriving at the college level I could compete. I guess it gave me a certain amount of pride...but then I knew I wasn't that good! As time went on I had great pleasure from working out the x's and o's, planning special defenses, etc. The strategy aspect was intriguing."

Looking back, Ted realizes that a certain sense of heroics, undoubtedly born from the wartime atmosphere, filled his youthful self-image. This was the era of great deeds with many valiant effort embedded in the imagination of young men nationwide. From the brave marines raising the flag on Iwo Jima to Douglas MacArthur telling his troops, "I shall return', the examples flowed. Seen from an adolescent view, far from the reality of death and suffering, the possibility for greatness and recognition intoxicated even the most logical mind.

Ted readily admits to being drawn in. "I read a lot of Ralph Henry Barber books such as Clint Frank of Yale, Fourth and Goal, Ninth Inning Heroics which were full of imaginary heroes. It was the Knute Rockne of Notre Dame kind of thing. That was what we had in our heads to a certain extent. Because it was the war years and there weren't big crowds at the games we were sort of the gladiators fighting for the girls. We thought we were something doing our battle. It wasn't really much but we had sort of a dream aura. World war II added to that. Idealism was rampant and certainly added to the glory aspect of those days."

The ever present possibility of injury slightly dampened the heroic images. Players lacked such protective gear such as mouth pieces, face masks, and personally sized helmets. To a great deal, they also went without immediate medical attention. Battlers such as Ted dealt as best they could. "We didn't have a trainer except Stan Sutton. No doctors at practice. If someone got dinged at practice we just sat them down. I got boils on my neck because of the dirty helmet. It did something which pushed into my neck and I got infected and had to get them drained at the infirmary."

The rash of injuries led Norm Berson to draw the following analogy in his column in the GS News, "The Buff football squad looks like a team Notre Dame just got through with. There isn't a man on the squad who has not been injured at some time this season. Someone was heard to remark, ``There is enough water on Mike Swayne's knee to float the battleship Pennsylvania'."

As with most players, Ted accepted injuries as part of the game. Though certainly not desirable neither injury nor loss weakened his love for football. He maintained that all-important sense of perspective. "There is too much of that finger-raised-in-victory today. A victory is nice but if you play a hell of a game it's more thrilling. That's a lesson I learned at George School. It's a lot of work and joys but life goes on after football."

George Ewing, quarterback on the '43 and '44 team, definitely agrees that the shared experience does not always have to end in victory to be meaningful. "The thing I remember most about GS football is the confidence the coaching staff showed in you. They were fair, wanted action, but were not very critical. We were asked to produce and when we did we felt very rewarded. When we didn't-well they were kind. Our coaches were outstanding because of their honest ways and excellent teaching ability. We knew that certain games were more important and more fun. We lost more games than we won. We did have some very good players but we were limited in number. Those we played with in the same winning spirit in a fair manner became close friends-some for life. Jack Mason was my best friend. We even roomed together and took care of the third and fourth floor of Orton."

1945 saw a change in the George School coaching order. Dick McFeely stepped down after a very successful string of Cub football seasons. Rees Frescoln also decided to take a one year hiatus from the football wars. His assistant, John Carson, assumed the duties of head coach. Perhaps inspired by the rebuilding and revamping going on worldwide at the end of the war in '45, "Long John" decided to try a different type of offensive strategy. Switching from the single wing, coach Carson installed the new T formation which featured a sliding, ball handling quarterback who took a direct snap from center.

Understandably, the Men in Brown were more eager than adept. The new system opened the potential for a good deal of deception, mis-direction, and passing plays. It also allowed for an equally large degree of confusion and error. The yearbook best summed up the resulting 1--7 season. "Handicapped by the lack of experience in the T formation, Coach Carson's squad dropped all but one game. The backfield, lighter than usual, completed many passes and thanks to the receiving of Captain Saurman and the ends, passes accounted for half the total points scored during the season."

GS scored 61 points total for the season, 31 of which came in their lone win, a 31-13 crushing of the Peddie B team. Captain Jim Saurman accounted for three tallies in the victory. Reflecting an attitude expressed by so many of the past GS gridiron greats, Jim took both victory and defeat in stride. He feels that the games "were all big. I loved the thrill of competition. Football appealed to me because it was a contact sport as well as a chance for team-work and fellowship."

The competition was intense as the Buff and Brown warriors encoun-tered many a behemoth-laden team. The George School News sympathized with the plight facing the Carsonmen. "In other games the team seemed to play all right for the first half, but would bog down in front of strong opposition in the second half. This was due to the bigger and more mature players on the opposition, forcing our smaller players to weaken."

In 1946 the Georgians somewhat balanced the manpower issue. Not only did Rees Frescoln return as head coach but two ex -G.I. 's, Fritz Wiedeke and Stanley Shoemaker, returned to GS and added muscle to the line. Reinforced by such seasoned vets, the Frescolnmen opened the season by tying a rugged Langhorne team 6-6. Employing both a single wing and T formation attack, GS was held scoreless in the first quarter. Down 0-6 in the second period, the stout hearted battlers, unlike the previous season, refused to fold. According to the GS News, "George School came back in the second quarter with a 51 yard march that culminated when captain Jim Saurman bucked through the middle for the last foot."

The second game of the season brought Friends Central to the home of the Buff and Brown. GS was determined to stop this potent foe who had crushed them 65-6 the year before. Though not quite turning the tables, captain Saurman and his cohorts certainly proved a worthy opponent. The yearbook noted their spirited effort. "Most heartbreaking of our defeats was the Friends Central game, in which time gave out with GS on the two yard line in enemy territory. Such games as this served to make the season very satisfactory from the spectators' point of view."

Even more satisfying were the team's three wins, 39-7 over Lambertville, 6-0 over Germantown Friends, and 18-6 over Bensalem. Captain Saurman again assumed the role of hero in the Germantown game. The two Quaker forces fought to a 0-0 tie with only minutes left in the contest. Then, "Art Henrie's 26 yard run set up a Saurman TD from the two yard line to climax an 80 yard, fourth period drive." (GS News)

His scoring heroics earned Captain Saurman the praise of the Newspaper staff who summed up the season saying, "Jim Saurman led his teammates with his hard playing and scoring ability."

The play of the resurgent Buffians might also have inspired the distaff side of the student body. The October 31, 1946 edition of the GS News reported that an unofficial addition was made to the girls' athletic offerings when a group of spirited coeds, undoubtedly led by some "ambitious members of third center (Main Hall)", took to the varsity football field on a Sunday afternoon. Using a ball provided by Art Henrie and employing Charles Kushell as referee, the girls set out to experience gridiron warfare first hand. The News recounted the brave ladies' exploits. "Even as in professional practices there were mishaps during the surprisingly well-organized game. As Ginny Kauffman went down after a swift 20 yard dash, almost knocking herself out, she hollered that Lee Arnett's western boots 'got mixed up with my goalie's shoes!'" The result of Nancy Bearisto's rather powerful tackle of unsuspecting Janet Korbeck was one deeply shadowed left eye...Korbeck's that is. Audie Wetzel and Molly Wood were the lone scorers of the first game." The lack of further reports indicates that the girls of the gridiron abandoned their pursuit after the inaugural affair.

The 1947 version of Buff and Brown football once again succumbed to the most tenacious opponent facing any team...injuries. Jack Witherington, who doubled as a player and reporter, described the aftermath of the Georgians' opener against Langhorne. "Mr. Frescoln claims he knows two people who didn't get hurt at the Langhorne game. When asked the names, he answered, 'Coach Thode and I.'" The Big Buff, as they had come to be known, finished with a 2-6 record. The highlight of the season was a 13-12 win over previously undefeated Lambertville High School.

Being held scoreless in five of its games did not lessen the Big Buff's worth in the eyes of the Newspaper, "This year's team will not be ranked among the great G. S. elevens but it would be hard to find one that had more spirit."

Undoubtedly stung by the previous season's misfortune and determined to reverse the outcomes, the 1948 team assembled a squad which could be considered one of the "great G. S. elevens". Bolstered by the addition of such promising sophomores as Jimmy Seabrook and Charles "Dusty" Scudder, the Frescolnmen rolled to a 6-2 record. Outscoring the opposition by a 148-61 margin, the Big Buff rocked Friends Central and Lambertville by identical 24-0 scores before crushing Church Farm School 35-6 and Frenchtown 34-7.

The most satisfying win came in the season finale when GS took on Bryn Athyn in the twenty-fifth anniversary of their heated rivalry. As is so often the case when arch rivals meet, one miscue cost the game. In the first period, GS recovered a fumble deep in Bryn Athyn territory. On the first play from scrimmage, GS quarterback Charley Stewart dropped back and lobbed a 20 yard touchdown aerial pass to Jimmy Sailer. As they say, the rest is history, with the Big Buff bettering the Men in Red 6-0.

Jack Witherington, captain and wise reporter, though not offering Isotoner Gloves to his front seven, credited the men in the trenches for the team's success. "Orchids of the week go to the GS line. These seven blocks of granite have allowed an average of only eight points a game to be scored against them while tearing opposing lines to shreds to allow George School backs to score on the average better than 18 points a game. (GS News December 2, 1948)

Even greater than the victories was the camaraderie developing among the players. The 'fraternity born from battle' again provided many GS gridders with their most cherished and lifelong rewards. Dusty Scudder, president of the class of 1950, lists such friendships number one among the lasting benefits he received playing football at George School. Most appealing was, "Working hard with a great bunch of guys and getting lots of recognition. It gave us an opportunity to excel in an activity that I found exciting and rewarding. I learned the value of teamwork and how hard work can pay off. Also, I formed close friendships, three of which, I am in regular contact with today- Bill Loucks, Jim Seabrook and Jack Williams."

Jim Seabrook ('51) echoes his friends' sentiments. "I had a great time playing football at George School. My senior year playing football was the fall of 1950. I had two roommates who also played football and were co-captains that year, Bill Loucks and Dusty Scudder. We were good friends on the team, which was the most important thing. I suppose we only won half our games but it was fun."

Jim's recollection of the won-lost record in 1949 proved close. The Big Buff finished with a solid 4-3 mark, including a 32-6 win over Sanford Prep, a 26-15 conquest of Germantown Friends, and a convincing 27-6 thumping of Frenchtown High School. All of the impressive play really served as preludes to the season finale, a showdown with the boys from Bryn Athyn.

It promised to be a classic match-up with GS pitting its single wing offense against Bryn Athyns deceptive T formation. Prior to the game Coach Frescoln said, "I would rather play any other team in the country. This game will be a humdinger."(GS News Nov. 18,1949)

The coach's trepidation probably came as little surprise to his men. Dusty Scudder well-remembers his emotional coach. "Coach Frescoln was very emotional and would sometimes weep during halftime. I, for one, can remember playing harder after seeing a grown man cry. During bus trips to away games, assistant coach Ed Thode would put magazines in front of Rees to try and calm him down. Frescoln would only look at them for a few moments before pushing them away and returning to his worrying."

It's not documented how many tears coach Frescoln shed at the Bryn Athyn game but he probably was not crying when the final gun sounded. As the '50 yearbook, with its new title Opus, stated, "Closing the season, the team put up a tremendous fight against Bryn Athyn, the traditional rival, resulting in a victory of 2-0"

Coach Frescoln went out a winner, turning the head coaching assignment for the 50' season over to Francis Brown. The Men in Brown literally became the Men of Brown. More importantly, the single wing gave way to the T formation as Coach Brown opted for a more wide open attack. Initially the strategy worked. The Brownmen walloped Sanford Prep 19-6, leaving the coach feeling confident. "The football team brought out just what coach Frank brown said in his talk at the Pep Rally; that they have no outstanding stars

but that every member is a star. The new T formation brings a sharp attack."
(GS News)

Come game two, however, trouble set in. Confused by the new system, the gridders lost their next three outings. The last, a 7-53 drubbing at the hands of Bordentown caused a strategy reevaluation. The single wing was back and GS regained its winning ways.

The yearbook accurately chronicled the turnaround saying, "In his first year as football coach, Mr. Francis Brown masterminded the team into a winning season. The squad started with the T formation which functioned well against a weaker Sanford Prep eleven as the Buff and Brown won the first game. They then lost three games and went back to the single wing."

Dusty Scudder and his teammates were relieved to return to the more traditional scheme. "Coach Brown changed us over to the T formation at the start of the 1950 season. We lost a couple of games and I remember feeling good when he decided to go back to the old familiar single wing."

The Brownmen showed their pleasure by beating Germantown Friends 30-20. Bob Maust led the attack, making it to the GFS end zone three times. Dusty Scudder rounded out the scoring, tallying twice. The "Buff T-men" were single wingers again. With Jim Seabrook leading the way by scoring 22 points, GS recorded a sound 34-13 win over Swarthmore the following week giving momentum to the Brownmen as they prepared for the season wind-up against Bryn Athyn.

350 loyal fans from school boarded the Bryn Athyn special at the train station and invaded the home of the Men in Red. The GS gridders gave them their money's worth. Bob Maust scored first for GS. After runs of 19 and 38 yards, he plunged in from the one yard line to give the Big Buff a 6-0 lead. After the hometown team tied the score, the Brownmen struck like lightning in the third quarter.

Jim Seabrook recounts his version of the "big play", saying, "The game I remember most, we were playing Bryn Athyn and it was raining and overcast and neither team seemed to be able to move the ball. Bill Loucks was also our punter and his good punting kept us in the game and then out of nowhere, late in the third quarter, Dusty Scudder carried the ball up the middle 66 yards for a touchdown and that was the game."

Dusty Scudder has a more modest memory of the dramatic moment. "The blocking back in the single wing seldom carried the ball. My senior year against arch rival Bryn Athyn Academy, wing back Jimmy Seabrook called for a "3 buck" inside the ten yard line and I was lucky enough to score the winning TD."

The school newspaper ran this account in their season summary. "G. S. right halfback Dusty Scudder cut off tackle, broke into the clear, and raced 45 yards for the final and winning tally."

Whether it was, 10, 45, or 66 yards, the most important fact remains. The Men of Brown had given their first year coach a fine season-ending gift, a 12-6 victory over Bryn Athyn.

The celebration which took place at the traditional closing banquet held at the Temperance House honored more than one big game. The players who gathered for their final team meeting relished every moment from the tangible scores to the personal contacts.

There were the good natured pranks such as the one Dusty remembers playing on Coach Brown. "Mr. Brown drove a tiny Crosely station wagon. One day we spotted it parked behind the kitchen near the exit from the store and about six of us picked up the front of the Crosley and left it propped up on two steel barrier posts about two feet off the ground. He never acknowledged that it happened. I think he had to hire a wrecker to get the car back on the ground. We liked coach Brown but he happened to have the only car on campus that we could do that to."

There were tales describing the neophyte years when scared freshmen got their first taste of gridiron wars. Dusty still remembers the traditional intramural game played by the cub team. "One team was led by the varsity coach at the time, Rees Frescoln, who had the nickname of "Wimpy". The name of his team was the McWimps. The other team was led by someone in the music department and was called The Oprestissimo. In 1949, however, the new Headmaster Dick McFeeley was coaching the Oprestissimo. At assembly, Mr. Dick made the following announcement. 'There will be a meeting of all McWimp supporters in the phone booth in the main hall.' We came to enjoy Mr. Dick's great sense of humor.``

They also came to worship both his courage and total support of the football team. Dusty readily lauds Mr. Dick's strength of character and determined nature. "Mr. Dick was a great athlete before being stricken by polio. His son Dick and I would often carry him up the stairs to the assembly room. His arms and upper body were so strong that he could support himself with just his arms. Once while bringing up the big wrestling mat in the gym, we accidentally knocked away one of his crutches. Before the remaining crutch could turn him sideways, he threw it away and went down straight with his hands flat on the floor. Asking for his crutches, he held one in each hand and climbed back up using them like ladders. We were in awe of his ability. Mr. Dick made a point of visiting the teams during practice and often called encouragement to the football players from his electric cart. The recharging station for his cart was behind the main building. In the morning, he would walk from Sunnybank up to Main, using his leg irons and crutches. I admired his persistence."

Another teacher gaining the admiration of the youthful gridders was Stan Sutton who actively supported the team. He still provided many life lessons just by his own reactions. One was to take the unexpected in stride. According to Dusty, "Edgard Able Franco-Ferreria was an end on the football team. His parents called him Edgard, some people called him Ed, and some called him Gard, but to us, he was 'Mudguard'. He was very clever at building things and made a giant yoyo, about two feet in diameter with fifty feet of clothes line for string. The best place to try it out, of course, was from the fourth floor of Drayton. We had to hold on to Mudguard's feet so that he could lie out onto the roof and reach over the edge of the gutter. When the giant yoyo hit bottom, we could feel the shock in his feet. It was working ok but he couldn't get it to climb all the way back. Suddenly we were all (except Mudguard) aware of the imposing presence of Mr. Sutton. We yanked Mudguard back into the room and he dropped the line and yoyo. Stan was puzzled and asked, 'WHAT was that going by my window downstairs?' We explained and he told us not to go out on the roof again. Before he left, he said, 'Son I have lived in this building for 26 years and seen many things go down, but that is the first time anything has gone back UP!'"

One source of humor undoubtedly brought up at the closing banquet was the need for some new equipment. Bernie Marshall, football player and columnist for the school paper, described Dusty's attire in the paper. "Dusty Scudder is setting the new style on the football field with adhesive tape pants held together with a little cloth."

The scenario proved sufficiently severe to prompt Jimmy Seabrook's dad to donate blankets to the cause. Dusty and his teammates welcomed any contribution. "Jim Seabrook's father, Belford Seabrook, was one of our most loyal supporters. After one particularly cold game where we all sat shivering on the bench, Belford donated special blankets for the whole team."

From admiration to good natured ribbing, Dusty basked in the entire aura of the football experience. He will not soon forget that final Victory Football Dinner. He was dating Min Parker at the time. "Stan gave everyone a gold football. They were tiny but mine sure looked good on a chain around Min's neck. I was proud to give it to her and she was proud to wear it. It was a great romantic time of my life that I remember with fondness, and football was a BIG part of it."

With the graduation of three fourths of the starting backfield, Coach Brown faced a rebuilding year in 1951. Not surprisingly, the Brownmen experienced growing pains, being shutout in their first three games. The learning process paid off as GS captured three straight games, beating Haverford 36-14, Swarthmore 24-7, and Bryn Athyn 32-0. The finale would turn out to be Coach Brown's last game as head coach.

As Sure as God Made Little Green Apples

O ther than an occasional Red Scare or the construction of a bomb shelter, relative peace marked the early fifties. Dwight Eisenhower sat in the White House. Gary Cooper waited for "High Noon". Robert Young demonstrated "Father Knows Best". Elvis Presley had yet to get America' "All Shook Up". And Bob Geissinger assumed the head coaching duties of the George School football team.

Where the last fact may not have shaken the International Balance of Power, it would positively impact the lives of many young GS men for the next three decades. Some contend that being color blind Geis wound up at a Quaker boarding school when he confused route 413 with 322 on the map and ended up in Newtown instead of State College. More likely, he tired of waiting for Notre Dame to call so, seeing a window of opportunity open when Francis Brown left to teach at Media High, he jumped at the George School offer.

From the GS viewpoint, athletic director Stan Sutton knew a good bet when he saw it. Iron Mike, as he was called at Springfield College, packed all the credentials. As both quarterback and defensive back Geis was well versed in offensive and defensive strategy. His gridiron exploits were heralded in the November 17, 1948 edition of The Springfield Daily News. "Bob Geissinger, a quarterback from Huntingdon, Pa. became the Maroons most consistent passer when he completed two out of three against the Aces to give him a record of five completions in six attempts over the season. His passes have gained 78 yards for the Massasoits and have been responsible for one touchdown." Now, those stats probably did not leave Johnny Unitas and Otto Graham shaking in their cleats, but they did show Geis knew what to do with a pigskin in his hands.

He undoubtedly developed a good deal of his football savvy prior to entering Springfield. Like so many young men in the early forties, Geis answered his nation's call and, after graduating from high school, enlisted in the army. At the time, military football ranked among the best brands of ball played anywhere. Teams blended the talents of eager youths, ex-All Americans, and professionals taking time off from their careers to serve their country. Geis was right at home with this impressive gathering of talent and experience. In 1945, his running and passing exploits helped the 65th Signal Battalion go undefeated and capture the VI Corps football championship.

Indicative of the 65th's dominance, they shut out their first five opponents while averaging over twenty points a game on offense. Articles in the weekly military newspaper, The Beachhead News, showed army football went beyond any "four yards and a cloud of dust" thinking. Plays were complex and required a really open and creative approach. The following describes just one of the many successful offensive assaults staged by the 65TH. In a game against Ordnance 48, "Ed Songin passed to McEwen for 25 yards and then he passed to Geissinger, who lateraled to Billy Fink who lateraled to John Kaslauskas for a gain of 47 yards. Geissinger and Don Schaefer smashed through to the 11 and then Songin passed to Geissinger in the end zone." Later in the game, "Geissinger, on a reverse, passed to McEwen, who took the ball on the five and raced over to score." Such innovative plays would help Geis in the coming years as he tried to help his often outnumbered and small George School charges as they battled more massive foes.

In addition to his gridiron expertise, Geis was a veteran of the 'teaching wars' who possessed a sincere belief in the value of each student he encountered. Prior to coming to George School, Geis taught History and Health, and coached three sports at Saltillo High School. The short stint at Saltillo undoubtedly helped mold the young teacher's philosophy, one he lived by until retiring in the spring of 1990. His words reveal that a young man's growth counted more than any gridiron exploits. "I think the sport of football has always been of value to GS because it has provided an outlet for a lot of red-blooded kids who did not have a say in picking the school. It also provides an opportunity for kids who have never played the game or thought they could, to learn the skills, gain some needed self-confidence, and make a varsity team in their junior and senior year. The game is a unique team sport because on every play each player has a definite responsibility where his effort or lack of effort directly affects ten other teammates. The value of teamwork is quickly evident and the players gain confidence knowing their efforts are a most valuable part of the team's success. The positions in football give an opportunity for boys of all sizes and shapes to play the game and win some recognition. I never looked at it as any more than part of the curriculum but an important part due to the lessons in self-discipline and the inherent lessons that come from playing a team sport. I have always tried to adhere to the philosophy of Ossie Solem, my college coach, who stated that the coach should aid the players to defeat their faults both individually and collectively to the point that they would have no regrets from having played the game."

The 1952 season certainly tested the young coach's faith. Denied any preseason practice time, Geis found himself in essence directing a squad of players whose personal and physical qualities were unknown to him. Not surprisingly, the Buff and Brown battlers got a sound thumping in the season opener, a 0-29 loss to Pingry.

Game two looked even more foreboding as Germantown Academy, a team boasting at least 13 recruited players, came to Newtown. The thought of their potency did not exactly instill confidence in the GS gridders. Burt Powell, in his column in the GS news, described the Drayton Building Meeting where dorm head Stan Sutton tried to inspire the boys. "During the meeting a slight murmur arose when he mentioned the upcoming game with GA. Mr. Sutton looked surprised and asked, 'Where's Gummy? Gummy, how much do you weigh?' Gum replied, '129'. Again, a little murmur. Mr. Sutton said, 'Look at that! Gum only weighs 129 and is playing varsity. And you're worried about getting hurt. Gum won't get hurt. You know why? Because he's too fast and shifty and won't stay in the same place long enough to get hurt'." (GS News, October 29,1952)

"Gummy" was quarterback Peter Gum who coach Geissinger described as, "a great competitor and leader with real poise in competition." Unfortunately, the 129 pound QB was not invincible. He broke his ankle in practice the week before the Germantown game, an injury he would long remember. "What comes back to me the easiest are my battle scars. The only broken bones I ever had, I got playing football at George School. I was on crutches for six weeks with a broken leg. How did it happen? In practice would you believe, on a sweep around the right end, foiled by an opposing classmate who made a fine tackle that sidelined me for six weeks. That was early in the season, so I got back in the game toward the end of the season, just in time to break the little finger on my right hand. I went around for some time with tongue depressors taped to the finger. Minor stuff, and brings a smile to my face thinking about it."

At the time, Geis was probably not smiling, a mood only enhanced by the fact that his entire offensive backfield would be sidelined prior to the Germantown invasion. The school news described the 6-41 loss. "George School was handicapped considerably by the loss of the entire first string offensive backfield, Bill Scheffer, John Battin, Pete Gum, and Burt Powell." (GS News October 15, 1952)

Always a class act, Geis showed none of the crudeness of a Buddy Ryan in his post game comments, "They were the best team in Philadelphia. We did well and we will not have any more games like that." Little wonder that Geis taught a Human Relations class, a course instructing young people in the art of proper social decorum.

The course, unfortunately, did not cover the ways of handling the frustration of losing your first five games while scoring only two touchdowns. Geis would discover this secret on his own. "One of the players on the team was John Battin. He was a real free spirit. Well into the season with no wins I excused the team early to watch the JV game. By the time I got up to the field Battin had substituted himself into the game. When I discovered it, I chased him down into the locker room. I caught up with him outside the showers by the coaching lockers and proceeded to have a Meeting for Worship where I did all the talking, screaming, and shouting while reading him off. Mr. Sutton's dressing room was directly above and he heard it. Next day he asked me how I made out with Battin. I told him great. I finally got two months of frustration out of myself. I said I was tired of pushing these guys to the limit and was going to let up and have fun during the rest of the season."

The very Mr. Battin who was subjected to the wrath of Geis undoubtedly realized what so many of us came to recognize in our George School football careers. While our adolescent bravado bristled at being 'read out', deep inside we knew Geis held us to task because he cared. Today John Brattin writes that, "We did nothing if we did not build character in 1952. The friendships that we formed on the football squad have lasted a lifetime. I always look forward to seeing Coach Geissinger and his lovely wife, Mary on Alumni Day. Coach Geis and Mary took a special interest in us and their support and friendship were greatly appreciated."

Geis's Meeting For Worship with young Mr. Battin had an immediate effect on November 7th, 1952. John well remembers how he and his team-mates helped Geis log his first coaching victory. "We loaded on a bus on a cold overcast Friday afternoon, and motored down to Germantown Friends. Coach Geissinger was anxious for his first win at George School, and we got it for him, thanks to a terrific team effort."

The final score read George School 13, Germantown Friends 7. John Battin described the game action, saying, "Germantown was up 7 to zip at the half. John Rahshenbush raced for a 31 yard touchdown late in the third period. The conversion failed so Germantown was up by 7-6 going into the fourth period. Co-captain Bill Scheffer solidified his position as our premier player by an interception and 28 yard romp to make the score GS 13-Germantown 7. The team held on to the lead for the victory. We had our first win, and Geis's first win at George School."

Not disheartened by his 1-7 'first' season, Geis used it as a learning period. He quickly identified the dilemma facing every George School coach. There is woefully little time to prep the players either in preseason or during the school year. Where other teams bask in the glory of four week summer camps and daily three hour practice sessions, the Buff and Brown men got only two or three days before school opened and then about an hour and a half for daily workouts.

Considering the nature of a boarding school and the need to house and feed players during any early sessions, Geis decided his best plan of attack was not to argue for a longer preseason but to adjust by simplifying the amount to be digested. "I went to the split T offense my second year to get some practice time. We had to emphasize our defense and kicking game in the first week while evaluating our personnel. I always felt it took three weeks to build an offense with a threat and decent timing. The split T was easy to teach with lineman using splits to set up plays and they could signal the running back which direction to run. The same plays were run left and right. Unfortunately, it was a lousy passing offense because you couldn't get any decent pass protection with the wide splits in the line."

Undoubtedly buried in the new offense were a few quick kicks, an alumni day special and a flea flicker. Geis always liked to be prepared for any situation. The players obviously found the new strategy very acceptable. After a close season-opening loss to Pingry, the Georgians went on a tear, winning four of their next five games. Newark Academy fell first when Hap Miller plunged into the end zone to give GS a 12-7 victory. Friends Central succumbed to the revamped warriors with a 50 yard Pete Gum pass to Hap Miller being all the scoring the Geissingermen would need to take a 7-2 conquest.

The fourth contest of the season against Swarthmore was hardly a study in perfection. George School scored five times in the fourth quarter but only two made the scoreboard as they pulled off a 12-0 win. An 80 yard pass interception and lateral from Gum to Harry Hoyt was nullified by a clipping call. A similar violation brought back Burt Powell's 60 yard TD jaunt with an intercepted pass. An illegal motion penalty negated Jack Purdy's scoring bomb to John Briscoe. A four yard TD run by Jon Lippincott and a 30 yard scoring dash by Gum, however, did hold up. Germantown Friends was next to feel the Georgians' wrath. The GS defense allowed only 28 rushing yards in toppling the city Quakers by a 13-6 score.

The season finale with archrival Bryn Athyn showed how far the Georgians had progressed. The yearbook described the excitement best. "The Bryn Athyn game brought the campaign to a sensational climax. Two great goal line stands by George School and a touchdown pass from Hap Miller to Ed Walsh tied the score at 6-6."

Ted Wright, back to assist Geis as the line coach, vividly recalls the dramatic goal line stands. "Bryn Athyn was first and goal on the 8 yard line. Finally, it got to be fourth down and about two feet. I had worked with Rudy Japchen on submarining and, by hands, frantically signaled to him to remember how to do it now! I can still see his head come up under a Bryn Athyn pair of legs and then rise up to stop their attack."

In his typical no frills manner, Geis again handled the press with style, succinctly summarizing the team's 4-3-1 record. "We had a vastly improved team this year and we should do much better next year." (GS News 12/16/53)

Though an accurate account of the team's progress and the coach's enlightenment, the capsule summary does not touch upon the real victories, rewards Geis values above any notches in the win column. Peter Gum would gladly suffer through the annoying injuries for the chance to grow. Reflecting back on his gridiron days, he says, "Sports for young people potentially confer a number of benefits on the participants. In my case, I gained confidence in myself. I gained a better understanding of the inner rewards of achievement. Examples of the benefits of teamwork registered on me. The process of setting and striving for goals, in this case aspiring for varsity status, made an impact on me. Not to be overlooked of course was the plain old camaraderie of the situation, also another context for the development of social skills."

Sounds an awful lot like the wisdom of George Walton, Stan Sutton and Bob Geissinger was echoing in the sentiments of the new breed of Buffian warrior. As quarterback, Peter also relished the strategy of the game. To the neophyte it's a show of push and grunt; to the gridiron vet it's a carefully choreographed chess match. According to Pete, "I don't remember particular games so much as I remember incidents. In one case we were in a game where both sides had scored, and so it was a genuine contest of fairly matched opponents. Late in the game the running back grabbed me after a play and told me that their left tackle looked really winded. So, we called a running play over that position. We gained ground, and called another play right over that position. More ground. We won the game, by exploiting the observed weakness. A smile to this day."

Ed 'Mundy' Dawes, Peter Gum's teammate and a player Geis describes as being "really consistent on both offense and defense", maintains a healthy perspective about his gridiron days. "I entered George School in the fall of 1952. I tried out for the team and played a very, very slow center and linebacker. I missed several games in both years because of a torn up knee I suffered in 1952. No arthroscopic surgery in those days and it was decided not to operate. Lots of sitting on the edge of a desk lifting sandbags to strengthen it. Sports were the most important part of my life at GS. You can look at my academic record and realize I must have been more interested in something than my studies. I still have my wreathed G letter, I think we called it a Pi letter, hanging on a bulletin board as I write this...I do think sports and team participation helped make me a better person and for the rest of my life for all the reasons associated with sports. It's the people that were important, not the game. Now that I'm retired, I miss the people, not the work."

No question, injury is an ever present possibility on the gridiron, one that almost enhances the team aspect of the game. If you mess up, not only won't you score but your teammate might get hurt. Joe Brewar, halfback and defensive end on the '53 team, knows the pain associated with the sport. "I have several injuries that have come back to haunt me as I grow older. The injuries that I refer to are all post college injuries. That's when the game gets really rough."

Joe knows of what he speaks. His GS football exposure inspired him to continue playing at Lafayette College, then in the army, and finally with the Baltimore Colts. Here he relished not only being razzed as a rookie and listening to Webe Ewbank's jokes but catching a TD pass in practice from Johnny Unitas.

Though the competition grew stiffer, the rewards remained the same. Life lessons learned on the GS gridiron proved lasting for Joe. "Football was not the most important thing to me. It was the only thing that mattered to me at that stage of my life. I loved to run with the ball. Need I say more? I learned to compete no matter what the score. That helped me all through my career as an independent self-employed business man."

For Geis it was back to the drawing board in 1954. The departure of such proven players as Brewar, Gum and Dawes opened the field for the new, untested aspirants. The school news offered an accurate analysis. "This year's team is a mixture of youth and experience, and is constantly improving, especially on defense. The line is light, although it partly makes up for the weight disadvantage in speed."

Unfortunately, the Georgians lacked sufficient quickness to get into the end zone, being shutout in their first two games. The Buff and Brown did show promise in game two, a 0-6 loss to Newark on Parents Day, "Ends Joe Hancock, John Briscoe, and guards Bill Pickering and Bill Cadwallader were outstanding men for GS." (GS News, 10/20/54)

The losses did not overshadow the learning taking place. The new players were starting to get the hang of the game's finer points. Ted Wright, line coach, remembers teaching Joe Penrose the art of self-discipline. "Bucky Penrose played defensive right tackle. We were to play a team that ran traps and a weak side reverse and Bucky had difficulty staying home when motion went away. We went through the drills time and time again and finally he got the hang of it....look to the inside, stay low, and wait for action coming back. The play might be fifteen yards down the right side but Bucky was back there, on his one knee, back at the post, waiting for the reverse or trap, all by himself."

Bucky was not the only student adjusting his game. Geis, though only in his third year as head coach, had already learned the need to be flexible. As the man in charge you have to make key decisions. If they do not pan out, check the wisdom of your moves before condemning the players. The first big reversal for Geis came in his choice of QB for the '54 season. "Ken 'Hap' Miller was a free spirit and a natural halfback with some speed and great moves that made him hard to tackle. I made the mistake of trying to make him a QB in the split T. I wasted a lot of time. He was really a quality competitor whom I would hate to play poker with. I finally gave up and switched him back to halfback."

With Miller back in his natural position, Geis turned the signal calling responsibility over to junior Mike Kosoff, a true leader who Geis says, "would have been a Hall of Famer if it weren't for his lousy coach." For the young QB it was a dream come true. "I had played football before going to GS. I always liked it, particularly calling plays, and the strategy of deceiving the opponent. I seemed to have a natural ability to pass a football and call plays."

Ted Wright would readily accept Mike's self-appraisal, "I remember we were playing Germantown Friends in the rain. It was a terrible field. Mud all over the place. After we got first and goal, nothing was working. Mike called the plays. He called an inside reverse and he told the players, 'Guys, if this doesn't work my rear is in a sling so let's push it across.' And it worked and we won. This story may be enhanced by time."

The records show any embellishment was minor. GS did capture its second victory of the season by a 28-13 margin, with Hap Miller scoring on runs of 60 and 70 yards.

By the end of the season, the raw rookies of game one had melded into a tough and competitive team ready to take on arch-rival Bryn Athyn. 350 fans boarded the Bryn Athyn special at the GS train station and set off to support their gridiron warriors. The Geissingermen did not let them down. George School took an early lead when Harry 'Demi' Hoyt returned the opening kickoff to his 40 yard line. From there Mike Kosoff took control. Utilizing the running of Bob Hahn, Hap Miller and Demi Hoyt, GS moved to the Bryn Athyn 13. Hoyt did the final honors scampering 13 yards to paydirt. The 6-0 lead held up until later in the contest when the home team recorded its first score. Facing possible defeat, the Georgians showed the heart of a champion with Harry Colson breaking through the line to block the extra point kick, thus preserving the tie.

Ironically, the Bryn Athyn game Mike Kosoff remembers most was his senior year (1955), a game he never played in. "I remember Bryn Athyn my senior year. I had been hurt almost all season and couldn't play but had great pride in my teammates, and the manner in which they came from behind to win. We lost only one game that year."

Mike's words reflect the greatest reward garnished from playing ball at George School. You learn your own relative importance and how valuable working with others really is. "The most memorable part of my GS football career was the people. We had what we felt to be an excellent team my last year at GS. I continue to stay in contact, albeit abridged, with members of that team, and of course the coach, Geis. I can honestly say that it was my experience with football and those teammates that I really learned teamwork, and putting the team ahead of personal ambition. This has stuck with me throughout my entire professional life. I retired at the end of '99, and I know that I have placed others and companies ahead of myself."

Where injury can dishearten many an athlete, it also has the potential of being highly instructive. Mike readily acknowledges that his gridiron mishap helped in his transition from a brash self-oriented kid to an understanding team member. "I would make note that the tremendous disappointment I had when I got hurt so badly that I almost didn't get to play my senior year taught me, I believe, to feel an empathy for others that I never would have obtained. I thought it was 'the end of the world'- but surprisingly the sun continued to rise and fall, and likewise I went on."

Mike's well-directed, selfless approach did not go unnoticed by his peers. Andy Nighswander in his school newspaper column, wrote after Mike had been hurt in an opening game loss to Pingry, "however Mike has been elevated to an honorary coaching position where the benefits of his experience and spirit will not be lost. During the practice sessions he teaches many of the finer points of the game to the less experienced players and during the game he can be seen yelling and pacing the sidelines in typical coach tradition."(GS News 11/4/55)

If Mike used Geis as his model he would doff a Bear Bryant hat, raise his voice a few octaves, and tell at least one referee to "Take that call and put it up your rectum." He would also show the insight of taking one player's heartbreak and somewhat assuaging it by making him an assistant coach. Where some coaches lose interest in a player once he is injured, Geis never stopped caring. He knew there was still much to be gained by staying active in some capacity or another. Mike's response to his senior year certainly supports this thinking.

The wisdom of Geis, however, carried beyond his players' needs. He was also an ace in dealing with unforeseen adversity. In '55 a Dr. Watts made a generous donation to the school to have the Varsity Field turtle-backed in honor of his son who was killed in the war. The hope was to improve the drainage of the field. Everything went according to plan except for one slight flaw. The contractor found he could get the dirt quickly and cheaply from the site of the new Acme store in Newtown. As they soon discovered, the dirt was mostly clay. Every time it rained the water drained into the turf but stayed there like a wet sponge because it could not drain properly through the clay.

Geis did not despair. He solicited the aid of science teacher William Craighead, who devised what appeared to be a biological and environmentally sound solution. Collect all the night crawlers that could be found on South Lawn after a heavy rain, spread them across the football field and let them solve the drainage problem by burrowing through the clay barrier. Enter the master tactician. The night of a heavy rain, Geis gathered 120 Draytonites after study hall, armed them with flashlights and pails, and directed them to South Lawn. The volunteers were paired up with one guy holding the flashlight and the other picking up the worms. This proved to be a most popular activity with everyone having a good time except the faculty in Main who had problems keeping the girls from joining the party.

While awaiting the outcome of the ill-fated "Crawler Experiment", Geis moved the football operation to the cub soccer field where the Buff and Brown men played all their home games in '55. Though the end zones were short and the goal posts close to the banks, the spectators did get a great view of their Buff and Brown battlers.

The players must have found the new 'stadium' to their liking as they went on to post a 5-1-2 record. Jack Templeton, filling in for the injured Mike Kosoff, led GS to a 25-12 upset win over Newark in game two of the season. Joe Hancock got the Geissingermen on the scoreboard catching a 5 yard pass from Bill Strandwitz. Jim Thompson followed with a 25 yard scoring run. Second half tallies by Thompson and Keith Eveland iced the victory. The most satisfying aspect of the big win for coach Geissinger was the poise displayed by his young QB. "This was a tight group of seniors who had been at GS for four years and it took a mature kid like Jack to replace Mike and earn the respect of these guys."

After tying Friends Central 6-6 in game three, the GS offense exploded, beating Swarthmore 21-6, Hun School 26-6 and Germantown Friends 38-0. Jim Thompson emerged as the main offensive weapon against Germantown, carrying the ball across the goal line four times.

In a perfect case of 'saving the best for last', GS met Bryn Athyn in what has become the oldest prep school rivalry in Eastern Pennsylvania. Where every meeting of these two teams is special, the 1955 encounter served as the first Trophy Game. After the contest, administrations at both schools agreed to create a trophy which would be kept by the winning team each year. The design included a bronze shoe from each of the opposing captains. Gayle Smith earned the honor for Bryn Athyn. Harry Colson provided the GS shoe with Bill Cadwallader contributing the shoe strings.

Geis felt both players were most deserving of the recognition. "Harry was a quiet guy and the most respected player. He was the strongest player on the team and we used him at right tackle and ran all or most of our offense over him. We used a split T and spread the lineman to get a one-on-one block for Harry in front of the dive man. We also double teamed and cross blocked with him on power plays by the halfback off-tackle. I loved the guy because he gave everything in practice and games. We had him at left tackle on defense and he took away the strong running plays of our opponents. Bill Cadwallader played guard beside Harry. He was a fine player, quick, and also played both ways."

The game itself proved a classic showdown. Geis describes it best. "On Saturday, it started snowing about noon and by gametime the field was covered with about three inches of wet snow. The snow continued throughout the entire game. On each time out, we had crews with brooms sweeping off the lines. They had to be swept before the measurements for each first down. We had scored first and had the game under control until George Pickering, a junior, tried to field a punt of Bryn Athyn's own four yard line and fumbled. BA recovered and scored. Then we controlled the ball with a sustained drive to score in the final minutes on a dive play by Keith Eveland."

The 13-9 win also ranks high in the memories of the young quarterback, Jack Templeton. "My most lasting memory of George School football was the extraordinary end-of-the-season football game against Bryn Athyn in a raging snowstorm in the fall of 1955. We won that game. The blizzard conditions were so substantial you could not see from one end of the football field to the other. Nevertheless, we won on a crossed halfback pass play. Because of the snow, I think that our receiver could not be seen by the defenders. He was all by himself when he caught the ball and ran into the end zone. The winning touchdown came after a long drive and a final four yard plunge across the goal line."

Though a fine capper for the seniors on the 1955 team, the Bryn Athyn victory really served as the beginning of a great career for sophomore Jack Templeton. He earned the total admiration of coach Geissinger, "Jack would be successful in any business or profession. Possessing ordinary build and abilities, he was a QB with all the leadership qualities who was very poised in competition. I could fill pages describing his efforts."

One of Jack's contributions was taking a supposed 'building year' in '56 and turning it into a most successful one. For the record, the '56 footballers racked up a 3-4-1 record. Though losing their first three games, the young players learned the necessary lessons and roared back to win three of their next four games. Key to the success was the increased maturity of the line which included in its ranks such tough competitors as Bill Houghton, Mike Hoyt, Joe Haines, and Dan Hancock. Geis never underestimated the worth of these stalwarts. "Bill Houghton, though small in stature, was a great competitor and the ultimate team player. Mike Hoyt played center and linebacker. He's a really tough kid and a certified human being. Joe Haines was a big strong guy who played tackle. Dan Hancock's physical condition left something to be desired but not his competitive efforts. The Good Lord doesn't make any better human beings than Dan-even his ex-wives have only kind words for him!"

Leader of these trench warriors was Asa Cadwallader. Geis needed only one example to highlight the power of this individual. "He was the strongest guy I ever coached. He was an outstanding guard who just kept coming at people. His senior year, Harry Franks of Neshaminy called and asked us to scrimmage them. They had a young team with Harry Schu at fullback (a 240 pound sophomore who became an all-pro). I told Franks we only had five practices but agreed to play defense most of the afternoon to give them a workout. We put Asa and Dan Hancock directly in front of the fullback and told them to submarine and grab legs on every play to counter Neshaminy's double teams. Dan came out and needed some rest but Asa played every down and really took their fullback plays away. The Neshaminy coach did a lot of screaming at their players but had nothing but respect in their comments about Asa."

Working behind these rocks of granite, quarterback Templeton engineered three decisive wins, 20-7 over Swarthmore, 33-6 over Hun, and 26-0 over Haverford. A young sophomore, Bill Wilson starred in the conquest of Hun, scoring on runs of 43, 28 and 44 yards, a game that would rate as his biggest memory. "I'll always remember playing against teams with bigger players but I loved the contact and physical conditioning that was necessary. The biggest game was beating Hun School my sophomore year, a game in which I scored three touchdowns."

Wilson's exploits did not surprise Coach Geissinger, "He was a great athlete and a fine halfback with real moves- yet he could still be a punishing runner when you needed extra yards."

Though losing their finale 0-13 to Bryn Athyn, the graduating seniors walked away feeling a good deal of satisfaction about their accomplishments and their GS gridiron experience. Mike Hoyt says he will always value, "Working with coach Bob Geissinger and all the friendships, teamwork and fun!"

With several key players returning, the 57 season started with a dramatic 19-13 conquest of Northeast High School. The game bore particular significance for senior Jack Templeton, "My senior year we played Northeast High School which the previous year had won the football championship in Philadelphia. To be fair, Northeast was split into two schools the next year. Nevertheless, they were a bigger team than we were with a better reputation. Our passing and running game, however, caught them by surprise and we won on a long-distance pass with a winning touchdown."

The winning touchdown was a twenty yard aerial from Templeton to Terry Spruance with only three minutes to play in the final quarter. Unfortunately, the next game against Friends Central proved less fortuitous for the gifted signal caller. GS not only lost the game 0-19 but the services of Jack Templeton. "I was tackled as a safety, running back a punt. I was hit in the chest, at the ankles and at my knee. As a result, I have massive tears of cartilage in my knees which effectively ended my playing career."

Losing a quality leader proved disastrous for the Buff and Brown. They were shutout in four of their next five games. Finishing his career with a disappointing 2-4 record did not diminish Jack's belief in the rewards he gained from football. "Football was very appealing because of the individual physical challenges, the exhilaration from successful teamwork, the mental intricacies of the game-all in the context of sportsmanship and living within the rules. I learned the importance of endurance and character as a contributor to success in sports or any other activity. I learned that often significant sacrifice and delay of gratification is necessary in order to make substantial achievements. I also learned the value of endless practice and disciplined team work in which each player makes an individual and meaningful contribution to the success of the group. Also, as a result of self-sacrifice and hard work I realized the truest reward which was self-esteem which comes as a result not of 'feeling good about yourself', but from true achievement."

Jack's words could well serve as an anthem inspiring any future GS football prospect. They also reflect the teaching of Geis, Stan Sutton and all those who saw the potential in bringing football to George School. Every kid should have the opportunity to succeed and truly feel good about himself.

The 1958 season would certainly test the "feel good" benefit. Having graduated several key players, the GS gridders found the early going tough. Northeast arrived on campus with full regalia and an ardent desire not to let the Quakers humiliate them again. Bob Hardy noted in his school newspaper column that, "Northeast brought an armada to the game. There were more people in the band than in the Philadelphia Orchestra." Undoubtedly awed by the invaders' strength, GS lost 0-16. A 0-6 loss to Friends Central in game two did little to boost the Buff and Brown confidence.

The Geissingermen finally hit paydirt in game three. Though scoring only once on a pass from Andy Fleschner to Billy Wilson, it was all they would need to walk away with their first win, an 8-0 conquest over Archmere. The magic did not last as the gridders lost to Germantown Friends School 14-18 in their next outing. The game did end on a positive note when center Dave Johnson lived out a lineman's dream by falling on a fumble in the end zone to record the final GS tally.

Dave's valiant effort was undoubtedly inspired by coach Geissinger who provided motivation in a number of ways. "Geis would throw his hat down when he became upset. That was colorful! I think Tom Landry tried to copy Mr. Geissinger and his hat years later with the Dallas Cowboys."

Dave may have feared being the target of a flying fedora or he might have ardently wished not to become a subject of one of Geis's practice maneuvers. "Geis had two GS ladies participate in a practice in 1958 to demonstrate how easily someone could run the ball if the blocking was as it should be. One of them was Patty Hammerstein and the other was Heather Halliday who was Mary Martin's daughter. They ran a couple of off tackle plays."

The play was undoubtedly the 32 or 31 dive, or something similar taken from the carefully crafted, hand drawn blue ditto playbook Geis distributed at the beginning of each season. The pages increased with each game as Geis personalized the plays, giving them easy to remember names such as The Germantown Special or Marshall's Jock. Some argue these have become collector's items, going for big bucks at antique auctions.

Whatever tactic Geis used before the sixth game of the '58 season worked to perfection. GS utilizing two touchdown runs by Billy Wilson and one by Henry Kay exploded to beat Swarthmore 24-0.

The Swarthmore game demonstrated another side of the coaching etiquette and sense of fair play Geis preached. As the school paper noted. "George School was leading Swarthmore 18-0 as the third period ended. At this point, Coach Geissinger took out the entire first team, putting in his second eleven. Henry Kay scored from the five to put the final score at 24-0." Never one to embarrass an opponent, Geis also remembered what it felt like to be on the losing side. Nothing is gained by running up scores and overwhelming an already beaten foe.

George School did not fare as well in the season finale, losing a tough game to Bryn Athyn 0-12. Dave Johnson, realizing the more important values he gained, was not disheartened by the team's 2-5 record. As he readily states, "Regardless of the team's won and loss record, I will remember the strong intensity and dedication among all who participated, the discipline and the basics. The real appeal of football for me was the chance for individual accomplishment in a team environment. Making a key block or beating a double team gives you a great feeling. My experience was positive. Anyone who would suggest the program could have been improved probably missed the point. It was an important part of growing up."

As is so often the case in high school football, records take on a cyclical nature. A strong team graduates leaving the younger, less experienced players to pay their dues and learn the vital lessons all over again. Eventually, these neophytes mature and develop. An increasing number of victories becomes the outward manifestation of their growth. The 1959 season saw several of the '58 rookies putting it all together to compile an impressive 5-3 record. After losing the first two games, the GS offense led by quarterback John McDaniel, found its rhythm and reeled off five straight wins. Key to most of the conquests was the running of the dynamic backfield duo of Robert Hunt and Andy Fleschner.

Geis quickly recognized the potential these two brought to the football field. "Andrew Fleschner was super intelligent, mature, and poised in competition. He was a respected leader who was not afraid to tell other players they weren't doing their jobs. Rob Hunt was a tremendous athlete. This guy was big and fast."

Fleschner's name lit up the scoreboard in the Buff and Brown's big wins over Hun and Pennington. His two touchdowns were all GS needed to upset Hun 12-8. He scampered across the goal line three times in the 20-0 beating of Pennington. Hunt emerged the hero against Germantown Friends. The GS News wrote, "Thundering halfback Rob Hunt celebrated his birthday by scoring two touchdowns and gaining over 200 yards in the 26-0 victory over GFS. He broke loose for a 45 yard TD run on the second play of the game."

In some ways Rob's achievements on the football field were quite understandable. A transfer from Moorestown High School, he had played in a highly competitive program. He was never sorry he made the move to GS. "Compared to my public school experience, football at George School was very low key. There were no big crowds, newspaper articles and photos, pep rallies and bonfires, or adulation from the fans. At Moorestown there were 150 football players and seven coaches. At GS there were thirty players and two coaches. I enjoyed playing at GS because I love the game itself a lot more than all of the 'hoopla'".

Tellingly enough, the game that sticks in Rob's mind most was the 14-25 loss to Bryn Athyn in the season finale. "The Bryn Athyn game was the biggest game I played in. I don't remember very much about the game except for the last play before halftime. We had driven the ball to their ten yard line. I broke through the right side of the line and one defender was between me and the goal line. Unfortunately, he made a nice tackle and time expired before we could score."

Geis had a slightly different version of this game. "Against ANC he broke loose for about fifty yards and that could have been the winning TD but he was grabbed by the ankles. He twisted to get away and really sprained it. On first down inside the ten his sub fumbled and ANC recovered and that was the game."

In some ways, Geis was lucky to have Rob's services for any portion of the game. He played most of the season trying to compensate for a painful injury. "I played the entire season with a separated shoulder. Besides being painful, it prevented me from catching a pass and reduced my tackling ability. I learned to make the most of a bad situation and how to play with a painful injury. These lessons would prove to benefit me during difficult situations in the years to come."

The final whistle ending the Bryn Athyn game also brought the conclusion of another decade of GS football. More lessons were learned, more memories made, and more young boys took a step toward manhood.

The Sixties- a Time of Questioning, Turmoil, and the Arrival of Dusty

The beginning of the sixties was like the calm before a storm. Kennedy was elected, bringing his vision of Camelot to the nation. Chubby Checker encouraged young teens to "Do the Twist". Sixteen year old Bobby Fisher successfully defended his US. chess title. Julie Andrews sang her way through the Austrian Alps. And Dale K. Miller joined the George School football staff.

Now on the surface this new addition appeared a kind and gentle soul, not prone to fits of violence nor dependent upon vague platitudes. Geis knew better. He realized that after six years as head coach at Council Rock High School and a short stint as coach of the Pendell Aces, a semi-pro football team, Dusty was his man. He could instruct even the most hard-nosed and unteachable youth...if he could only remember their names. He was a pure fundamentalist. One of his former players and soon to be coaching colleague, Mike Zettler, used to tell a story about his playing under Dusty at Council Rock. Apparently the young and innocent Mike, manning the defensive end position and wanting to impress his new mentor, asked Dusty which foot he should push off of when rushing the quarterback. Dusty, in his own poetic manner, said, "Son, I don't care if you run or crawl, just get the hell over there and hit him!" Truly this was the type of reflective being every Quaker school seeks.

The combination of Geissinger and Miller worked magic during the 1960 season. After losing their first game by a narrow 6-0 score to Friends Central, the Buff and Brown men came together, winning their next three contests. They followed their 21-0 win over Perkiomen by soundly drubbing Solebury 49-0. In a true offensive explosion, six GS players reached the end zone. Tom Palley, who Geis described as a "free spirit, a great fullback, and a power back with real athletic moves", started the assault scoring on a 40 yard run. Norm Ziegler then pulled in a twenty yard TD pass from John Syrett who followed suit by scrambling 20 yards to pay dirt

Syrett's productivity came as little surprise to Geis. "John was even smaller than John McDaniel but cut from the same mold. He was intelligent, poised, and a real competitor. His left handed passes often looked like a dying quail but John probably had a higher percentage of any of the quarterback's when we needed a play on third down to keep a drive alive."

Rounding out the scoring against Solebury, Lloyd Betts tallied on a twenty yard run and Horky Townsend rumbled 10 yards for the fifth TD. Sophomore George Corts made his varsity debut sneaking in from the five yard line. An aspiring football player never forgets these first moments in the limelight. According to George, his lasting memory of GS football was twofold. "I remember as a sophomore, getting in a game and scoring my first varsity touchdown; also scoring in the fourth quarter to tie Hun School on Parents Day."

The following week, GS only put six points on the board but it was enough to come away with a 6-0 win over Germantown Friends. A heartbreaking 20-22 loss to Pennington and an 8-8 tie of Hun set up what would be a convincing finale with Bryn Athyn. Tim Aston scored first for GS on a 60 yard run. Lloyd Betts then caught a short pass from Syrett to climax a 55 yard drive and give the visitors a 12-0 halftime lead. Palley would widen the margin on a four yard TD jaunt early in the third quarter. Norm Ziegler iced the game with a 20 yard reverse run to put GS ahead 26-0. The rest, as they say, is history.... GS 26- BA 8.

Undoubtedly, Geis and Miller were as animated in victory as they were in defeat. In fact, Phil Brick, senior defensive and offensive back who Geis called a "real fine athlete," did not hesitate when asked to recount his most lasting memory of George School football. "Geis! He was my first real coach in a sport and although he yelled and screamed, he showed me I could do better. I wanted to please him. He wanted to win and I liked that. I liked him."

Phil, as with so many players before, carried away the real benefits. He sensed any screaming at him aimed to make him a better person, "I loved the sport of football well before I got to George School, but to play it on an organized team was a tremendous and wonderful feeling. The biggest reward was being a member of a team, which has stayed with me to this day. I enjoyed the contact, the hitting and the chance to throw that touchdown pass or to make an interception and return it all the way. Most of all I liked the chance to prove myself- to challenge and test myself. I had no desire to play any other fall sport except football and I wanted to perform, if not excel, and gain respect as I was both younger and smaller than any others in my class that played."

Having logged two straight winning seasons, the inevitable fortunes of GS football wars caught up with the Buff and Brown in 1961. Graduation once again depleted the proven vet pool. Though possessing several quality athletes, Geis realized the learning process would start anew. The first big problem faced by the coaching braintrust was the lack of bulk. As George Corts good naturedly recalls, "I developed a slogan for our team of 1961, 'We may not be big but we're slow.' And how about calling us the 'Earthquakers'." The records show that GS averaged 164 pounds in the line and 152 pounds in the backfield, not the kind of figures that would strike fear in the hearts of such opponents as Haverford School and Hun School.

Pete Taylor in his column in the GS News dissected the GS strategic approach, saying, "Captained by a 138 pound Merit Scholarship semi-finalist, the team is trying to make up for its lack of size by befuddling the opponents with some scientific razzle dazzle. So far they have developed a "shotgun offense" with a "slotback". As soon as they can find time to work in a lonesome end, some deep double reverses, a smattering of 'halfback options' and a few 'Statue of Liberty' plays, they will have attained the zenith of erudite football."

The acclaimed 'scholarly' approach failed to produce a touchdown in the first three games as the Georgians lost to Haverford School, Friends Central and Perkiomen School. By game four, the Quakers were hungry to take on their city counterparts, Germantown Friends. Playing solid defense, GS shut down every offensive attempt by GFS. A third quarter 15 yard scoring strike from Harby Norris to George Corts would be all the scoring the Geissingermen would need to capture an 8-0 win in front of a large Parents Day crowd.

After tying Pennington and losing 6-28 to a loaded Hun team, Geis prepped his charges to take on Bryn Athyn in a season ending 'make or break' game. Key to success for the Buff and Brown battlers would be stopping Bryn Athyn's mammoth runner, Bruce Gladdish. George Corts developed his own personal strategy. "It was the last game of the season as tradition would have it, and Bryn Athyn was loaded. They had a running back that was bigger than anyone on our team, and to complete the analogy to my slogan, he was fast. I was playing (strong?) safety. It seemed every time he touched the ball, he chewed up yardage while our guys took shot after shot at him. To my great dismay, he always managed to get to our last defender: me. That day I made a career decision: hit him high- around the shoulders- and ride it out. After all, he had already picked up 8-10 yards by the time he got to me. What's five more? It was actually suggested by the coaching staff at half-time that perhaps I should consider hitting him low. Hey, I had the pros to consider!"

In actuality, GS managed to contain Gladish for all but one scoring play. Thanks to a six yard touchdown burst by Horky Townsend, the "Earthquakers" completed the tough season in grand style, holding Bryn Athyn to a 6-6 tie.

Unfortunately for George it would also be his last game as an active player. A serious neck injury sustained in wrestling sidelined him for the 1962 season. Typical of Geis, he knew how upsetting such a setback can be to an athlete of George's caliber so he enlisted his aid as an assistant coach his senior year. Such awareness on Geis's part did not go unnoticed by his charges. As Steve Gessner, tackle on the '91 team, says, "I have tremendous admiration for Geis who was a thoughtful, supportive, kind but determined coach."

This author (John Gleeson) was one of the kids lucky enough to benefit from Geis's insight and get to perform for a player I had greatly admired in George Corts. George good naturedly recalls some of my youthful unskilled antics. "After being sidelined with a neck fracture during a wrestling match, I was asked to help out with the younger football players the following season. I actually coached an away game solo, no other coaches. That is where I saw the greatest individual play (stunt) of all time. This kid named John Gleeson ran a pass route. He had double coverage and the ball was thrown a little high. John batted the ball higher in the air and simultaneously got sandwiched by the defenders, crashing to the ground. Instantly, he popped back up and, incredibly, caught the ball. It's a true story, print it."

Obviously, George's injury was more serious than the doctors had at first determined. He suffered from hallucinations. What he probably saw was me desperately grabbing for one of my bodily parts that had been dislodged by some behemoth opponent. My actual entry into the GS football wars was humble at best. I remember, in the fall of '61, standing in line dressed in white shorts and a T-shirt while Stan Sutton asked those of us who had scored sufficient points on our PE test what sport we wanted to play. I had no option. In addition to a strong desire to test myself, I also had a sister who was a senior cheerleader. I feared that I would have been pompomed to death if I selected any other activity. When I said football, Mr. Sutton just looked at my scrawny, muscle free, 111 pound body and made a notation on my chart. Later that spring Stan Sutton retired and, to this day, I wonder if he had not looked at me and thought, "If this is the future of George School football, I better call it a career."

Having eagerly put on whatever pads I could figure out, I awkwardly maneuvered myself in the direction of the cub football field. There I met Dusty and his faithful companion, Mike Zettler. Miller stared me in the eye and said, "MacGregor, I think your pads are on backwards." It wasn't until later that I realized he was not staring at my eyes but the label on my helmet. Shortly thereafter, Dusty also retired from football coaching.

Geis must have been made of sterner stuff. He not only fathomed my presence in football but he survived an 0-7 season in 1962. Though featuring some big rugged lineman in Ted Nichols, Tom Turner, Sam Sullivan, Dave Pusey, Will Aufderhyde, Dale Adkins and Randy Cleaver, as well as a capable backfield with Lance Rembar, Marc Acuff and John Ambler, the offense could never get in rhythm. Close losses to Perkiomen, Friends Central, and

Germantown Friends by a total of ten points indicated the hard luck encoun-tered by the Buff and Brown men.

One emerging star who weathered it through the 62 season was soph-omore Steve Hancock, son of Joe (30) and brother of Joe, Jr. and Danny. Unfortunately, Steve felt the pressure to succeed in a personally unfamiliar territory. "In most respects, I played football because of tradition. My dad played it, my brothers and cousins played it. I didn't want to let that tradition down. My sophomore year they put me in a lot of varsity games. I really wanted to play more J.V. games and not have the responsibility. That sophomore year was hard. I played as I was told but got roughed up pretty bad."

The 140 pound running back grew and matured from his experience. Most importantly, Steve gained a greater self-awareness. "I certainly learned about myself and my capabilities, good or bad. If I hesitated on a crucial play, whether on a tackle or carrying the ball, my team and teammates were affected directly."

For a young neophyte, no matter how tough or genetically graced, the world of football can be a scary place. Just learning where to stand, let alone what to do if a play comes your way can be confusing at best. Steve learned under 'varsity' fire. "I did learn about myself a lot, especially under the pres-sure of half a dozen guys coming around my corner while I was on defense. Geis kept telling me, 'all I want you to do is turn the play in so they don't go wide. Just go five or ten feet in and stand there'. I never could really get the concept. I kept going for the ball, and sure enough, they went for the side line and down field. I realized fast enough, I didn't have the 'killer instinct', nor did I ever really fancy too much contact. However, I did find myself, often to my surprise, placing myself in the way of certain pain when I knew I was between the ball carrier, two or three blockers and the goal posts. I have found myself doing that same thing as an adult, not literal pain but confrontational stuff, like at my work or at my former school board activities. I always recognize the situation and basically respond to it that way."

In addition to the 'making' of a top varsity player, two other major occur-rences did come about during the tough '62 campaign. Stock in Old Grand Dad soared, with major sales coming in Bucks County. Also, the Penn Jersey

League formed. For the first time GS could compete for a championship and all-team recognition in a well-balanced league of seven teams. Joining GS were Solebury, Perkiomen, Friends Central, Germantown Friends, Pennington Prep, Hun, and Bryn Athyn Academy.

In 1963 several of us on the '62 Junior Varsity joined the now seasoned vet Steve Hancock on varsity. Bob Waters came on board to help coach the line and teach the "Bird dogs" a few tricks. I had buffed up to a robust 138 pounds and was forever grateful that very few strong winds blew across our field or I might have ended up in the middle of a Bordentown Military Academy practice. We lost our season opener to Solebury 12-14. In actuality, the score was GS 12- Bryant Mitchell 14. We scored first when Ian Vickery hit Scott Griscom with a six yard pass. Mitchell retaliated with a 60 yard TD run. Fred Craven dived in for the two point conversion giving Solebury an 8-6 lead. In the third quarter, I lived out a kid dream when Rick Griscom and Will Aufderhyde opened a hole in the Solebury line allowing me to score from 12 yards out. Mitchell retaliated again, this time for a 65 yard TD jaunt.

After being bested 0-16 by Perkiomen, the Buff and Brown ended its twelve game winless streak by upending Friends Central 12-0. The school newspaper described the first tally saying, "After a scoreless first period Vickery marched his team brilliantly to a touchdown. The running of fullback Rob Lyons and halfback John Gleeson spurred the drive. The team hit pay dirt when Vickery dropped back and fired a 20-yard scoring aerial to (Buzzy) Marshall." (GS News Oct. 25, 1963) Steve Hancock iced the victory going in for a score from ten yards out early in the fourth quarter.

The victory only seemed to whet our appetites. The following week we faced Germantown Friends in our big homecoming game. According to the GS News, "Halfback John Gleeson, sprung loose by tackle Dale Adkin's block, raced 70 yards for a touchdown, in the opening minutes of play. Steve Hancock accounted for the other score on a 10-yard end run." (GS News Nov. 1963) Who says fear is not a prime motivator? Unfortunately, GFS doubled our output to win 28-16. Three more losses closed out the season and left us with a good deal to ponder over the next nine months.

As seniors we returned in the fall with a mission, bring gridiron respect-ability back. As co-captains Steve and I were to provide the leadership. Ian Vickery, or Big Vic as he called himself, was to supply the brains. Carl Croft, Scott Griscom, Jeff Pearlman, and Rob Lyons were to spark the offense. The only problem was who would supply the bulk. Big Vic drew double duty, weighing in as the heaviest kid on the team at a whopping 170. The line only averaged 167 pounds. Thanks to Vic, the backfield averaged 164.

The season started with two disappointing last second losses to Solebury 13-14 and Perkiomen 18-20. In both cases our opponents rallied late in the game to pull out a win. Against Friends Central in game three, the Buff and Brown decided not to let history repeat itself a third time, scoring early and often. Steve Hancock tallied first, racing around right end for a TD with only four minutes gone in the game. In the second quarter, "Ian Vickery hit pay dirt on a 15-yard keeper over the middle" (GS News, Oct. 1964). Though weighty, Big Vic must have been stealthy. Rob Lyons powered his way for a fifteen yard TD. Vickery hooked up with Scott Griscom for the final GS score, assuring the 26-6 win.

In our next game we ruined Germantown Friends' homecoming when we rallied to score two TDs to take a 12-6 victory. A late breaking edition of the Philadelphia Inquirer reported that, "George Gleeson (30 yard run) and Ian Dickery (one yard plunge) tallied George School touchdowns." The Buffians were always favorites with the local press. Bruce Evans of the Bucks County Courier Times presented a more accurate, if somewhat colorful account. "The second play of the fourth quarter produced George School's first touchdown. Gleeson gathered in a Vickery swing pass from his left halfback position and raced 34 lengths for the score. After holding Germantown following the kickoff, The Buff and Brown of Coach Geissinger began a march on their 43 yard line that produced the deciding victory. Vickery, whose mother teaches Russian at George School, looked like Khruschev evading the new regime as he scram-bled around while seeking to find open receivers. With two men holding on to his midsection, and while falling to the ground, he lofted a long pass that was hauled in by Gleeson, who duplicated the wizardry by catching the pass while falling backwards with a man on him." (Bucks County Courier Times Oct. 1964) From here, Big Vic needed only to wave his magic scepter and transport himself one yard into the end zone for the winning score. It's amazing that two GFS defenders figured out that his weak spot was his Achilles waist.

The taste of victory must have proven pleasing as we thumped Pennington 19-7 the following week. Again, Bruce Evans of the Courier was there to pen his flowing prose. "'Give us Vickery or give us death.' George School fans led this prophetically-tuned historical retort Saturday afternoon on their campus as Ian Vickery along with colonial namesake Steve Hancock, led their revolutionists to a 19-7 'tar and feathering' of visiting Pennington School." (Bucks County Courier, Nov. 1964) The GS News offered a more direct report. "Behind the power of Steve Hancock's ground gaining, GS rolled over Pennington Prep 19-7. On the fourth play from scrimmage, Hancock romped 32 yards to give the Buff and Brown an early lead." (GS News Oct, 1964) Obviously, the scared kid of two years earlier had gotten a good feel for the game of football.

Despite a sound 6-27 thumping at the hands of Hun the following week, we were eager to do battle with Bryn Athyn and avenge the 6-42 loss of the previous year. Our spirits dimmed a bit when Steve broke his ankle during practice and was deemed unfit to play in the game. Trying to convert disaster into motivation Geis told us that if we won we would give Hancock the game ball. All agreed!

The showdown, staged at Bryn Athyn in front of a crowd of over 600 fans, proved a classic. BA featured the hard charges of star running back Ivan Willie. But we had Big Vic. Willie scored first on a 36 yard first quarter run. George School countered when Vickery plunged into the end zone on the first play of the second stanza. Willie opened the second half scampering 68 yards for the Swedinborghian's second tally. Not to be denied, on the first play from scrimmage following the ensuing kickoff, Vickery found Scott Griscom for a 66 yard pass and run touchdown. Willie retaliated again, scoring on a two yard run.

With only a few minutes left in the game Big Vic went to work, guiding the Buff and Brown warriors down to the Bryn Athyn five yard line. From there, "the Russian field general tossed five yards to Nicky DeGraff for the final score. Then he hit Griscom on a look-in pattern for the decisive score." (Bucks County Courier Times November 1964)

Geis will always relish this moment. "I always thought I missed an opportunity in the spotlight in the ANC game. When we scored, I called time just to make sure we had the right play going for two. ANC people filled the other side; our whole school on ours. TV cameras focused on the GS quarterback and coach- going over the play decision. Vickery walked over and I met him at the thirty yard line. I said, 'We go with the Salem pass!' Vickery replied, 'No sweat!' and walks back to the huddle. He didn't need a drink because the only time he ran on a football field was from fright! The whole scene may have taken 10 seconds. So much for time in the spotlight."

With the 20 to 18 win, we finalized our record at 4-3, George School's first winning season in four years. Coach Geissinger was succinct in praising our efforts. "Of all the teams I coached, this is the one I was most proud of." That was all the reward most of us needed...that and the blessing of Big Vic.

By the time the 1965 season rolled around, the dramatic win over Bryn Athyn undoubtedly moved to the category of history as the new Buff and Brown gridders prepared for battle. The first most notable change coming about was the adoption of a new mascot. Thirsting for a more inspirational battle cry, the student body opened up a poll welcoming any possible suggestions. When such names as "Fighting Quaker Bonnets" and "Friendly Persuaders" failed to ignite the masses, the school turned to the animal world, eventually agreeing upon the "Cougars".

History of another sort, however, was taking center stage. Changes were rapidly consuming the nation. Kennedy's assassination in '63 shocked the American public and blasted the round table right out of Camelot. Racial strife tore the country apart with riots in Watts leaving 35 dead and 40 million dollars in property damage. Students protested vehemently against the war in Vietnam leaving singers such as Bob Dylan telling us the answer was "Blowin' in the Wind". Obviously, the order and discipline of gridiron wars took second billing.

Sturgis Warner, a GS sophomore in '65 and a player Bob Geissinger dubbed "a prince of a guy and the ultimate team player," captured the tone of the times in his recollections. "It is hard for me, after 32 years, to separate my George School football experience from the overall experience. Certainly, I cannot imagine a more interesting three years in terms of the cultural change.

My sophomore year was the last in the long reign of Richard McFeely. My junior year James Tempest was interim headmaster. And senior year was the first of many for Eric Curtis. The Vietnam war was raging and reaction to it changed dramatically from September 1965 to June of 1968. Civil Rights, too. Martin Luther King was assassinated on April 4th of my senior year. Robert F. Kennedy, too, just two days before graduation. Our class had the very first George School drug bust. Eleven students were severely disciplined and two kicked out for smoking marijuana at an off-campus party. School literally stopped for three days as the administration struggled to come to grips with this terrifying and extremely threatening crisis."

For a young teenager football provided some focus during a very uncertain time. Sturgis recognizes the real importance the game played for him. "I came to George School because it had a football program. Also, because it was co-ed, unlike many boarding schools of that time. Like many, I had a particularly rough junior high school experience and wanted to go away, someplace, anyplace, where no one knew me or my past. A clean slate, a fresh start. In junior high, I was the kind of kid who in a desperate attempt to move up the pecking order would say the wrong thing at the wrong time and get lambasted for it. One day in ninth grade, I decided not to say anything at all. And I didn't. I became very quiet and was so for many years until theater experiences in college started bringing me out of myself. But football I loved. My high school choice had to have it. Westtown, one of the few co-ed boarding school options, was out of the question."

As for so many GS gridiron aspirants, Sturgis started his Buff and Brown career on the Cub level, in itself a humbling experience. "I remember cub football my sophomore year. Getting the crap beat out of us 0-42 by a public school JV team (Council Rock). I played safety. Their fast, muscular backs flicked us off like flies, running any place they damn well pleased. It was cold and rainy that day and I can't remember a more miserable time on a football field. Coach Dusty Miller was as disgusted as I ever saw him--not because we lost, but because we gave up. And we did. We were true prep school pansies that day."

As history proves, the Cub "pansies" would transform into a ferocious breed of Cougar over the next two years. But first they had to wait their turn, watching the '65 varsity post an impressive 3-3-1 record. After losing their first two contests, the Cougars sharpened their claws against Friends Central. Locked in a 0-0 tie for three quarters, GS erupted for two final period tallies. According to the School News, the gridders beat Friends Central 13-0 on "touchdowns scored by offensive spark plugs Chip Stone and Nick DeGraff. With eight minutes left in the game Stone scored on a four yard run off-tackle to give GS a 6-0 lead. Five minutes later, DeGraff with legs kicking like pistons went fifteen yards around end for the home team's second TD." (GS News Oct. 29, 1965)

Liking the taste of victory, the following week the Cougars treated an Alumni Day crowd with a convincing 26-7 thumping of Germantown Friends. Ken Strehle dashed 9 yards for the first tally. Junior quarterback Jed Monego then hooked up with Jim Heisler and Chip Stone for two TD aerials. Stone finished the scoring rushing 55 yard to pay dirt.

The Cougars ran the win streak to three games, beating Pennington 12-6 on a Ken Strehle 1 yard run and a 19 yard pass from Monego to DeGraff. The GS News credited the offensive line for their part in the victory. "Offensively the interior line, Dave Pratt, Dave Miller and Bryant Musser provided good pass protection and crisp blocks on running plays."

Come 1966, many of the victims of the Cub Football Council Rock slaughter had perfected their skills and gained the necessary confidence. They were ready to test their mettle on the varsity level. The move proved as exciting as it was scary for Sturgis Warner. "I remember my junior year. Making the varsity. Heady accomplishment in itself. One year earlier the varsity guys seemed so big, so tough, so good. And here I was starting at end."

The season opener served notice that these new Cougars packed a gridiron wallop. No fewer than five Buff and Brown men crossed the goal line as GS amassed 341 yards of offense in besting Solebury 37-0. Ken Strehle, Roger Eareckson, Doug Stevens, Chris Stark and Elliot Altman all scored for the home team.

As far as assistant coach Dusty Miller was concerned the touchdowns came from Hamilton, Spaulding and Riddel. Names were not his forte. Apparently, his Air Force boxing career affected him more than anyone suspected. Jed Monego described Dusty's dilemma in his column in the GS News,

"A visitor to practice would be quite shocked when Dusty calls for "Wilson" and Doug Stevens comes jogging in. A few such nicknames which have stuck are "Shlockmeyer", and "Steelwagon" for Stu Steelman, "Widdington" for Jim Waddington and "Staley" for Ken Strehle. If he cannot think of a name, Mr. Miller simple mumbles "Wadamar" under his breath and forgets the whole thing."

Getting a nickname from Dusty almost served as a medal of honor. You had been lifted from the depth of anonymity. As Sturgis Warner relates, "Dusty could never remember names. He dubbed me "Humphrey", a name that stuck with my teammates and others the rest of the year. I liked it. A lot. Much preferable to the derogatory ones I had been called in Junior High."

His new moniker would not be the only thing that would stick to the young receiver. He demonstrated a real penchant for catching passes. The school newspaper summed up the Cougars' second victory of the season saying, "Jed Monegos' two TD passes to Sturgis Warner led the Cougars to a 14-0 win over host Germantown Friends October 28. Monego completed six of 13 passes for 204 yards and two touchdowns of 50 and 23 yards to Warner."

Sturgis will long remember this game. "Roger Eareckson was the other end and the team's star player. Our big threat. "The Eareckson Special" was the bomb play called many times, often with success. Against Germantown Friends, "The Warner Special" was called because of double and triple teaming on Eareckson. It resulted in my first George School touchdown. I caught another one that day in a 14-0 win."

The following week "The Eareckson Special" took over as Roger caught two Jed Monego passes in a big victory over Pennington. Roger's catches of 70 and 53 yards led the way as the Cougars romped to a 25-7 win. The scores came as no surprise to Geis. "Roger was a split end who could run all day. He was our big threat on offense. Jed had a great touch throwing the ball deep to Roger."

Not all of Geis's evaluations were positive, a fact Sturgis Warner put into perspective. "The next game, I believe against Hun, I somehow ended up at cornerback--I think because of an injury. They scored twice on me, their end blowing straight by me both times on bombs. Geis was livid after the second one -- screaming and carrying on in front of everybody. You learn to take the bad with the good. I never played cornerback again."

Falling to arch-rival Bryn Athyn 24-30 in the season finale did little to nullify a good season. Like Sturgis, the Cougars basked in the glory and learned from their mistakes. The following season would prove just how far they had grown as the Cougars made GS history becoming the first undefeated football team. Geiss knew the prospects were excellent and solicited Dusty Miller and Mike Zettler to make the most of the talent. "This team was composed of a lot of big guys with above average ability. Dusty and Mike Zettler really helped me challenge these guys. All of them came to play on Saturday but needed to be pushed to develop their skills during the week."

The push made a definite impression on Sturgis' cranial cap. "I remember training camp my senior year. Geis brought Mike Zettler in to work with the line. Mike, then in his early twenties, had gone to George School for a year or two, left, and ended up playing football at Council Rock. Mike was a big part of our success. He worked us like we had never been worked before--yelling, prodding, threatening, challenging our limits, our wills, our psyches, berating us with humor and tough love. We hit the dummies like we had never hit dummies before. His sessions were brutal, but we loved working with him. We knew how good he was for us. Mike had other obligations during the season and was only able to make a few of our games. But after the season we all chipped in and bought him a bowl engraved with our names thanking him for our undefeated season."

David Allison, tight end and defensive end on the '67 team, shared Sturgis' appraisal, "My most lasting memory was certainly the fact that the team my senior year was the first to be undefeated in the school's history. Mr. Geissinger, Dusty Miller and Mike Zettler were a wonderful coaching threesome."

The coaching trio recognized the individual talent on the team. According to Geis, "Glenn Betts was an outstanding athlete who was great in competition. Guard Sam Holden was a tough competitor. Stuart Steelman was the biggest, gifted athlete at GS. David Allison was an outstanding tight end and defensive end who could have made division three or two teams. Quarterback Sig

Hersloff was a free spirit but was most poised in competition and had a great touch throwing short or deep. Doug Stevens was a bright guy and fine athlete who had outstanding stamina and could run all day. Dusty and I used to say, 'Just run Stevens, don't think'."

After tying Wilmington 6-6 in the opener, Stevens and his teammates did run...like wildfire. They bested Solebury in game two 46-0. Stevens tallied three times. Eldon Foster scurried 88 yards for another TD. Sturgis Warner and Steve Waddington each hauled in TD bombs from Hersloff.

Game three proved a bitter-sweet affair. Stan Sutton passed away on Wednesday October 11th. On Saturday the Cougars faced Perkiomen, a team that had whipped them five straight times. The game ranks high in Sturgis' memory. "I remember a game halfway through the season. Former George School Athletic Director Stanley Sutton had just died. Geis had to miss our game to attend the funeral. None of us had known Mr. Sutton. But assistant coach Dusty Miller gave us a speech before the game that sent us out on the field as up as any team I've ever been a part of. He talked about how much Mr. Sutton had meant to Geis, how he was Geis's mentor, he talked about Sutton's values, he talked about Geis and what a truly special person he was, and how it was our duty, our obligation to go out there and play some football. We charged out there sky high, full of piss, vinegar and adrenaline. Our first offensive play I steamrolled the defensive back covering me even though the play was run to the other side of the field. The other team didn't know what hit them."

For the record, the final score read GS 7- Perkiomen 6. Sig Hersloff's 42 yard pass to Mark Hollowell followed by Glenn Betts' extra point kick provided the margin of victory. Hersloff completed 7 of 13 passes for 102 yards. "Vicious tackling by co-captain Dave Williams and Stu Steelman led the Cougar defense." (GS News Oct. 20, 1967)

The victory over Perkiomen proved inspirational as the Cougars went on to outscore their next three opponents 93-12. The Cougars beat Friends Central 33-6, Germantown Friends 34-6, and Pennington 26-0. Against Pennington, GS gained 234 yards of offense compared to 44 yards for the Red Raiders. The only obstacles standing between the Cougars and history were Hun and Bryn Athyn.

Always a tough opponent, Hun School gave the Cougars a real run for their money. Hun scored first to take a 7-0 lead. Late in the first half, Doug Stevens scored on a five yard run bringing on Glenn Betts to try to tie the score. Dave Allison recounts the dramatic moment, saying, "I can remember Glenn Betts missing an extra point kick to tie the game. He rekicked it due to a penalty and that time he made it." Stu Steelman added more heroics to preserve the tie when he tackled the Hun quarterback on the Cougar one yard line late in the fourth quarter.

For a season finale, the Cougars had to take on Bryn Athyn on the Lions' home turf. The night before the game the entire student body gathered to give the team support at the pep rally. As co-captain Sturgis, would be called upon to address the adoring fans. "I remember the bon-fire rally the night before the Bryn Athyn game, 1967. Dave Williams and I had to come up with a skit depicting what we were going to do to Bryn Athyn the next day. I remember little about it except I had to die a particularly gruesome death which I did quite realistically. Afterward, Geis told the large, cheering crowd that he hoped we played football better than we acted. I felt a tiny part of me feeling hurt because I thought I did a pretty damn good job. It was my first performing experience. Two years later I started acting in college and have been doing it ever since-- although now I'm mostly directing."

Where Geis, the movie critic, failed to appreciate the subtleties of the young actor's performance, he undoubtedly gave two thumbs up to the Cougar's 13-0 win over Bryn Athyn, a game featuring a 52 yard TD jaunt by Doug Stevens. The undefeated season was official.

Where being undefeated undoubtedly bears a special place in the players' recollections, it's the intangible rewards Sturgis Warner values most. "In retrospect, George School had the perfect program for me. The level of play was challenging but not overwhelming. It was a level where I and others could have some success. Kids who had some other interests could have success. We didn't have to dedicate our entire lives to the game just to make the team. Football, like other team sports, can teach a kid the concept of teamwork. Of ensemble. The sense that a unit, when really meshing together, can always go further than the sum of the individuals that make it up. It teaches focus, grit, determination, success, failure, and never taking anything for granted. And, hopefully along the way, it's fun."

The 1967 team proved a tough act to follow. Trying to match the success of the undefeated Cougars obviously would be a difficult task at best. Though proven leaders such as Sturgis Warner had gone the cap and gown route, Coach Geissinger, having a good pool of talent from which to draw, felt optimistic. Some of the lessons learned in '67 would surely carry over. Unfortunately, the luck of being injury free did not. The first bad news came when quarterback Sig Hersloff reported to school with mono, an illness that would sideline him his entire senior year. Geis still recalls Sig's courageous attempt to get some playing time. Sig ``bugged me every day to play. He had his dad call to give him permission to play but Blaine Gardner (the school physician) said as long as that spleen was enlarged, he could be seriously hurt in a contact game like football. This guy was special. He could have carried this team."

Sig was not the only starter to taste misfortune. After an opening loss to Wilmington Friends, GS found itself without the services of Sam Walmer, Mark Battersby, Ray Hatchett and Ken Cleaver. To highlight the plight of the injury-prone Cougars, Geis went through four quarterbacks before the season ended. The one seemingly invincible force was captain Dave Williams. According to Geis, "Dave was a really fine football player on both sides of the ball. He was a team leader who was poised and led by making plays in competition."

Not surprisingly, victories were hard to come by in '68. The team did manage to handle Solebury 26-9, and then take two close contests, 7-6 over Friends Central and 14-7 over Pennington. The final 3-4 record left Geis to muse, "This was a team of fine potential that never got off the ground. It seemed like we were starting over on offense all season after Sig and Sam went down. I really didn't have time to really sort out who would be best for the job and the team. My handling of the situation wasn't the best, probably due to the letdown of having the prospects of another great season crushed."

The agony of '68 turned to ecstasy in 1969 mainly due to the emergence of junior Ron Hancox as a real bona fide scoring threat. The Rocket, as he came to be called, managed to twist, turn and dance his way to a 122 point scoring effort, the best in all of Lower Bucks County. He was amply supported by twin brother Don, Larry Potter, Antonio Jackson and Jeff Meredith. Jay Griscom manned the all-important quarterback spot, earning praise from Geis. "He was the QB who came the farthest with his throwing touch on passes. He learned the whole position early in the season and proved to be an outstanding leader who had the complete respect of the team."

The line proved equally capable In Geis's estimation, "Mark Battersby, a guard, was a no-nonsense competitor. Pete Bowers was a great guy and a fine center. Mike Burlingham was a great guy and a very competitive lineman. Peter Moyes was a solid tight end who had the stamina to run all day. Tom Trowbridge was another great guy who gave everything he had every game."

After a 13-27 loss to the always tough Wilmington Friends, the Cougars went on an offensive tear scoring at least twenty points in each of their next four games. A 30-22 win over Solebury was followed by a bizarre 42-42 tie with Perkiomen. The Cougars owned the first half as the mercurial Ron Hancox danced, passed and dazzled the confused Perkiomen defense. In the second half, Perk's version of Fran Tarkenton dodged, scrambled and passed his team all the way back to tie in the closing minutes.

Undoubtedly maddened by the reverse of fortune, the Cougars took their frustration out on Germantown Friends the following week. With the Rocket working on all cylinders, GS swamped the unsuspecting visitors 42-14. Hancox alone accounted for 38 points in the game. Tony Jackson, split end and an individual Geis describes as being a "quality person and athlete" still remembers the Rocket launching, "The biggest game for me was when Ron Hancox scored at least six touchdowns. I played in several games during my junior year in which I was able to make several spectacular catches or caught a pass that won the game."

The GS News concurred with Tony's appraisal. "Our entire offense hinges around the quarterbacking of Jay Griscom and his passing and play calling abilities. At halfback is one of the county's best in Ron Hancox. Ron is leading all Lower Bucks schools in scoring and was selected all-County back of the week for his 38 points against GFS. Catching passes is the job of split-end Tony Jackson and he performs admirably. Underrated and almost unmentioned and virtually uncontrollable on the gridiron is senior Mark Battersby." (GS News Nov. 21, 1969)

The Cougars used their next game, a 22-0 win over Pennington, as a warm-up for their invasion of Hun, a team laden with several behemoths.

Where Hun was big, they were not agile enough to corral The Rocket. Mike Burlingham loved watching the speedster do his best Fred Astaire routine through the entire Hun defense. " Geis was the greatest. Much to my delight, he put in a tackle eligible play that QB Jay Griscom and I worked with considerable success on our befuddled opponents. A highlight was the big game with Hun School. We were overmatched, but Ron Hancox put on an awesome display from his halfback position. One play in particular stands out. He seemingly covered half the field, running back and forth, and eluding the entire Hun team until finally taken down. Wow!"

Hancox's heroics helped GS post a 28-18 upset, setting the stage for the season finale with Bryn Athyn. In a typically hard-fought match, GS bested the men in maroon 14-0 on touchdowns by Larry Potter and Tom "Touchdown" Trowbridge, who ran an intercepted pass in for the Cougar's second tally. The 5-1-1 season proved most satisfying to senior Mike Burlingham. "I guess I initially went out for football because I was eager to participate in a contact sport, with all the exhilaration of gladiatorial combat. I got a sense of pride and belonging and togetherness that was useful to my development. Not to mention all the fun."

All the lessons coming from football are not always a result of great plays or team camaraderie. As with Mike Kosoff and George Corts before, injury presented Tony Jackson with the kind of heart searching scenario no athlete likes to face and only the truly mature can handle. With the graduation of Jay Griscom, Geis entered the 1970 season searching for a quarterback with the physical prowess and leadership ability. Knowing Tony possessed all the essentials, Geis gave him a shot at this key position. Tony, responding with the expected poise and finesse, won the starting job.

Then misfortune reared its ugly head. In Tony's words, "my most lasting memory was without a doubt the devastating, season ending knee injury during my senior year. Like many of my teammates, I played offense and defense. I was the starting QB and defensive back. When I was injured I was playing defensive back and about to hit a tight end who had caught a pass in my zone. One of the Hancox twins hit him before I could and he rolled onto my left knee, snapping ligaments and tearing cartilage. The pain was intensely excruciating and I recall using language I never use to get my helmet off. My knee swelled and I spent a couple days in the infirmary before I had a cast placed on my leg (conservative treatment). I eventually had to have surgery after my first year at Amherst."

Time and a mature outlook allowed Tony to put the injury in perspective by accepting both the agony and ecstasy inherent in sports. "My senior year, Geis wanted me to play quarterback. I gave it my best shot because of my love and respect for Geis. I started out as third string and after several games, I was the starting QB. My lack of experience was evident and I think if I had another year I could have been very effective. It is often stated that sports help build character. I believe that my football team experience helped with the character building because of the parity and the challenge of starting as third string quarterback and becoming first string and then suffering the knee injury which was one of my life challenging experiences."

In some ways, the very paradox confronting the young quarterback marked the entire 1970 season. Against Wilmington Friends, Ron Hancox took the ball on the Cougar's first play from scrimmage and raced 60 yards to pay dirt. His heroics paid off as the Cougars roared past their straight T oriented visitors from Delaware to win 22-14. In the next four games Ron would continue to set a blazing trail. He rushed for 480 yards and averaged over 9 yards a carry. In an interview with school reporter Bernie Komer, Ron explained the secret to his success, "I'm always singing in my mind and playing games because I know that the other guy who is out to get me is only human and I shouldn't get scared because once you get scared you get hurt. My reputation has really helped me a lot, because it may make a man think twice before he hits me, and how he may hit me, and by that time I'm planning my next move for a long gain."

Even with the Rocket exploding, the Cougars could garnish victories in only two of their next six contests. A 44-0 shellacking of Bryn Athyn did help put a dramatic finish on Ron's GS gridiron career. It also brought about an equally dramatic announcement from Bob Geissinger. At least for a while, he was retreating to the comfort of the administrator's lounge. After nineteen years at the helm and hundreds of thankful players later, Geis decided his family had sacrificed enough. It was time to turn the head coaching job on to some young buck.

The Seventies- a Time of
Rapid Adjustment

T he unrest marking the sixties pervaded the seventies like fog covering a mountaintop. Americans, young and old, puzzled over the meaning of such disturbing events as the Kent State massacre, increased bombing in Indochina, and Watergate. Authority and allegiance became questionable forces. Rebellion and individuality were the call of the day.

Amidst the national confusion, the George School gridiron scene remained fairly steady. Young men were still afforded the opportunity of testing their potential in a most challenging environment. The primary difference in 1971 would be their chief mentor. Mike Heverin, '66 graduate and former GS gridder, assumed the awesome responsibility of following Geis as head coach. Mike filled his coaching staff with veterans of the Quaker football wars. Defensive coordinator Fran Bradley played high school ball for Friends Central before moving on to the unfriendly confines of Earlham College. I was the other coach. After graduating from GS, I went on to dazzle the twenty or thirty fans who attended games at Haverford College. Together, our biggest attribute was we had enough fingers to signal to our defensive captains one of Mike's many complicated 4-4 defensive schemes.

The combination of coaches seemed in sync as we hit the victory column in game one, a 22-14 conquest of Germantown Friends. Jeff Clark and Scott

Stein split the quarterbacking chores. Dwayne McKamey and Chris Johnson did most of the running following the blocking of Marc Colcord, Jay Cox, Tim Raynolds and William Forrest.

Any hopes of a Penn-Jersey championship, however, vanished in the next four games as we lost to the Pennsylvania School for the Deaf, Hun, Pennington and Wilmington. Coach Heverin showed veteran savvy in explaining the tough streak to the press, "We didn't lose any of those ball games. The clock just ran out on us". (GS News Nov. 10,1971) Dwayne McKamey remained a bright spot scoring 48 points in the first five games and averaging 5.2 yards a carry. The Cougars finished out the season splitting their last two games, a 19-12 win over Perkiomen and a 0-14 loss to ANC.

Whether winning or losing, the players remained spirited. John Mason, junior split end on the '71 team, relished the whole aura surrounding the sport. "The necessary combination of speed, agility and strength appealed to me. Of course, the team concept, with its associated camaraderie and sharing of common goals was important. I also adored the romance of football, clear, crisp autumn days in Bucks County; the crowd and the cheerleaders. It was very attractive to be the gladiator in the arena."

Every gladiator has to first master his trade. For John, the schooling started his sophomore year. "As a wide-eyed sophomore playing defensive end during a big game, I was beaten for a touchdown reception by the opposing wideout. Teammate, senior co-captain Larry Potter got right into my facemask. 'That's your outside responsibility!' he screamed. Then, immediately, 'C'mon Mase. You can play with anyone on this field!' On an ensuing defensive stand, a sweep to my side, the only players between me and their running back were three monstrous, pulling linemen...somehow, I managed to slip through and make the tackle for a short gain. Potter, again, was the first in my face, to lend a hand, 'Now you know what I'm talkin' about', followed by another healthy slap on the shoulder pads."

Needless to say, the young Cougar valued the advice, however terse, he got from the savvy vets. "The indelible values of teamwork and sportsmanship made their greatest impact during that formative sophomore season. Team leaders, Tony Jackson, Ron and Don Hancox, Potter, Jeff "Bruno" Meredith,

Hugh Oldack and Dave Bakkila were true sportsmen, very skilled football players, and, without question, exceptional young men."

A very good student, John also felt he benefited from the coaches' collective wisdom. "Of course, 'it all begins at the top'; to this impressionable fifteen year old, Bob Geissinger, Lew Watts, John Gleeson, and Mike Heverin were genuine, sincere... in retrospect, those coaches defined GS athletics and 'Mind the Light': Humble, hard-working humanists. Highly talented technicians. Ultra-competitive communicators."

In the '72 season, John's senior year, Coach Heverin used all his technical knowledge to help the Cougars log an impressive 4-3-1 record. John summed up the season, saying, "My memories are vague, but I believe my senior year was bookended by two fantastic victories. Dwayne McKamey ran back the opening kickoff for a TD, and went on to account for nearly 400 yards in combined offense in the first game of the season. And our final GS game was a come-from-behind victory over rival Academy of the New Church, with outstanding performances by Jeff Clark, Tim Raynolds, Chris Johnson and John Oldach."

The time may have altered his recollection of the "facts" but John's memory of the success is accurate. In the opening 22-6 win over Germantown, GS featured 17 returning lettermen as well as promising newcomer Tom O'Connell. The young sophomore scored the first Cougar touchdown on a two yard plunge. Scotty Stein hooked up with speedy Wayne Hudson to notch a 52 yard aerial score in the second quarter. Dwayne McKamey raced 26 yards to clinch the victory. The final tally showed GS with 223 offensive yards to only 88 for GFS.

After two miscues cost the Cougars a win against Mitchell Prep, O'Connell and company roared back against Pennsylvania School for the Deaf. O'Connell and Wayne Hudson scored early but the real heroics came late in the game. After PSD went ahead 14-13, "dependable O'Connell took a Scotty Stein handoff and ran into the endzone from the 9 yard line. O'Connell converted on the two point attempt and the Cougars held on to win 20-14." (GS News Oct. 20, 1972)

Losses to Pennington and Wilmington, followed by a 26-7 victory over Perkiomen, set up the season finale with ANC, the game John Mason will long remember. "In the first quarter, Bill 'Stumpy' Forrest picked up a fumble and trucked 34 yards for a TD. You know who...Tom O'Connell scored the extra point to give GS a lead of 8-0." (GS News) Jeff Clark raced 27 yards for another tally and then completed a 19 yard scoring strike to John Oldach. Scott Stein contributed three interceptions as the Cougars prevailed by a 28-6 score.

Coach Heverin decided to go out a winner, retiring at the end of the season to pursue a managerial job with General Motors. Waiting to assume head coaching duties was Roger Eareckson, another former GS grid hero. Roger relished the thought of the upcoming 1973 season. "It should be a good year. The six returning lettermen come in significant spots with all-conference running back Tom O'Connell, defensive tackle Wayne Matthews, and honorable mention defensive back Scott Stein. We can build around those men and the other lettermen Ron Downs, Craig Sotres and Jon Powell give us good leadership." (GS News Sept. 27, 1973)

What even the optimistic coach Eareckson could not foresee was the arrival of talented newcomers Dave Lehner and Matt Saunders. Lehner was a long legged speed merchant who bolstered an already strong backfield. Saunders, who transferred to GS his senior year, proved to be a solid lead blocker and devastating middle linebacker.

True to the coach's prediction, all the components for a great season were in place. The Cougars started strong, shutting out Penn-Jersey opponent Germantown Friends, 13-0. A tough loss to Mitchell in which O'Connell got the only GS score was followed by a solid 27-14 conquest of the Pennsylvania School for the Deaf.

The next encounter with Pennington proved crucial. A victory would place the Cougars in line for a shot at the Penn-Jersey League title. Ron Downs, tackle on the team who went on to play for the Naval Academy, knew the importance of this match-up. "I think the year we split the Penn-Jersey title every game was huge! But that year, I believe, '74 we had a big game against Pennington."

The Cougars dominated both sides of the line, surrendering only 63 yards and three first downs to the Red Raiders. Tom O'Connell provided the offensive spark, tallying on runs of 3 and 16 yards. Two weeks later the dependable workhorse would reel off TD scampers of 73 and 37 yards to lead GS to a 13-3 win over Perkiomen.

The season finale against ANC bore twice the importance as usual. A win kept the coveted shoe trophy at George School. It also earned them a co-championship in the Penn-Jersey League. On Friday, the entire school let out at noon and boarded the fan buses waiting outside of Main Building. Just as the bus drivers were getting into gear the disheartening news reached the Dean's Office. The game was scheduled for Saturday. Coach Eareckson and the fired-up Cougars had arrived at ANC only to find the team practicing and the cheerleaders setting up the evening pep rally.

The one day delay ironically acted as an inspiration. The Cougars dominated play from the opening kick-off with many players contributing to the 30-6 win. According to coach Eareckson, "What made the win all the nicer, in addition to winning the co-championship, is the fact that it was a team victory. We scored five times and each TD was by a different player."

For the record, Tom O'connell scored on a 1 yard run, Matt Saunder on a 2 yard plunge, Jon Powell on a two yard sneak, Jim Seabrook on a 32 yard pass from Powell, and Scott Stein on an 89 yard run.

To a young sophomore, the season was special. Jim Seabrook will never forget the feeling. "Looking back I'm most proud of being part of one of the few league championship teams. The game I recall most was from that season. It was a home game. I don't remember the team we played nor the score. The remarkable thing was the people who attended. They ringed the entire field. Usually, I was focused on the game and didn't notice the sidelines but I remember being on the field and slowly looking around at all the people. I was thinking, ``This is really cool that they are all here to see us."

Any dreams of repeating as co-champs in 74 received an early dampening. A sound 6-42 thumping at the hands of Wilmington and two 8-8 ties left the Cougars winless after three games. In both of the tie games, GS put points on the board only to have them nullified by penalties.

After a little searching for the inner gridiron light, the Cougars rallied, winning four of their next five games including a 30-7 conquest of ANC. As satisfying as the climax of his senior season proved, it's the intangibles Ron Downs values most. "I remember the feeling of running out onto the playing field with usually a sparse crowd on hand but having the feeling that anything was possible. I also remember the relationship between the players as well as the players and coaches. From football, I learned how to compete and to win with dignity and lose with dignity. You carry that with you on and off the field. I loved it as a kid and only dreamed of playing varsity football. I grew up watching high school football on Friday nights. Playing college football was beyond my dreams."

Jim Seabrook would certainly concur. His senior year, 1974, the Cougars did not fare well in the win column. Their only victory was a 13-0 win over Saint Gabriel in the season opener. Quarterback Kurt Bergland scored on a 7 yard run and then found split end Don Rice for a TD pass. After the opening game coach Eareckson installed a two platoon system as well as a wishbone offense. The transition appeared tough for the Cougar players as they were shutout in five of their last six games.

Despite the losses, Jim Seabrook still valued what football offered him. "Sports in general and certainly football gave me self-confidence and made me feel good about myself. Being a valuable part of a team working toward a common goal is a skill that can apply to any situation. Football appealed to me also for its combination of physical and mental explosiveness. Everything pointed to that moment of contact on every play. So many people at George School excelled academically and creatively in the arts that I was glad to have one area of my school life where I excelled. Being named all conference flanker and middle linebacker told me that others appreciated my hard work."

Ron Downs and James Seabrook hit upon the real intangibles of a George School football career. Every gridder suffered the physical pain inherent in the sport, the agony of losing a close encounter, and the humiliation coming from one's own mistakes. Yet, the rewards were great. The main one included the knowledge that you were not alone. Whether raising your hand in victory or walking humbly away in defeat, you shared the experience with your teammates. Many became lifelong friends. Above all else, you came away with a feeling of self-confidence. You had survived in a physically and emotionally challenging arena. It helped instill in you a feeling of self-identity. George School is a very diverse place, featuring many talented students, each excelling in their own field of endeavor. Football gave many of us our own testing ground, a place to discover our own particular skills and abilities. The feeling went way beyond just participating in what was increasingly becoming a national pastime. It was a very personal expression of your own self-worth.

The lessons James had learned from his Cougar gridiron days obviously impacted his younger brother Wes. In the 1976 season Roger Eareckson moved south to assume a position as coach and athletic director in the Maryland school district. Though undoubtedly not relishing leaving his retirement from the sidelines, Geis answered the call and once again assumed the head coach position. Fortunately, having a young quarterback of Wes Seabrook's caliber undoubtedly eased the pain of long nights of preparation and any postgame soul-searching Geis would experience. In the first two games of the season Wes ran for 176 yards and passed for 95 more as the Cougar's defeated Germantown 14-0 before losing 8-16 to Mitchell Prep. Don Rice was the recipient of two of those touchdown aerials. After the opening victory Geis was quick to credit the play of his unsung heroes upfront. "The entire line played well, especially Russ Haines. He had several unassisted tackles in that game."

Willie Twyman, one of the linemen earning the head coach's praise, took special delight in the team's success, particularly the efforts of the younger Seabrook. "On kickoff returns, I was Wes Seabrook's blocker. During the game the kicker was laying his kicks down ten yards in front of Wes. There were a few times when I handled some of the short kicks, but Wes was definitely faster. So, I finally told Wes to move up ten yards and when he got the ball to follow me straight up the field. When the ball was kicked it landed right in Wes's hands. I turned and started to run as fast as I could straight up the field. At some point it seemed that I made it through the heavy traffic and slowed up to see where Wes was. As I turned my head, Wes went running past and straight into the endzone for a touchdown. I felt damn proud and smart that day."

The wins did not come easily in the next three games with the Cougars losing close contests to Pennsylvania School for the Deaf, Pennington and Friends Central before finally capturing a well-deserved 22-0 win over Perkiomen. At the end of the 1976 gridiron rainbow sat archrival, The Academy of the New Church. Though falling behind 12-0 in the first half, the Cougar's did not lose heart, a spirit that Geis lauded. "The first half was my fault but the boys refused to quit and played a good second half." ANC would eventually prevail by a 21-6 score.

The final loss did not dampen Willie's appraisal of his George School football experience. "Everybody who played football at George School weren't always the greatest athletes, including myself. First, being in a small school allowed me to get a chance to play football. Then I had to really work hard to get a chance to play. I saw other students who had to work harder at it than me. I thought it was really cool to see someone elevate themselves to a level that they probably never thought they could achieve." Though overly humble in his self-appraisal, Willie's words echoed the experience of so many former George School gridders. Win or lose they all felt a sense of accomplishment.

The 1977 season proved to be a time of dramatic change for the Cougars. Bob Geissinger decided to hang a "Gone Fishing" sign on his tenure as head coach, turning the post over to Steve Radanovic, his new assistant athletic director. Steve's credentials included a stellar career at Ursinus College and Upper Dauphin High School. Such a background, however, would not prepare a fledgling coach for the trials facing anyone assuming a head coaching job. Fortunately, Bob "Papa Cougar" Geissinger was still in the wings to offer comfort and insight into the complexities of the game and the George School gridder. The season started on a high note with the Cougars reeling off two straight wins, a 21-14 squeaker over Germantown friends and a 12-0 shutout of Mitchell Prep. The remaining five games proved less satisfying with the Cougars only managing to score 14 points en route to five straight losses.

The won/loss record did not dampen the spirit of Steve Miller, Dusty's son and defensive halfback on the team. "In all my years of playing football we were not what one would consider a powerhouse. There were many frustrating games and moments, but by far, the most frustrating was when we were losing a game and basically collapsed as a team. I think it was a good life lesson that it's not who is better than you or who you think you can beat, but the integrity and effort with which you play the game,"

Steve also showed another trait undoubtedly passed on by Geis. Do not lose your perspective and maintain a sense of humor. "There are so many memories of GS football but one afternoon stands out. Andy Alexander decided to test out his punting abilities. He got off a real nice line drive but unfortunately coach Geis was right in front of him and got hit squarely in the hind end. There was a long silence that seemed to last forever while everyone digested what happened. Then Geis let loose in a voice several octaves higher than normal and said 'Jeeeesus Christ Alexander, what the hell do you think this is, the Yardley YMCA? We're trying to run a football program here.' I think even the coaches were snickering as Andy took several laps around the track."

Whether genetically influenced by Dusty or simply sharing many a youngster's desire to step on the gridiron, Steve was thankful George School provided him the opportunity. "As a kid I had always wanted to play football, but weighing 98 pounds as a freshman was rather limiting. At George School size was less of a factor and I am still grateful that I got a chance to play on an organized team."

The opportunity also brought a sense of accomplishment to the young Cougar. "Bryn Athyn was always the big game. I remember one year we were down by two touchdowns late in the fourth quarter and had yet to score. Wes Seabrook took the kickoff up the middle all the way down for a touchdown. We lost the game but for that moment we were proud as hell."

The 1978 campaign started off on a real positive note as the gridders blanked Germantown Friends 8-0. One of the key plays was Ross Hunter trapping the Germantown quarterback in the endzone for a safety. He was ably supported by defensive tackles George Frew and Leonard Whitmore. The sack proved very consistent with the inner psyche that fed Ross. "I like running into people. (I still do, now I just do it verbally…not as much fun.) I liked the running, the speed. I liked all the equipment too."

Ross valued the other intangibles even more than mere physicality. "I loved it. I still think about how much fun it was. I developed friends I would not otherwise have. Nate McCollum and Seth Rosenthall became good friends."

The Cougars extended their win streak through the second game of the season when they defeated Mitchell Prep 14-6. Nate McKee, wide receiver who revived the old lonesome end style of play, well remembers this tussle. "On the last play of the game against Mitchell Prep, quarterback Bill Bald threw a thirty or forty yard strike to me in the endzone. This marked the first time we ever beat Mitchell."

The two victories would be all the Cougars could garner for the rest of the season. Despite the 2-5 record, Nate, who later became dean of George School, took away the more important principles inherent in the sport of football. "I learned that a group of players working as one unit can develop great work ethics and long-lasting personal relationships. I also learned that playing your best day in and day out doesn't always yield a win on Saturday. However, it makes you a better player and tests your commitment to the sport."

Ross Hunter good-naturedly remembers another of football's many lessons, one he incurred in a 8-22 loss to Saint Josephs of Camden. "I remember playing a game in Camden on a field covered in broken glass. I still have a scar from a cut I got on my finger. I taped it during the game with white tape so I wouldn't get taken out. It took a lot of stitches later."

The following season, 1979, proved a veritable testing ground for several up-and-coming GS gridders. Though winning only two games, a 28-0 victory of the Pennsylvania School for the Deaf and a 19-0 triumph over Gil-St. Bernard's School, the Cougars would flash signs of a real offensive potential. Mike Etzrodt manned the quarterback position. Mike had a trio of sure-handed receivers in Steve Boccado, Dan Broad and Scott Kramer. They also showed real line strength in the presence of Asa Cadwallader and David Wertz.

A man of true insight, Geis spotted the team's potential and returned to the varsity sidelines to serve as offensive coordinator in 1980. The move proved fortuitous as the Cougars ran up a 5-2 season and just missed winning a Penn-Jersey League title. The team started out on a strong note defeating Hun School 14-6, Saint Gabriels 20-0 and Princeton Day School 12-0. Against Hun, Scott Kramer and Dan Broad earned top honors, both scoring on passes from Mike Etzrodt. They would duplicate their success against Saint Gabriels with Kramer scoring on two aerials and Broad adding a third touchdown pass reception. Against Princeton Day, Asa Cadwallader and Kramer provided the scoring punch.

A 0-14 loss to Pennington Prep did little to dampen the Cougar's spirit as they roared back to defeat Friends Central 13-6 and Jenkintown 13-6. Coach Radanovic seemed most pleased after the Jenkintown game. "We've been getting good defense all season yet I thought I would need more offense today." Mike Etzrodt helped provide that offense, completing 12 passes for 143 yards.

The victory set up a classic duel between George School and Bryn Athyn. Not only would winner take home the coveted shoe trophy but they would emerge as champion of the Penn-Jersey league. The game proved a real defensive battle with ANC scoring first and taking a 0-7 lead into halftime. The Cougars would not strike paydirt until less than a minute remained in the game. Etzrodt hit Steve Boccardo with a six-yard scoring strike. The school newspaper described the play saying, "Bocarrdo's amazing one-handed grab gave George School an 8-7 lead with about 40 seconds remaining."

Unfortunately for the hometown Cougar fans the lead did not hold. Choosing to avoid a long kickoff return, the coaching brain trust opted to try an onside kick. ANC recovered the ball on the Cougar's 42 yard line. A long pass netted 22 yards and set up a last second field goal from the 19 yardline. The kick sailed through the uprights, giving ANC its second straight Penn-Jersey title.

Though obviously disappointed, coach Radanovic praised his team's effort. "I just can't believe how much heart my kids played with today. They just stopped our passing game and that was it."

Despite losing most of its potent 1980 offensive weapons to graduation, the 1981 squad showed it still packed plenty of firepower. Dave Cadwallader saw double duty as defensive linebacker and offensive running back. Tim Pesce manned the quarterback spot and took aim at receivers Scot Bald and Elvin Padilla. The line, though young, was anchored by Asa Cadwallader and featured Eric Levengood, Rob Lowers, Matt Etzrodt, and Jung Kim. The team jumped out to a quick start, beating Hun School 13-0 and Youth Development Center 17-0. Against Hun, Dave Cadwallader scored on a 31 yard run and Scott Bald tallied on a five yard sprint.

The big win over Hun held special meaning for Jeff Freedman, a junior transfer student. "I had just transferred into GS from Hun and lo' and behold our first game is against my old teammates. I remember running out of the locker room onto the field and past the Hun team and as they were stretching, they were yelling 'Kill Freedo'. No wonder I transferred out of Hun...ha,ha! I played defensive back, punter, punt returner and kick off returner that day. As the D-back I covered my friend Martin Summners who I had known since I was 8 years old and with whom I had played countless sandlot football games as we grew up in Trenton together. We knew each other's moves inside and out. Needless to say, luck was with me and GS as we went on to defeat Hun 13-0."

Jeff could not help but glory in the moment. "My most vivid memory was having two interceptions and after the second one in the fourth quarter up 13-0 and time waning, running the pick-off to the Hun 7 yard line and handing the ball to my buddy Martin and telling him to 'put the ball in his trophy case'. I was still new at GS and the Quaker principles had not yet been instilled in me. After I handed Martin the ball, we both laughed and slapped each other on the helmets. The amazing thing is nearly twenty years after this game Martin and I still talk 'trash' to one another about this contest."

While friendly bashing an old chum, Jeff was also learning the importance of bonding with his new teammates. "I remember on this day Radanovic and Geis coming up to me along with several teammates after each interception and high fiving me. It's amazing how athletes can make you feel accepted and part of a community. Prior to that game, I was still new as a transfer student. The victory against Hun was one of my most memorable moments in athletics. The indescribable euphoric feeling I had that day has only been matched on one or two other occasions. We all play sports to achieve this feeling which is so hard to describe and explain."

The euphoria was a bit short lived. After the Cougars suffered two close losses to Pennington and Pennsylvania School for the Deaf, they managed a 13-13 tie against Penn-Jersey League rival Friends Central. They finished out the season with another frustrating loss to ANC by a 0-20 score.

In 1982, senior Dave Cadwallader was determined to succeed in the sport he loved with a victory over ANC being tops on his list. "I love the game. Practice was the best time of the day. I just loved to play football. I am tempted to walk on every fall but everyone should have the chance to play. I loved the contact, hitting, tackling and running."

Unfortunately, graduation once again had depleted the available talent. The Cougars started on a rough note losing their first four games. Hun School pounded the Cougars in the season opener by a 8-32 margin. Jeff Freedman good naturedly ate a bit of humble pie. "This time we got crushed. I played quarterback and punter and I think I got sacked at least a dozen times. I think my offensive line was the master of the 'lookout' block that afternoon. Every time I was sacked the Hun players would say 'hello from Mr. Quirk', Hun's head coach. Also on this day, one of my punts went backwards and I still don't know how. Twenty years after this woeful punt, my buddies from Hun and GS still talk about it."

After another tough 0-20 loss to Princeton Day School, Coach Radanovic said, "We just need a little more experience. There is not a senior on the line. We have two sophomores and the rest are juniors."

The Cougars proved to be quick learners as they came on strong in the fifth and sixth games of the season, beating Friends Central 45-0 and Saint Andrews 38-13. Against Friends Central, John Jorgenson scored 4 touch-downs. Jeff Freedman hit on a 37 yard scoring pass. Jorgenson was equally effective against Saint Andrews rushing for 194 yards. Dave Cadwallader almost matched the feat, gaining 127 yards on the ground.

The victory string, however, did not carry over to the season finale. Once again, the Cougars fell victim to their archrival ANC by a 0-14 score. David viewed this as the biggest disappointment of his entire football career. "Every game was the biggest game of my life. ANC was always the game to win. My most lasting memory, however, was the frustration of never beating ANC/Bryn Athyn."

Though undoubtedly sharing Dave's 'football grief' over not vanquishing ANC, Jeff Freedman carries a more important memory from his senior quarter-backing days. "The amazing thing about football is that I can still vividly recall everyone's face from both the offensive and defensive huddles I was involved in. I still keep in contact with Richard Ray (1985). He was in my wedding and we attended law school together. I also keep in contact with Dave Cadwallder (1983), the toughest player I ever had the privilege of playing with."

The following season, 1983, started slowly as Coach Radanovic faced breaking in a whole new batch of promising recruits. Shawn Buki took over the quarterback spot. He relied heavily upon running backs Antonito Merritt, R.J. Wiley and John Uyeki. The line featured Matt Etzrodt, Mike Jones, Aaron Sexton and Kirk Fredendal. Facing a rugged schedule the Cougars lost four straight games to Hun, Chestnut Hill, Princeton Day School and Pennington Prep before finally starting to gel in a tough 14-16 loss to Friends Central. Shawn Buki completed 7 of 12 passes for 153 yards and one touchdown. Coach Radanovic's squad finally tasted victory in a 20-0 conquest of Saint Andrews. The big win saw Antonito Merritt tally on a 29 yard run. Shawn Buki hit Rich Ray with a 21 yard scoring strike.

Over the next two seasons victories were equally tough to come by. Again facing a tough 1984 schedule of most worthy opponents, the Cougars could manage only one win, a 13-12 squeaker over Gil Saint Bernard. They suffered lop-sided losses to Bristol High, Chestnut Hill, Pennington Prep, Wilmington Friends School and the Academy of the New Church.

The 1985 season proved equally difficult with the GS gridders going winless. They lost several heartbreakers, 9-13 to West Nottingham, 6-7 to Jenkintown, 0-12 to Princeton Day School and 0-17 to Chestnut Hill. Though obviously a disappointing campaign, the Cougars took hope in the fact that many of the players on the team had logged a 5-1 record on the junior varsity. Given a little more seasoning, such talented players as Phil Hardy, Clarence Jaspar, Chuck Minter, Matt Caruliccio, Phil Caputo, Morgan Esser, Neal Cheskis, Dave Brumfield, Ted Hackman and Enis Cosby would definitely find gridiron success.

The Nation Strives for
Upward Mobility

After a tumultuous Vietnam War era, the nation wanted a return to normalcy in the eighties. Ron "the Gipper" Reagan introduced his Reaganomics. The upwardly mobile Yuppies replaced the socially conscious Hippies. E.T. just wanted to phone home. Madonna crooned about being a material girl. And I became the ninth head coach of George School football. Now that news may not have rivaled the end of the Cold War but it proved monumental in my life.

Early in the summer of 1986 Steve Radonavic left gridiron coaching to assume the position of head swim mentor at West Windsor High School. That left athletic director Bob Geissinger in a quandary. Should he resume the duties of head coach or find some last-minute recruit to fill the vacancy? Lacking the time to run a thorough job search, Geis opted for a more convenient outlet. He went across campus and asked me if I was interested. Initially I balked, thinking I lacked the total knowledge of the game's complexity. Geis assured me that he had already hired a football man in Ron Dilks, a University of Miami graduate and former assistant coach at Cheltenham and Hatboro Horsham, to be defensive coordinator. Though not convinced I was the right man, I reluctantly agreed but added it would only be for one season. Trying to add more comfort to my decision, I hired my friend and former head coach Mike Heverin. At least that way the players would benefit from his expertise.

I also took heart knowing Geis was still in his office in the Alumni Gym. His presence served as a constant reminder of his very meaningful philosophy of football coaching. As he later wrote me in a letter, "Part of the organization story of GS football was a decided source of pride. The pride comes from coaching the kids that come through the gate each year. Many came out for the sport without previous experience and were able to earn a letter and a starting position in their junior or senior year." In terms of recruits or postgrads, Geis was an ardent believer in playing the hand you're dealt. In other words, teach the youngsters who show up to practice. Allow them to grow and mature in a demanding sport. In Geis's words, "During my tenure, we won some and lost some but I never had to explain to parents of a player who had practiced and played for two or three years why he had been benched to allow a better player who came in as a junior or senior to play his position." This credo certainly resonated with me and spoke of the days I enjoyed playing for Geis.

The 1986 season started when 18 players showed up for our three day preseason. What they lacked in size and numbers, they made up for in athleticism and tenacity. Many of the players had logged a 5-1 junior varsity record two years earlier so I knew they could be successful. Dave Burton, a young sophomore lineman encapsulated my thinking when he said several years later, "In life, there are very few instances in which success comes from being the fastest, strongest or biggest; however, there are many instances in which success comes from perseverance, consistent effort and personal responsibility. John Gleeson provided his football players with an opportunity to engrain these qualities into their character. John Gleeson by example taught me more about managing people than I learned attending General Electric's renowned executive training programs. John set clear expectations, did not micromanage and held players accountable but also enabled players to move past mistakes."

Philosophy intact, I needed to tend to the actual X's and O's. When designing an offensive scheme, I decided not to force a system on the players but to allow their talents to dictate the attack we would employ. We settled on an I formation with two wide outs and a tight end. The primary objective was to attack the perimeter, basically stretching the field from sideline to sideline and from endzone to endzone. Then we would try and run or pass in the gaps. On defense Coach Dilks designed a 4-4 scheme that showcased our aggression and made it difficult for the opposition to know just where we were attacking.

One performer we definitely knew we had to utilize was stellar two-way threat, senior Paul Burke. Paul had found sports a saving grace in his early school days. In an honest self-appraisal thirty-six years later, Paul would write, "One of my fondest memories of life at George School was my participation in the football program. You look back at specific time periods in life and some periods became stamped into your memory as the most indelible periods of your life...being a member of the Cougar football team, the lessons learned and of course what I personally learned from Coach Gleeson. My experiences learned from Cougar football as well as Coach Gleeson were lessons I transferred over into my life as a parent and a citizen in my community."

He further explained that, "Confidence socially was not something I possessed as a child born with a hearing impairment. I was shy and quite introverted. Social confidence was very limited growing up. I would avoid large social gatherings and as a result it limited my interactions. Sports was an outlet for me and I participated in many different sports including one year in pee wee football. My experiences at George School, the friends and the participation in programs like the Cougar football program helped considerably in my development. It developed confidence in me both socially and individually."

Allowing the player's individual skills to dictate what system we employed, suited a multi-talented player such as Paul. "Coach Gleeson took over the program and things changed rapidly for the betterment of the program. Not only did we win more than lose, we came together as a team. Coach Gleeson developed chemistry. Players bought into their roles and our energy level as a team was vastly improved. A major lesson I learned from Coach Gleeson was the ability to adapt your roster. Players were put into positions to succeed based on their skill set as well as masking their deficiencies. This has a positive impact on the chemistry of a team as players are more motivated with their personal positive impact on the team. Many coaches have their systems and lose sight of the skill set of the players that do not fit into their system. Coach Gleeson understands that and made major changes to each player's role on the team."

I was quick to spot that Paul was a natural at middle linebacker and blocking fullback. He readily adjusted to his new positions. "In prior seasons I was utilized on both defensive line and offensive line. My senior season Coach Gleeson dramatically changed my role on the team. He inserted me into the roles of fullback and interior linebacker. I to this day have some lingering physical reminders of my playing days from that season. I certainly loved blasting holes for Clarence (Jaspar) and was always amped when he made a big gain. Defense was my favorite unit to play on and playing alongside Chuck (Minter) was always fun and memorable."

After two weeks and one controlled scrimmage against Hill School, the Cougars were ready for their home opener. They took on West Nottingham Academy, a team that had just upset a solid Pennington Prep squad. The game turned out to be a fledgling coach's dream as we turned back the Maryland invaders by an 18-0 score. Dave Chapman of The Courier Times began his recount of the contest, saying, "A single word could be used to describe the season opener for the George School Cougar football team. That would simply be intensity." (Courier Times, September 1986). I readily concurred. "I would attribute the win to the aggressiveness of the kids. These kids want to play football this year. They don't consider themselves a losing team. They haven't thought about it since they came back this season. Last year was last year. They are ready to turn things around." (Courier Times, September 1986)

The Cougars presented a balanced offensive attack passing for 108 yards and rushing for 111 yards. Phil Hardy teamed up with quarterback Matt Carluccio for scoring strikes of 34 and 37 yards. In all, Hardy caught 6 passes for 100 yards. Clarence Jaspar added 49 yards rushing. The defense shared in the glory, holding Nottingham to a total of 101 yards and only four first downs. Junior Ted Hackman picked off an errant pass in the first quarter and carried it in for a twenty-yard tally.

After tough away losses to Morrisville 0-7 and Jenkintown 6-26, the Cougars showed real resiliency by thumping Princeton Friends School by a 36-8 score. I summed up the game action, saying, "It was a pretty convincing win. Everything was going right for us. The passing game and the defense were really working." (Courier Times, October 1986) Ennis Cosby opened the scoring by recovering a blocked punt for a touchdown. Cosby later caught a forty-yard scoring strike, one of three touchdowns thrown by Matt Carluccio. Phil Hardy caught touchdown aerials of 8 and 16 yards. After each TD, Hardy would face the game camera and assume his signature move, raising his hands to indicate another score.

Thinking the head coach job description included stadium maintenance, I decided to spruce up Cougar field for our big homecoming game against a tough Saint Andrew squad. The ancient scoreboard gracing the Route 413 end of the field served as a sure target. This relic had undoubtedly overseen many a mighty gridiron contest but had fallen into disuse over the past years. No one volunteered to sit on its rickety scaffold and change both the time and score by hand. I decided to replace it with a bold brown and gold plywood banner boasting "Cougar Pride". I also deemed it appropriate to hang a similar display on the fence near the field, showing action photos of our proud senior warriors, Paul Burke, Phil Hardy, Phil Caputo, Clarence Jaspar, Neal Cheskis, Chuck Minter, Morgan Esser, Ennis Cosby, and Kenny Tate. This would surely arouse any Cougar player as well as all the parents passing by on the way to their scheduled teacher conferences.

The intended effect worked for Dave Burton. "1986 was the first year of more than three decades of the Gleeson era. John introduced the concept of Cougar Pride. Posting signs around campus with pictures of the players and Cougar Pride. No one had ever told me to have pride in anything and it was quite a feeling."

The Cougars proved the extra incentives worked. Dave Chapman of the Courier Times aptly summarized the game. "George School's football team certainly knows how to treat a Homecoming crowd. Saturday afternoon, a partisan crowd of 300 left the Newtown campus very satisfied. The Cougars came up with another top-notch performance to defeat Saint Andrews 26-12 in a non-league affair." (Courier Times October 1986)

In a highly physical game, the Cougars relied on the driving runs of Clarence Jaspar who rushed for 118 yards on 18 carries. Though completing only three of nine passes, quarterback Matt Carluccio managed to find Phil Hardy for scores of 7 and 30 yards. Hardy, who doubled as kicker, took off on a 70-yard touchdown jaunt on a fake punt. Defensively, the home team alertly jumped on four of Saint Andrews' fumbles. Middle linebacker Paul Burke made a key interception to thwart a final Saint Andrew scoring drive. After the game the team carried the photo display to Marshall Center for all to see. Cougar pride was definitely back!

Not one prone to superstition, I did take note that we had won all three of our home games and lost both of our away contests. Our next game was a travel date with Newark Academy, a team sporting a 5-1 record and boasting a Division One caliber quarterback. The opposition definitely presented an awesome front. Fortunately, our loyal booster club led by the Hackmens, Jaspers, Minters, Brumfields and Caputos came up with an answer to calm any jitters. They decided the best way to a warrior's nerve center is through his stomach. Armed with frying pans, spatulas and barbecues, they camped outside the Alumni Gym and prepared a hearty sendoff meal for the Cougars. The strategy worked.

The Courier Times once again praised the Cougar battlers, saying, "Going into Livingston, N.J., for their contest against Newark Academy, the Cougars of George School had to be considered heavy underdogs, The Cougars, it was thought, could not handle the 5-1 New Jersey team despite compiling an impressive 3-2 start to the season. But if the Cougars were supposed to lose, somebody forgot to tell them." (Courier Times October 1986)

Clarence Jasper spearheaded the attack following solid blocking by Paul Burke, Neal Cheskis and Chris Kelly. Jasper racked up 128 yards on 23 carries and tallied two touchdowns and an extra point run. Cheskis got into the scoring act, blocking two punts and returning one 14 yards for a TD. Matt Carluccio opened the offensive attack, hitting Phil Hardy with a 44-yard touchdown aerial.

Phil Hardy summed up the convincing 30-0 victory, saying, "Everybody is psyched for each game. We have a new coach (Gleeson) and I had him sophomore year when I played JV. He's fair and he teaches us to have fun. Last year we had a problem going out and doing that." (Courier Times October 30, 1986)

Though the Gridiron Gods saw fit to end the funfest with two convincing season-ending losses to Chestnut Hill and The Academy of the New Church, few among the Cougar faithful seemed disheartened. Phil Hardy earned first team honors on the Courier Times Golden 30 Football Team. Hardy finished second in the area in pass receptions with 32 catches for 448 yards and nine touchdowns. He was just nosed out by two points for the Bucks County scoring title. Matt Carluccio finished fourth among local passers, completing 48 of his 120 aerials for 631 yards and 10 touchdowns. Clarence Jasper finished sixth in Lower Bucks County toting the pigskin 99 times for 497 yards.

More importantly to me, after a year as head coach, I could more fully understand what Geis meant when he said. "The always special challenge of taking a group of guys in the fall and attempting to mold them into a cohesive unit was the ultimate high for me. I felt the most important thing I did as a coach was placing the players in positions that complimented their abilities and skills." Each player on the team, whether a stellar athlete or willing sub, played a role in our team's success. I knew that just one year of coaching such fine young men was not enough. I was hooked.

My second year, I recognized yet another bit of Geis wisdom when he lamented not having enough time in preseason to test and instruct his often-inexperienced charges. I decided to rectify that situation. I bartered with the administration to grant the football team a week of preseason practice in exchange for some hard labor. In essence, the plan was to have three two hour long practices a day. Players would check in on Monday, sleep over on the wrestling mats at night, eat cooked meals provided by Barbie Gale and myself, and then work for three hours at whatever task the head groundskeeper Vince Campellone could devise. The plan sounded great. The practical application proved a bit scary. It was somewhat daunting to see Nigel Smith and Derek Minter emerging from the wilds of the outdoor auditorium wielding machetes. I also got to sleep in the gym to supervise the troops. In the morning I noticed one brave sophomore, Kassem Lucas, would go around and wake up all the exhausted athletes. I figured he was either a born leader or he was criminally insane. Halfway through the week I decided the players needed some fun time, relaxation at night. I sent two members of the team to go rent a film from Blockbuster. Now I did not expect them to come back with "The Sound of Music '' but I did not anticipate "I Spit on Your Grave" to be the movie du jour. Mike Heverin merely laughed and said, "Well you wanted to bring them together." Nothing like an x-rated horror flick to bond a team!

Ted Hackman, co-captain of the 1987 squad well-remembers both the agony and ecstasy of preseason. "Most of my memories come not from the games played but from all the other experiences associated with the football program. I believe we started the August camp program when we started practicing before the fall semester. Sleeping in the gym overnight. Doing chores for Vince to 'pay' for our week. The 'killer' practices when I could hardly stand anymore."

Dave Burton added another torturous moment to the list of memories or nightmares, "Coach Gleeson created a torture devise that required bear crawling around stakes in the ground connected by a rope that would catch any player who tried to stand up. When the ground got wet it became even harder to traverse the device in the mud, which was a reason for Gleeson to order the team through the device even more. The drills may have worked. Junior BJ Lowe was covering a kick-off. He tackled the ball carrier very low and the ball carrier ended up in the air and flipping over and over. When the play was over the referee came up to Lowe and told him that was the best hit he had ever seen in a football game at any level."

We made it through the rugged week without spitting on anyone's grave and then prepped for the regular season. Being a brash, young coach, I over-looked another credo of Geis, "At GS, when a group of kids play together for two or three years, the schedule should be of teams that they will have a shot at a winning season." I started the 1987 campaign with a scrimmage against Wyoming Seminary, a team that sported eleven seniors who were earmarked to play at the Naval Academy. I sensed some difficulty when the first four guys to enter our locker room outweighed anyone in our line. The coach happily told me they were the managers.

Having emerged relatively unscathed from the Wyoming debacle, I felt the Cougars were ready to tackle our first two opponents, Caravel Academy and the Hun School. Both teams outnumbered us and featured post grads and fifth year seniors. Not surprisingly we lost 6-30 to Caravel and 6-34 to Hun. Our next foe, Princeton Day School, looked more compatible. The game proved to be a cliffhanger that was not decided until the last minute. The Cougars took the lead with 3:46 left in the game when Andrew Farmer recovered a fumble in the PDS endzone. A Matt Carluccio to Ted Hackman pass for the two-point conversion gave the Cougars a 14-12 edge with 2:20 left to play. Ted recalls that play, "I told Matt Carluccio to throw me the ball in the endzone. Luckily, I caught it for a lead late in the game. Unfortunately, we lost in the last seconds." The margin did not hold as PDS scored on a last second pass.

Though disappointed, the Cougars refused to give up on the season, winning the next three games. We notched our first victory with a 30-6 conquest over Maryland's West Nottingham. Chris Dixon sparked the Cougar offense, scoring on its first possession from seventeen yards out. He would end up with 72 yards rushing to assure the victory. Senior Les Lewis carried the offensive torch in the next game, a close 20-13 conquest of Newark Academy. Lewis chalked up 171 yards receiving and scored on passes of 25, 18, and 1 yards. GS completed the three game win streak by defeating a tough RCA Youth Center 20-14. Ted Hackman rumbled in from two yards out to cap off an eight-play 41-yard drive on our first possession. Carluccio teamed up with Les Lewis on a 20-yard scoring toss on our next possession. Carluccio completed his 127 yard passing performance with a fourth quarter 18-yard toss to Nasheet Waits.

Despite season-ending losses to Chestnut Hill and ANC, the Cougars had fared quite well. Les Lewis earned first team honors on the Courier Times Golden 30 Football Team. Lewis led Lower Bucks County with 30 receptions for 500 yards and six touchdowns. Matt Carluccio finished out his Cougar career with 67 completions for 894 yards and 10 touchdowns. Ted Hackman picked up 130 yards on the ground.

For Ted, the Cougar football experience meant more than just rushing yards. As he would later reflect, "Sometimes it's hard to reflect back on certainly one of the best experiences I've had so far. The friends made, the dedication spent, the lessons learned, the triumphs and defeats are still very clear in my mind. "

Ted relishes a plethora of Cougar football memories. "I have lasting impressions of the pre-game meals the parents prepared for us which really psyched us up for the games. Other specific memories are playing nose tackle in a varsity game my sophomore year. Getting my pants pulled down on a runback in a JV game. I was only about 130 pounds. Gaining two player of the game awards and attending the BCCT (Bucks County Courier Times) weekly banquets. Driving to the biggest game of our senior year (ANC) in Drew Farmer's Mustang because Geis forgot to call the bus company. The memories go on and on, but maybe the lasting memory was the relationship with the coaches and coach Gleeson in particular. Coach taught me discipline, the importance of teamwork and hard work. We didn't have the most talented squad but through his coaching we were able to put GS football on the map." It's little wonder I decided to stay on for a third year. The bonds developed between a coach and his players are lasting ones.

Three of the biggest challenges awaiting any scholastic football coach are graduation, changes in the coaching staff, and injuries to key players. The 1988 season featured all three. Eight Cougars went the Cap and Gown route which in a big program would seem miniscule but when you only field twenty-some players it carries greater impact. Our defensive coordinator Ron Dilks moved on to assume the head coach job at Morrisville High School. I solicited the aid of Tom English who was currently head of the George School history department. Having played at Dartmouth, Tom knew all about the skills requisite for solid line play. He also was a storehouse of historical references though at times I became confused as to whether we were playing Hun School or fighting the Battle of Trafalgar. Initially Tom's only flaw was his sideline attire. Our tri-captain Nigel Smith rectified that situation, suggesting Tom not wear argyle socks to the game. Nigel would later suffer a serious season ending injury to his wrist, one not due to his work as fashion coordinator.

Dave Burton, by then a polished and efficient lineman, greatly valued the addition of Coach English to the staff. "It was Tom English's first year as the line coach. Coach English was of the view that offensive lineman needed to be agile. This included somersault drills in full pads, which is not something you see being tested at an NFL combine."

The season started with a close 6-14 loss to RCA Youth Center. Nigel tallied the only score for the Cougars on a 24-yard run. The losing ways continued for four more games with losses to Hun, Pennington, Princeton Day, and Newark. The one bright spot was the emergence of Kassem Lucas at quarterback. A converted tailback, Kassem passed for 148 yards against Princeton, including a 20-yard scoring toss to Smith.

The game against Newark proved more costly than a mere loss. Nigel Smith ended his playing days with a serious wrist injury. Years later he would reflect on this moment. "Sadly, my most lasting memory is when I shattered my arm while playing Newark Academy in October of 1988. I have a substantial scar on my right arm and have lost feeling in my right thumb due to nerve damage. It was on the opening kickoff and it had been raining and when I went to tackle the return man, I put my foreman on his helmet and the rest was history. I remember staying in the game for a few plays and might have even made a tackle or two. I knew I was hurt but didn't want to come out of the game. I was able to convince Irv (Miller), the Trainer, that it was just a bruise or sprain."

Nigel always played all-out regardless of the situation. He did remain in the game and even tackled the quarterback on a blitz. However, the injury proved too serious for even Nigel Smith to continue. "My last play for GS football was a few minutes after Irv's diagnosis when we had a four-and-out offensive series and I needed to punt the ball. I remember telling Derek Minter to snap it softly because I could only catch the ball with one hand. I think my kick went nine yards. My career best."

Losing a player of Nigel's caliber could disrupt any lineup but when a team only has 24 players listed on the roster it becomes tough to adopt a next-man-down attitude. Fortunately, the Cougars flashed real determination as they prepped for a home encounter with West Nottingham. Tri-captain Derek Minter volunteered to assume Nigel's running back position. The move proved fortuitous as the Cougars chalked up their first victory of the season. Minter combined with senior Rad Stafford for a combined 258 rushing yards to help the GS gridders capture the 34-0 victory.

Dave Burton noted the adjustments the Cougars willingly made. "Two players stepped up to fill Smith's shoes at running back and kicker. Minter was the team's most effective offensive weapon as a receiver with most of his yards being earned after the catch. He moved to running back, which meant it was easier to get the ball in his hands. Senior Jeff Vernon who was 6'4" and playing football for the first time stepped in to be the punter and placekicker. Vernon also played defensive end. He described his job as defensive end as to beat up whomever lined up opposite him, which he was pretty effective at. But the job arguably has something to do with tackling the ball carrier too."

After a sound thumping at the hands of Morristown Beard, the Cougars prepared to take on The Academy of the New Church. Determined to end a 14 game losing streak to their archrival, the Cougars struck first. Recovering a fumble at midfield, GS took nine plays to reach the end zone with Kassem Lucas scoring on a two-yard plunge. A twelve-yard ANC pass in the second quarter knotted the score at 6-6. The Academy would finish the scoring on a 45-yard pass from Quarterback Rick DeMayne to capture the 12-6 win. After the game, ANC coach Andy Davis would say, "I gotta give George School a whole lot of credit. They've been whipped by us a lot of years in a row. But not today." (Courier Times, November, 1988)

Ten years later, a reflective tri-captain Dave Brumfield still felt responsible for the loss. "I remember falling to my knees and crying after time expired in my final game, a 6-12 loss to ANC. I remember being on the 35-yard line looking around the field thinking I had let down all of my teammates. I kept thinking I should have, and could have, done more."

Dave's remorse, though undeserved, stemmed from what he later learned after becoming an All-American and Academic All-American while playing for Ithaca's Division III national championship team. In looking back, Dave, "Realized, mainly from the loss to ANC my senior year that I had wasted my last two years of high school football. I had decided that since I was the biggest and strongest guy on the team, I did not have to work on getting any better. I did not work on getting any better. Though I was strong I did not develop my back or leg strength that I later learned was so important. Finally, despite the fact that it severely limited me, particularly on defense, I did not put forth the required effort to improve my speed."

Dave would later apply that wisdom to the ANC game loss. "When I got to Ithaca and realized how far I still had to go, I was devastated. Because now I had to ask myself, 'If I had put forth the effort could I have made a difference in the ANC game?' I was two steps from DeMayne (ANC's quarterback) when he threw the second touchdown pass. If I had worked harder, could I have sacked him before he got the pass off? I accept my college losses because I know I did the best I could, but I will always be haunted by questions and regret about ANC. Hopefully as a result I have learned that if it's something you care about, it's something that deserves your best effort." David had obviously converted an important lesson learned on the George School gridiron into a highly successful collegiate career.

Nigel also put his Cougar football days in perspective. Any physical scars did not dampen his love of the game. "Football is the greatest game. There is the 'bonding' when you play a game that physically hurts. You give your all on the field to get a first down or make a tackle for not only the team but also the entire school. Unlike baseball, football is dangerous and you can get hurt but you know your friends are out there sacrificing themselves for the team to succeed. It's the closeness with your friends I'll never forget. Football is planned confusion. You know that you're supposed to get to 'point A' but someone is trying to stop you and you just have to figure it out."

The big hit concept provided Nigel with many a lasting memory, "When I was on the JV team, we'd scrimmage the varsity every once in a while, and most times we held our own. I'll never forget coach Dilks yelling at me after I hit QB Matt Carluccio pretty hard. I think I even surprised myself. The very next play while we were on offense, Chris Dixon leveled me. It was good stuff."

The bonding concept applies not just to teammates but includes coaches. In Nigel's appraisal, "I'd say Coach Gleeson was a major part of my GS football experience. He, both on and off the field, helped instill some confidence in a teenager who struggled with schoolwork in general. Clearly, I was a much better athlete than student but the lessons on the field helped translate to the classroom and beyond. Alums always talk about the faculty and how committed they are to helping shape and nurture each student. I'd say Coach Gleeson had a major influence in how I turned out as an adult."

Who could walk away from such relationships? My one-year promise to Geis was turning into a lifetime commitment. The 1989 season provided yet another opportunity to be a part of a great group of young men. Many of the players experienced an undefeated junior varsity season three years before under the tutelage of Bob Geissinger. They were determined to reverse the won/loss record of the previous varsity season. As a newcomer to George School Rick Piechota wavered as to whether playing football would prove worthwhile. "I'll never forget my first practice in the fall of '89. After playing for a 4A team in Tennessee, I didn't know what to expect from such a small school.

Most of the guys told me that the team record from the previous season was not impressive, and that they didn't expect to do well again. I recall such words as, "We really suck!". I thought about turning in my pads and trying out for the soccer team instead. After about two weeks of practice, I was glad I stayed with the team. I finally got to meet the guys who did care about playing and those who were determined to win, guys like Dave Mittleman, Kassem Lucas, Oscar Carrero, Eli Papatestas, and Judd Cain."

The team's determination paid off. Backed by a solid defense, the Cougars logged a 5-2 season. Senior captain Kassem Lucas described it in the school newspaper. "Since I've been here, this has been the best and most successful team in terms of teamwork. I've never played on a team that has worked so well together." (George School News, December 18, 1989)

Chris English of the Courier Times lauded the defense. "Stingy might be too soft a word to describe this defense. Through six games of the 1989 football season, the George School "D" has been impregnable." (Courier Times November, 1989) The statistics validated the writer's praise. The Cougar's captured five of their first six games. Over that span, they allowed only two touchdowns. They shut out RCA 12-0, Pennington Prep 28-0, West Nottingham 28-0 and Morristown Beard 12-0. Their only loss was a 7-0 squeaker to Newark Academy. I quickly attributed the 'impenetrable' defenders to our defensive coordinator Mike Heverin. "He's done a great job. He puts together a good package. The defense has been keeping us in a lot of those games. Eli Papatestas just plays a solid game the whole time. He's a key and Lance Hulack, the nose guard, is really an aggressive kid." (Courier Times, November 1989)

Rick Piechota noticed another unusual aspect of his new team. The Cougar quarterback had complete control of the game. "Some of the highlights of that year (1989) Kassem called the plays from the huddle. That was absolutely unheard of at the high school level. An excellent defense which allowed only 14 points in the first six games. Blanking Pennington Prep 28-0. And ending up 5-2, the school's best record in 10 seasons."

Kassem had already spotted my offensive philosophy. He was quoted as saying, "With the team we have, that's basically what we have to do. We are small and quick and John's philosophy is he looks at the players and sees what the team can do and we fit that mold." (Courier Times September 11, 1989)

Spotting Kassem as a born leader counted as a no-brainer for me. After the Nottingham victory I said, "We wanted Kassem to call his own plays. And after the first drive we let him call the rest of the game. He made some great calls. He can see things on the field I can't." (The Philadelphia Inquirer, October 30, 1989)

Kassem noted that he had matured in his role as quarterback. "Last year was my first real work at quarterback. I played a little as a freshman. But I didn't learn how to read defenses that much. This year I want to learn how to read defenses. Improve on that." (Courier Times, September 11, 1989)

The awareness manifested itself in the 28-0 win over Pennington Prep. Kassem ran for two touchdowns and threw for two more. In all, he accounted for 77 rushing yards and 125 passing yards. After his second touchdown run, he and flanker Kapr Bangura broke into an endzone celebration they called "The Running Man". Though not rivaling one of Fred Asataire's numbers, the routine showed why Kassem would later count the Pennington game among his favorite football memories. "Beating Pennington 28-0 my senior year. It was great to stick it to them."

For the season, Kassem completed 42 passes good for 491 yards and 5 touchdowns. He added 141 yards rushing. Showing his true versatility, he was named to the Courier Times first team Golden 35 defensive team as a linebacker.

All the accolades aside, it was the intangibles that Kassem as a player and later as a GS coach would remember. "The overall experience of playing and coaching GS football has been one of the most rewarding of my life. My experience with GS football and the pledging to my fraternity (in college) have been the two things that I have put the most into and gotten the most out of. The 7-1 season (1999) was the highlight of that experience."

From these gridiron moments Kassem gained the following lifetime rewards. "Hard work, resistance, learning the game, maturity, resilience, discipline. The list goes on."

The only downer of the 1989 season came with an 8-30 defeat at the hands of the Cougars' old nemesis, ANC. Lance Hulack felt that proved a tough finale to an otherwise great senior season. "Losing to ANC was a lasting memory. It was very hard to accept after having such a great season. You play hard and you practice even harder the whole season just for that game."

The following year the Cougars experienced a rough start both on the scoreboard and on the injury front. Before the campaign even got underway, we lost the services of Rick Piechota, a player who had rushed for 184 yards and a 4-3 average in 1989. A dedicated performer, Rick faced the unfortunate fate possibly awaiting any player strapping on the pads. "My senior season was a little discouraging, but still a memorable one. The team was young after losing about 10 seniors, but they were still committed to winning. I remember tearing the ligaments in my left knee on the third day of preseason practice and having surgery a week later. We lost Judd Cain that year also to knee surgery. I remember sitting on the sideline for the first few games watching us lose and wishing I could be a part of the team."

Lacking such proven starters as Cain and Piechota, the Cougar offense sputtered. We were shutout in our first three games to RCA, Princeton Day School and Pennington Prep. The opposition focused most of their attention on stopping our two remaining offensive threats Kapr Bangura and Joel Wennick. Bangura rushed for 76 yards against RCA and 93 against PDS. Wennick would go on to tote the pigskin for a season total of 436 yards.

With the available troops dwindling, I sought help from the junior varsity. One aspiring gridder, sophomore Sam Laybourne, showed a good deal of promise. As he recalled thirty years later, "I remember playing on the JV squad at the beginning of my sophomore year, my first year at the school. It was a blast because I had a bit more experience than the other players as a kid who came from a big New Jersey football program that started in seventh grade. I loved playing with kids my age as a wildly skinny middle linebacker, hustling all over the field, racking up tackles and helping fire-up the JV team."

Sam also loved the move to varsity. "I must confess I was happy when coach Gleeson called me up to varsity practices a month or so into the season. I was playing with juniors and seniors, which was an honor, if a little intimidating.

I had a lot to learn about the game, but I did have one early victory on my very first day practicing with the big boys. I was playing defense in a passing drill and I realized that I was lined up opposite one of the senior prefects on my hall. My prefects were great guys but they were definitely tough on us and enjoyed wielding their power in Orton Dormitory. Out on the gridiron, however, we were equals, so I saw the opportunity for a little role reversal. My prefect went out for a pass and I was lucky enough to time my hit in such a way that I laid him out flat on the turf. It was one of those tackles that sends someone's legs flying up in the air and defies gravity for a few comic nanoseconds. As this prefect looked up at me from the ground and all the other seniors reacted to the hit with winces, laughs and hollers, I felt like I avenged a lot of 'wedgies' and 'dead-arms' on the hall. I knew that I was going to LOVE being a Cougar."

The feeling went both ways. The Cougars loved having an athlete such as Sam on board. We played better in our next game against Newark and managed to score a touchdown when Rob Hardy blocked a punt in the endzone. The Cougars displayed a never-say-die attitude that led quarterback Kapr Bangura to say after the Newark tussle, "We did a lot of good things today that the score will not indicate. We are going to come back next week and give all we can to win our homecoming." (Courier Times, October, 1990)

Rick Piechota's return to action undoubtedly served as a rallying point. Rick remembers the moment well. "Finally, after four straight losses, I was cleared to play. I remember playing West Nottingham at Homecoming, and getting the first call on a tailback dive which broke for 30 yards. We scored on the first drive and eventually won the game 19-12."

Though our only win in 1989 Rick still had another lasting memory in our 12-30 loss to ANC. "There is another moment from that season I'll never forget. In the closing minutes of the ANC game, we were on the one-yard line going in for the score. I remember Coach calling timeout and coming into the huddle. He called for some sweep play to Wennick but Joel and Kapr told the coach to give the ball to me on a dive. I scored on a one-yard plunge for my first TD in two seasons."

Such team camaraderie certainly ranks as one of football's true rewards. Rick sums it up well saying, "Playing for GS may not have been as glorious as winning the Big 33 Classic, but they are days that I will always remember. Even though we were a bunch of undersized academic type kids, there was a lot of heart and guts on those teams."

As a coach, I would definitely agree!

Time to show up, suit up, and keep 'em choppin'.

The twentieth century's last hurrah featured a series of high and low moments for the nation. The nineties saw the Gulf War, race riots, school shootings, and the rise in domestic terrorism. On the brighter side Elmo wanted to be tickled. Dolly the sheep sought her family tree. Meat Loaf sang about doing anything for love. And the World Wide Web gave rise to an awareness of multiculturalism. Through it all Cougar football prevailed.

The Cougars entered the 1991 season filled with optimism. The team featured a group of eager young talent blended with a few savvy vets. Jon Allen, senior linebacker and defensive mainstay, awaited the new campaign. "I look forward to playing football. George School is built around a team spirit. We're a small team. Instead of using brute force, we have to use intelligence and agility." (Courier Times, September 5, 1991)

The combination proved effective as the Cougars opened with a 6-0 victory over RCA. They really flexed their offensive muscles in their next tilt against West Nottingham, capturing a 39-0 win. The GS gridders amassed 372 total yards, 322 on the ground and 50 in the air. Kudzai Jones led all runners with 108 yards on 8 carries. Sophomore Anthony Rogers-Wright contributed 47 yards, Sam Laybourne had 59 yards, and Stafford Woodley added 43 yards. The youth movement was in full force with quarterback Isa Clark completing 3 of 7 passes for 50 yards.

A 6-14 loss to Wardlaw Hartridge in the next game did not dishearten the Cougars. They eagerly prepped for a key showdown with Princeton Day School. The game was a proverbial back and forth affair that went down to the last 41 seconds before Kudzai Jones scored to assure a 32-26 victory.

The contest showcased several of the Cougars' rising talent. Sam Laybourne, who combined with Kudzai Jones for 124 yards rushing, recognized my offensive strategy. "One thing I loved about the way Coach Gleeson called games was that he dared the other team to stop things that were working. I remember the 34 Dive play where, as fullback, I would run the ball in the gap between right guard Glenn Davis, and right tackle, Sheldon Cummings. This was my favorite running play because I got to lower my head and just gut-out a few yards straight ahead. I was a pretty slow, lumbering runner, so this was my sweet spot. When the play worked, coach Gleeson would call the exact same play two times in a row- one time even three times. It was such a brazen and genius call because teams weren't expecting it at all. It was a mental chess move to just challenge the other team: stop this if you can. When the 34 dive was rolling, thanks to Sheldon and Glenn's expert blocking, we felt like an unstoppable train."

What Sam attributed to 'genius' was really just common sense on my part. I always believed that you ran a play until the opposition adjusted and then ran a counter move. It also helped to have our version of a Mr. Inside and Mr. Outside running game in the presence of Laybourne and Jones. After four games Sam averaged 5.1 yards a carry and Kudzai averaged 6.5 yards a pop. It made sense to me that two carries would usually net us a first down.

Sam added another weapon to his offensive arsenal. He devastated would-be tacklers with his blocking prowess. Reporter Todd Beckwith described our game-winning TD drive against PDS. "Laybourne also had a key block on the critical last drive as he flattened a Panther defensive end to free Jones for a nine-yard run and a first down to the 10 yard line." (Courier Times, October, !991)

Equally impressive in the PDS game, Isa Clark emerged as a bona fide passing threat. He threw for 175 yards and three touchdowns. The junior QB described his growing awareness. "I am still young and I am not the biggest player in the world but this game really gave me confidence. My line also kept me from getting sacked so they deserve a lot of credit." (Courier Times, October, 1991)

Isa often teamed up with his two favorite targets, sophomores Dwayne McCoy and John James. He hit McCoy with a five-yard touchdown and then hooked up with James for a 74-yard scoring strike to give the Cougars a 16-13 lead at halftime. Princeton Day school coach Mark Adams sensed James' potential. "We knew James was a real quality player, and if he got the ball, he would do something with it, and he did." (Courier Times October, 1991)

Unfortunately, Dame Gridiron did not smile on us in our next outing, a 10-26 loss to Pennington Prep. We not only lost the game but lost the services of Jon Allen, out with a severe ankle sprain. Two more defeats at the hands of Newark and Perkiomen bode poorly for a winning season. In our eighth game we tested our fortunes against Morristown Beard School. After Sam Laybourne hurt his ankle, we turned to sophomore Stafford Woodley. The young running back responded well toting the pigskin 12 times for 73 yards and two touchdowns. The output surprised even Stafford. "I think I carried the ball 15 times today (actually twelve) That's like double the amount I had in all the other games. I wasn't expecting to get the ball that much because I usually don't get the ball that much. It was a real shock when he (Gleeson) kept calling my play and I was happy about that." (Courier Times October, (1991)

The momentum did not last as we lost the season finale 8-30 to ANC. Though only a sophomore, young Ibrahim Fletcher, who a few years later would himself coach at Cheltenham and then Malvern, already sensed the importance of the ANC football game. "The 1990 team played hard but I'm not sure they believed they could win. When the game was over, guys felt frustrated that another class had come out and left without having ever beaten ANC. In 1991 the team seemed like they were optimistic they could win and they fought hard but it wasn't enough. After that game I sensed the guys were angry and tired of losing to them. What I noticed that was different was there was a resolve that next year, we were going to do whatever it took to defeat ANC and end the streak. Looking back on it now as a high school football coach. I believe this season was a major catalyst for the success of the 1992 team."

Despite the tough ending, overall, the season was one of outstanding achievements. The Cougars finished fourth in Lower Bucks County in team offense with 213 points. They also ended up fourth in team defense, surrendering only 211 tallies. First year signal caller Isa Clark was fifth in the area in passing, completing 60 passes for 710 yards and 7 touchdowns. Dwayne McCoy earned all Courier Times first team honors after intercepting an area-best 7 interceptions. John James finished third in receiving, hauling in 27 passes for 413 yards. McCoy was close behind with 24 receptions, good for 244 yards.

Some thirty years later, Dwayne McCoy, with typical modesty, summed up his ascension to the varsity level. "I guess Coach saw things in me that I didn't know I had. I didn't even remember what positions I played on the ninth grade team with Nate (McKee). In junior high school (7th and 8th) I know I played running back and linebacker, so how did I end up being 3 time Bucks County interception leader? It all started when we scrimmaged that school (RCA) for juvenile kids near Neshaminy Mall. It was just a scrimmage, I was only a sophomore with a few upperclassmen ahead of me. I think that game I had about two or three interceptions and from that point on, coach made me the starting safety. That year I finished with 7. We still lost to ANC that year. I developed a real hate for them and vowed that the 17-year losing streak would end during my time at GS."

With so much fire power and determination returning in 1992, spirits ran high. Ibrahim knew this team would not be denied. "Heading into the 1992 season, we had excitement and energy I personally had never experienced at GS. We were really good and we knew it. We had a sense of urgency during the spring workouts and before the season we got new uniforms and they were a big hit. The new unis resembled Washington State's jerseys at the time and had a new color scheme. They were brown and white helmets and the logo resembled a cougar. The material was much smoother and they had a paw print on the top of the shoulder pads. This reinforced the idea that this season was different, our team was different, and the on-field results would be different."

Matt Crocker, junior center, shared Ibrahim's optimism. "The 1992 season we were a powerhouse. We only lost two games that year. They were close too and that was the year we beat and shutout ANC for the first time in seventeen years. I still have the article. I will never forget Sam Laybourne walking into the locker room the first day of the season and telling us we were going to beat ANC that year. Everyone believed it and sure enough that team worked harder than I have ever seen to accomplish that goal."

Sam, who was a co-captain and proven veteran performer, put a more literary touch to the opening days. "I remember doing two-a-days in the late summer, before school started in the fall. During one especially intense practice outside the old fieldhouse, I remember Coach Gleeson quoting a passage from literature. I don't remember the exact quote, but the line that sticks in my head is "To a man." It was a challenge for us all to step up and find the inner strength necessary to finish the practice strong. It was a reminder that a football team only functions if the entire team is focused. It was a reminder that we were becoming men, a compliment and goal wrapped up in one single word. The fact that Coach Gleeson took this call to act so seriously, to the point where he elevated our work to literary level, fired us all up that day. But the truth is, Coach always found the poetry in football. And the way he honored the game with thoughtful, intelligent coaching made us all feel we weren't just chest pounding gladiators. We were playing for each other and creating a story on the field that had the potential to be bigger than us. It was an epic journey that we were all lucky to be on together."

My literary references were not lost on Sam who would go on to grad-uate Phi Beta Kappa from Wesleyan University as an English and American Studies major and later would work as a TV and film writer/producer. Between Tom English and myself, apparently the classroom teaching carried out onto the football field. Any player seeking a break from pure academics ran into tough luck attending our practice sessions. Tom and I were the only two varsity coaches in 1992, which meant he handled the line and I served as both offen-sive and defensive coordinator. That did present some interesting scenarios. In our away game against Wilmington Friend the athletic director asked where we wanted to put our assistant coach on the phones. We just looked at each other and said, "What phones and what assistant?".

The shortage of coaches did not deter the 1992 Cougars. 'Students of the game' such as Sam Laybourne and Dwayne McCoy being on the field, min-imized the need for coaching interference from the sideline. I had told the team in our first preseason meeting that we were going to a two split end offensive scheme, with a slotback and a split backfield. That way we could play perimeter ball as well as attack up the middle. Prior to any 'attacking' we needed to prep. That involved two weeks of hard-draining preseason in late summer weather. Linebacker Ken Andreson remembers those grueling sessions well. "What I remember most are those grueling summer preseason workouts under 95-degree August sun. We'd hit the sled with him (coach Gleeson) standing on it (preferable to Line Coach Tom English standing on it), growling down at us, "Keep 'em chopping...KEEP THE LEGS CHOPPIN"!" I've been through some rough patches in my life, and once in a while I still hear that John Gleeson mantra. Sometimes I think life isn't much more complicated than that: show up, suit up, and keep 'em choppin'."

The strategy and preparation worked as we beat Wardlaw Hartridge 33-19 in our season opener. Against Wardlaw, a team that had gone undefeated the year before, Dwayne McCoy and Isa Clark shared MVP game honors. McCoy caught seven passes for 148 yards and three touchdowns. Clark completed 14 aerials good for 226 yards.

Dwayne summed up the change in the Cougars' thinking in a newspaper interview. "We expect to win every time we play. We are capable of beating any team on our schedule. Last year, I think we were predictable. This year, we can beat a team with the run or the pass or with our defense. We have set high goals for ourselves and we went out today expecting to win." (Courier Times September, 1992)

Proving McCoy a prophet, the Cougars relied on their run game to dismantle West Nottingham 43-0 in their next encounter. The line of Sheldon Cummings, Mark Nadler, Matt Crocker, Bradd Forstein, Jack Ford, Glenn Davis and Ibrahim Fletcher opened holes all day for Stafford Woodley, Sam Laybourne, Anthony Rogers-Wright and Jim Dudnyk. In all the Cougars racked up 264 yards with Woodley accounting for 125 of them.

In our third game, a 13-6 victory over Princeton Day School, the third aspect of our three-pronged attack prevailed. The defense took control. In Ibrahim's words, "As the season started, we got off to a strong start and everything kept falling into place. Early in the season, a Danish exchange student (Tao Binslev) joined the team and he ended up anchoring the interior of our defensive line. He ended up being the last ingredient we needed to get over the hump. As the season went on, we kept winning and the community support increased every week."

The exchange student was Tao Binslev who wrote to me in the summer and said that although he never played football he was a "true Danish Viking". How could we go wrong with those credentials? Another valuable piece to a very aggressive defensive alignment came in the form of 5' 8", 140 pound Ken (Chip) Anderson, our outside linebacker. Though lacking the normal physical attributes required for a linebacker, Ken bore the necessary tenacity. Thinking back on his Cougar football days, Ken would say, "Coach Gleeson had that kind of selfless belief in us. I didn't exactly have the build of a starting linebacker. That didn't deter Coach Gleeson, who seemed to appreciate that I was disciplined, hard working and willing to take (and give) a hit for the team."

Against Princeton Day Mark Nadler stole the defensive spotlight. With the game on the line, defensive end Nadler started a one-man assault on PDS's quarterback. On four successive plays, he sacked the quarterback, forced him to hurry his pass, thwarted his attempt to scramble and then harassed him into misfiring on a fourth down pass attempt. In a postgame interview, Mark would say, "We knew we had the personnel. The offense didn't have as much success this week, but that shows the composure of this team. We all know everyone has to do their job to win and today it was the defense's turn. We just happened to make big plays.". (Courier Times, October, 1992)

The winning ways stalled in our next two games. We lost to Wilmington Friends 15-21 on two questionable calls by the referees. The first came on an illegal lineman downfield penalty on a TD pass. The second came on an inadvertent whistle call, coming when Wilmington misfired on an option play deep in their territory. The play, which would have set up a short Cougar scoring drive, was negated. The next game, a 7-6 loss to Newark Academy, the questionable call came from an overaggressive coach who would not settle for a tie. In the closing minutes of the game and down 7-0, Isa Clark hit John James for a touchdown pass. Rather than kick a tying extra point, I chose to go for the win. Newark tipped the pass, preserving the one point winning margin.

After the game I feebly defended my decision, saying, "If we had scored in the third quarter, I would have gone for the tie, then come back. But at the end, I'm just going for the win. A loss and a tie mean the same thing when you have a chance to win." (Courier Times, October 1992)

I apparently learned my lesson. The following week against Lower Moreland we found ourselves tied 6-6 with 14 seconds left on the clock. Rather than try a last-ditch pass, I put the game on the gifted toe of our placekicker, Seth Weigl. Seth's 30-yard field goal sailed between the uprights, sealing the 9-6 win.

In our seventh game, an away contest against Morristown Beard, we trailed the home team 0-6 at halftime. Matt Crocker remembers some of my halftime coaching theatrics which I later admitted to Tom English were staged. According to Matt, "There were plenty of times when we fell apart and didn't perform. I remember my junior year. I loved that year because I was the only underclassmen on the O-line. We were playing Morristown Beard, a team we usually walked all over and we spent the entire first half slacking, like we didn't even want to be there. I will never forget that colorful half-time speech Coach Gleeson gave us. He called us so many names I can't even remember. He was so disappointed with the way we were playing he wouldn't even talk about the first half. He told us that we had to think about what we were doing and decide if we wanted to play that day. Man, we felt like real idiots that day because after his yelling we went out there and scored a bunch of touchdowns. We came out a different team."

On the second half kickoff, Anthony Rogers-Wright hit the returner so hard he coughed up the ball on his own 22-yard line. Two plays later Isa Clark hit John James with a 16-yard scoring strike. Later in the fourth quarter, Stafford Woodley swept left end to tally six more points for the Cougars. A two-point conversion pass to Paul Zuber would assure the 14-6 win.

The big moment had arrived! All the preparation led up to the big game with our rival ANC. Ibrahim put the game in perspective. "By the time we got to ANC week, the school was on fire and Cougar Pride was on display everywhere on campus. Everyone believed that this year was our year and without a doubt the ANC home game was going to be the most anticipated game during my time at GS. That week in practice the buzz around the campus gave us more energy and we had an excellent week of practice. We knew when we took the field, to a man we were going to win. That game was without a doubt the greatest game I've been a part of as a player."

To defeat a strong ANC team required a good deal of thought and execution. In designing a defense, I felt the best strategy was to confuse our opponent with multiple looks. Fortunately, I had the talented players and a savvy play caller in Sam Laybourne. Basically, I used the multi-talented John James as an end on a 5-3 look, an outside linebacker on 4-4, and a safety on a 4-3-4. We also varied the line calls and used multiple slant and soft schemes. The strategy worked as we held a potent ANC offense scoreless. On offense, we knew they would try to take away our two outside threats, James and McCoy. Instead, we tried to pound the ball up the middle.

The game proved a heated affair. As Matt Crocker said, "The game was a knife fight." In essence we engaged in a defensive brawl. With 1:09 left in the fourth quarter Stafford Woodley scored from twelve yards out to put the Cougars up 6-0. One last defensive stand and the long losing streak was finally over!

The game will live in the minds of many a Cougar warrior. Ibrahim said, "It was a tight defensive battle but I never sensed any panic or worry on the team. I remember seeing the ANC players in shock that they weren't running over us. When Stafford scored late in the fourth quarter, we knew we needed a stop and we had achieved our goal. Once we got that stop and iced the game, the place exploded and that was the loudest I've ever heard a GS game. The streak was broken and we were ecstatic. We took a long victory lap with the long-coveted trophy as the fans showed their appreciation for our efforts. At the team's season ending party, we watched the film from the game and just soaked it all up. It was a beautiful day!"

Dwayne McCoy had lived out his pledge to defeat ANC before he graduated. As he remembered thirty years later, "My junior year was our best year. I think we only lost 1 or 2 games. ANC wasn't our best game statistically that year, but it was enough to get the job done, a 6-0 shutout. Most of the game was a blur to me except for 4 plays. The first was my offensive pass interference.

I think Isa (Clark) underthrew me and I pretty much grabbed the defender to prevent an interception. There was a play that ANC's #84 (always lined up with his back to the center) that almost had an interception at the line of scrimmage that could have set our fate. If he caught it, he could have walked into the endzone. Instead, he dropped it. The third was Staff's game-winning TD. Just seeing him will his way from the 2-yard line was epic. The last memory was my game sealing interception. It was the biggest interception of my career. I didn't think I caught it. If you watch the tape, you'll see me look at the ref for the call. As soon as he called it a catch, it was time to celebrate. Ironically that was my 7th interception that season. I guess 7 was my lucky number. There was no bigger moment in my athletic career at GS than winning that game. We finally, after 17 years, won the 'Super Bowl'".

As a senior captain playing his last game, the game held special meaning for Sam Laybourne. "Of course, I will never forget the team's victory over ANC, 6-0 in a hard-fought defensive battle my senior year. My teammate Stafford Woodley, scored the winning touchdown and I was honored to provide a lead block for him. This game, in many ways, was the culmination of my time as an athlete at George School – an almost inconceivably joyful storybook ending. We defeated ANC for the first time in what seemed like forever. (It was at least 14 years since we defeated our sworn rivals, but some folks say it was 18 years. All I know is the number keeps going up as we get older!) We so wanted to deliver a victory to Coach Gleeson, Tom English and the rest of the staff that the players pledged to shave off all of our hair if we were victorious …and we all wore our shorn looks as a badge of honor once we won."

One moment that both coach and player will long remember took place on the sideline after the game. Sam retells it. "There's an image from the end of the ANC game of me and Coach Gleeson hugging on the field. I was full-on sobbing tears of joy and we were locked in a joyous, vigorous bear hug – and it's one of the most meaningful images from my life. It represents what it feels like to collaborate with someone you love and respect and finally succeed in achieving an ambitious goal. Happy endings don't always happen out in life, but the fact that we were able to win that day, and defy the pull of history, is something I can recall whenever I need extra motivation in my life. To me, this image of a coach and player hugging represents the ideal of not just athletics, but of education as a whole. It's the desire to better oneself and to thrive under mentorship as a young person. I wanted to win that game for myself and for a coach who believed in me. A coach who challenged me, and my teammates to be the very best version of ourselves. To a man."

Sam's words hit at the heart of what football coaching had come to mean to me. It is the mutual bond between player and coach that touches more than just scores, wins or championship seasons. Both participants learn and grow from the relationship. As my mentor Bob Geissinger had written me, "I never looked at it as any more than part of the curriculum but an important part due to the lessons in self-discipline and the inherent lessons that come from playing a team sport. I have always tried to adhere to the philosophy of Ossie Solem, my college coach, who stated that the coach should aid the players to defeat their faults both individually and collectively, to the point that they would have no regrets from playing the game." Both coach and player grow and learn from the experience. Both suffer through the defeats, agonize over the injuries, and celebrate the victories. Such growth is a true and meaningful part of the educational process.

Looking back at age 45 Dwayne McCoy touched upon that relationship when he wrote, "Being a silent leader, I don't think I talked much as a hype man or motivational speaker, but let my play on the field do the talking. I left it all on the field and I attribute that to Coach. I remember in practice that he would do drills which motivated me and others to work harder. 'If I could just be half as good as Glees, I'd be great.' That would be my motivation to get through practices and games. If I worked this hard during practices, the game was always easier. I'm sure to this day he would be good for a game. Those three years playing varsity football were the best TEAMS I've played on. We always played as a team and rarely did we bicker amongst ourselves. We may not have been the most talented all the time, but we always played 100% from the traits Coach instilled in us."

The 1993 season brought a whole new set of challenges for the Cougars. They were proven winners and, despite the loss of several key components to graduation, still boasted an arsenal of explosive players. The twin towers, John James and Dwayne McCoy, still remained in their wide out positions. Stafford Woodley and Anthony Rogers-Wright anchored a solid running game.

The two questions looming as the season opened was whether Ben Walmer could fill the quarterback spot vacated by Isa Clark and could a line with only one returning starter in Matt Crocker hold up.

Now a senior leader, Ibrahim Fletcher summed up the plight facing the GS gridders. "Our senior year we lost a lot of talent from the '93 class. We had a rivalry with them and we wanted to prove that we had better athletes than they had. We were sluggish in camp and coach Gleeson ripped us the week of our first game. He managed to get our minds right and we had a very strong start to the season."

The first game, a 32-0 rout of Wardlaw -Hartridge, indicated the new-look Cougars packed plenty of potential on both sides of the ball. Ben Walmer answered the call, completing 8 of 10 passes for 132 yards and two touchdowns. James caught 4 aerials for 79 yards and a TD. McCoy hauled in 2 for 15 yards and a TD. Paul Zuber caught 2 for 38 yards and another score. Anthony Rogers-Wright rushed for 79 yards behind the revamped offensive line.

The second game presented a whole new series of challenges. Originally scheduled to play RCA, we had to scurry around to find an opponent when RCA canceled its football program. The only team with compatible openings dwelled three hours away in Federalsburg, Maryland. The three-hour bus trip seemed daunting. It did, however, guarantee the Cougars their first ever night game. Ibrahim described the excitement, "We played our first and only night game versus a team in Maryland. We were so excited to finally get a chance to experience the Friday night lights. In addition to that the team (Colonel Richardson) had a running quarterback who Coach Gleeson described as Randall Cunningham. We knew going into that game we had to keep him in check. We absolutely demolished them from start to finish in what was our most dominant game of the season. We found out during the game that their quarterback quit at halftime. They had a player who came into the locker room and asked if he could come back with us and be a part of our time."

Featured in the 36-0 rout were Anthony Rogers-Wright (7 carries foor 134 yards), Ben Walmer (9 for 19 passing and 129 yards), John James (3 catches, 54 yards, 1 TD) and Dwayne McCoy (3 catches for 49 yards and a TD). The new line, anchored by senior captain Matt Crocker, looked equally impressive.

Matt, foreshadowed the Eagle's Jason Kelce as the only center to snap the ball and then pull out and lead the running plays around end, valued his role as team leader. "I learned a lot about leadership and how to make things happen, how to motivate people and how to lead through example. I am glad that I was elected to be captain. I know I wasn't the best player on the team or had extraordinary talent, but I knew what we needed to do. Coach described me as a silent leader."

His leadership role blossomed after Matt graduated from George School to pursue a career in the military. "Things have changed for me since then. I am a little more outspoken in my leadership abilities now. I am presently a First Lieutenant in the United States Marine Corp and I know that GS football played a large part for me becoming a successful officer. GS football made me believe that any challenge can be met and just how hard you have to work to achieve goals that you set forth. Since I left GS, I have set many goals for myself and so far I have accomplished everything that I have wanted to do. There are more days than not that I feel my goals are too hard to reach, but I just work harder to get what I want. I definitely saw that while I was on Coach Gleeson's team."

After a tough 12-14 loss to Princeton Day School, the Cougars rebounded in their homecoming encounter with Wilmington Friends. Though down 8-13 at half, the Cougars managed to rally and pick up a 22-13 victory. Anthony Rogers-Wright sparked the comeback with a 2-yard run in the third quarter. In the final period slotback Paul Zuber stole the limelight and made an acrobatic catch to set up the Cougars final TD, a nine-yard slant pass to Dwayne McCoy. Zuber described his heroics in a postgame interview. "We eventually ran that sideline pass and I didn't run it that well. The linebacker really had me covered. I saw the ball coming and tipped it over him with one hand. He fell by me and I caught it and had the whole sideline wide open." (Courier Times, October 17, 1993)

As satisfying as the win seemed, it did not overshadow the loss of Dwayne McCoy, who suffered a season ending shoulder injury. Ibrahim described the plight of the Cougars. "As quickly as the start came, it went as we were decimated by injuries to key starters, many of which suffered season ending injuries. Others were hobbled and even though they played, they weren't able to play at their normal levels. We fought hard but it wasn't enough as it seemed like every week someone else went down with an injury. We were able to salvage some parts of the season including winning our final senior home game against Morristown Beard. The following week after playing hard and hanging around against ANC, we were just too depleted and in the fourth quarter ANC put the game away."

Ibrahim aptly described the Cougars' fate. After two sound thumpings at the hands of Sidwell Friends and Lower Moreland, the GS gridders rallied to capture a 26-14 home affair against previously unbeaten Morristown Beard. Anthony Rogers-Wright once again sparked the Cougar offense rushing 13 times for 106 yards and a touchdown. Walmer completed nine passes for 109 yards and two scores. John James, playing in his last home game before heading to the University of Pennsylvania, returned a punt 65 yards for a score and then caught the game clincher with a sensational fourth quarter catch. Don Beideman of the Philadelphia Inquirer wrote that, "The six-foot 4-inch, 225-pound senior, one of the leading receivers and scorers in Bucks County, simply went up over his defender to make a dazzling catch for his one touchdown. (Philadelphia Inquirer, November, 1993)

Despite closing out his varsity career with a 0-20 loss to ANC, Ibrahim still cherished the bonds he experienced in his days on the GS gridiron. "As I look back on those years, I miss being around the guys in the locker room, the rides to and from games with my teammates, the feeling of walking around school on Friday with our jerseys on. That time in my life was so special because I had the opportunity to play football at GS. What people don't understand about our game is that once it is done, it's done. In other sports you can get pick up games, while there may not be a crowd you can still play the game and compete. Once you take off the pads and helmet, you'll never be able to simulate that experience ever again. There hasn't been a year since I graduated when I didn't wish I could play one more year at GS for Coach Gleeson. I'm sure many of my brothers in sport who played football feel the same way."

Matt Crocker also put his Cougar experience in perspective, "I have to admit that the one thing I think of most when I look back on my experience at George School was football. I went on to play football at Gettysburg College where I was a walk-on. I found out that college ball is definitely a step up. It was challenging but not much fun. It felt more like a job than a sport. I found my college experience not to be nearly as rewarding as high school. I subsequently left the team after my second season. Many of my friends felt the same way and left as well. A lot of us did not get the attention we got in high school and felt like a number, especially as an average player. When I think of what a football team is supposed to be like I think of the teams that I was on during my time at GS."

The spirit extolled by Matt certainly remained strong in the years to come. Though the 1994 season saw many seniors go the graduation route, the new cast of characters bonded firmly. Jeff Haines, a junior lineman, echoed that feeling. "Playing football at George School led to a plethora of shared experiences, good and bad, on the field and off, and the mindset that you will do anything for any of your teammates at the drop of a hat because staying together was absolutely essential. If links are players, we never had a very long chain but it was strong and intact. For me, practice is where our relationships were forged, fortified, and what I will always remember as my favorite part of playing football at GS."

Despite listing only four seniors on the roster, the 1994 Cougars showed veteran savvy in their opening 20-0 victory over Saint Andrews. The defense, led by Rashon Thorne, limited the Delaware invaders to 136 total yards. Thorne, a defensive end, had 10 tackles, 2 sacks and one blocked punt. He would tell reporter Daryl Dobos in a postgame interview, "We were expecting Saint Andrews to run to my side and not pass a lot. After a while they started running away from my side, so coach Gleeson made some adjustments to allow me to get them deep in the backfield." (Courier Times, September 25, 1994)

On offense, fledgling quarterback Chuck Draper gave all the signs that the passing game of previous years was alive and well. He completed 5 passes for 82 yards and two touchdowns. Those numbers would only increase as the season progressed. Chuck would summarize his first game at QB saying, "The line did a great job blocking all day. I think our problem on our first few series was first game jitters, I was really nervous but with Antoine Speights' catching and Willie Lenzner (5 carries for 56 yards) and Eli Miles (14-75, TD) running real well, it made things much easier. It feels good to get that first win under our belt." (Courier Times. September 25, 1994)

The young line, featuring only one senior in Captain David Gonzales, played extremely well on both sides of the ball. The receiving core of Antoine Speights, Rashon Thorne, Kevin Edwards and Eli Miles indicated a real readiness to take over for the departed Dwayne McCoy and John James. Speights sealed the victory with his second TD grab in the third quarter. Antoine described the play to reporter Adam Gusdorff, "I was trying to keep the defender away with my left hand and I just stuck out my right hand and caught it. We were trying to come right at them and attack after the interception." (Philadelphia Inquirer, September 26, 1994)

The Cougar's Draper-to-Speights' combo would prove a lethal weapon all season. Speights earned Courier Times first team Golden Team honors with 29 catches for 561 yards and 9 touchdowns. Draper led all of Lower Bucks County, completing 67 passes for 1096 yards and ten touchdowns. Add Thorne to the mix with his 20 receptions for 315 yards and one could see why opposing forces feared "Air Cougar".

After a wake-up call 6-28 loss to Sidwell Friends, the Cougars regained their winning ways, downing Princeton Friends 6-0. The defense proved paramount as the bend-but-don't-break strategy limited Princeton's explosive running back Eric Boyd to 110 yards rushing and no touchdowns. Quarterback Chuck Draper plunged in from two yards out for the Cougar's only tally.

Another tough away loss to Wilmington (0-18) set up a home encounter against Bristol High School with their vaunted wishbone running attack. The game saw every offensive explosion imaginable from long runs, long passes, kick returns, to interception returns. Every time Bristol tallied, George School answered until the final whistle to put the Warriors ahead 48-34. For the home team Draper completed 10 of 20 passes for 226 yards and 4 touchdowns. Speights caught 4 of the bombs for 127 yards and three TDs. Adding to the fireworks, Rashon Thorne returned a kickoff 75 yards for a score.

After the game Rashon Thorne said, "None of us have ever been in a game like this. But we never quit. We always thought we could get another score to tie or take the lead, but we fell short. We won't hang our heads. There's nothing to be ashamed about this one." (Courier Times, October 23, 1994)

Bristol coach George Gatto reiterated Thorne's sentiments, "I'll tell you what, that's the wildest game I've been in. No question about it. George School came after us and did a great job. They didn't give us a moment of peace. We've had a bunch of games go down to the wire. It's about time we won one." (Courier Times, October 23, 1994)

The offensive shootout seemed to spark the Cougar attack as we won our next two contests, 6-0 over Lower Moreland and 24-0 over Wardlaw Hartridge. Against Lower Moreland it took a Draper-to-Speights 26-yard touchdown pass to seal the deal in the fourth quarter. The running game took center stage in the Wardlaw tussle. Eli Miles toted the pigskin ten times for 84 yards. Senior Jamil Brown rushed ten times for 49 yards and two scores. Not to be denied, the Draper-to-Speights' combo clicked on the game's first tally. Speights would later return a punt 42 yards to score.

The two victories set up our annual year-end fight against arch-rival ANC. The game proved to be another shootout with ANC earning the laurels with a 35-22 win. Despite Draper connecting with Speights (68 yards) and Thorne (178 yards) the Cougars could not match the Academy's running game which chalked up 266 yards. From my vantage point, the young Cougars had matured. I said to reporter Daryl Dobbs after the game, "Draper is the first quarterback that I can remember to go over 1,000 yards. He did an excellent job for a first-year player. Thorne has been hiding all year just waiting to come out. He is a horse with great hands. Both guys are going to be forces next year." (Courier Times, November 13, 1994)

Years later, captain David Gonzales would put the true meaning of his George School gridiron career in perspective. In a letter to me after the 9-11 disaster David wrote, "Hello Coach, I am sorry to have allowed a tragedy of the magnitude of the World Trade Center Crisis for me to write to you. You may or may not remember me, David Gonzalez Jr, but I most certainly remember you. I am writing to let you know that I am in New York and am suffering through this crisis on a first-hand level. I wanted you to know that what you taught us on the football field and in the classroom has helped me get through these trying times. You always spoke of getting through tough times and pushing ourselves past the point we believed we could go. I know this may seem a little odd, but coach, I just wanted to let you know you have had a tremendous effect on my life and I just wanted to thank you. God bless you and your family coach."

David's letter supports Sam Laybourne's earlier words and reflects that the bond between a coach and his players goes well beyond how successful they are on the field. Both players highlighted the true value of sports. The lessons learned on the gridiron are endless.

The Cougars returning for the 1995 season seemed a talented and determined lot. During their fledgling season they showed they could attack from both sides of the ball. This potential inspired a very rigorous preseason practice plan. The drills started with the running of the now infamous obstacle course, a series of maneuvers aimed at testing the players agility, determination and pure athleticism. We progressed through three daily practices with a good deal of running and skill work. Just when players started rounding into shape, we had what I called "Bang, Bang" Thursday, a day long affair reserved for hitting.

Where I thought most kids dreaded both preseason and regular season practices, Senior tri-captain Jeff Haines shed a different light on these sessions. "I loved football practice, especially as a senior when I was bigger than anyone else (save Rashon Thorne). Looking back, I think that football practice at GS formed so many of the good habits I now employ on a daily basis. Habits like accountability, dedication, comradery, communications, working hard so that I can make a teammate's job that much easier, proving myself to my teammates, coaches and myself...I can go on and on. If only my current routine could also incorporate all these habits but also be acceptable to blindsiding certain individuals to the ground."

With the grueling preseason finally behind us, we felt prepped to take on any challenge. Unfortunately, the football gods viewed life differently, showering us with seemingly constant adverse weather and injuries to key players. The week before our opening game, Antoine Speights injured his shoulder. It appeared he would be lost for the season. Another of our starting linemen transferred to Perkiomen School. With depleted forces we traveled to Saint Andrews and battled to a 6-6 tie. Our only score came via an Anthony Wade pass interception that went 40 yards to paydirt. Admittedly, the Cougar passing attack was off, accounting for only 8 completed passes. After the game I lamented that, "They did a great job in taking Rashon out of the game. With Antoine (Speights) injured we need to go to Rashon even more, but they wouldn't let us get him the ball." (Philadelphia Inquirer, September 24, 1995)

The following week against Princeton Day School, the Cougars regrouped. Spearheading the offensive attack was Stafford Woodley's younger brother Rashawn who picked up 125 yards on 21 carries good for 2 touchdowns. John Wadley added 69 yards and a score to the Cougar's output. Rashawn quickly attributed his fine play to the offensive line, bolstered by Jeff Haines, Will Adams, Randy Boyton, Bliss Holloway, James Wilson and Jaron Shipp. "All my yards go to my line. They really opened up holes for me. We had to step it up after last week." (Courier Times, September 24, 1995)

The next four weeks saw the Cougars battling not only tough opponents but an endless barrage of rainy weather, conditions not conducive to a pass- oriented offense. After losing to Pennington 0-6 and Wilmington Friends 0-12, we took on Bristol in our homecoming game. Bill Kenny of the Courier Times aptly described the prevailing monsoon season, "When it's been raining constantly for a day-and-a- half and the middle of the field looks more like Woodstock than a gridiron, football teams tend to simplify things." (Courier times, October 22, 1995)

Bristol got the best of the simplification process when fullback Reuban Ray plowed 20 yards through the muck and mire to give the Warriors the only score of the game. Chuck Draper did manage to complete 8 passes to tight end Rashon Thorne good for 64 yards, a feat that drew praise from Bristol coach George Gatto. "No question about it, that Thorne is a heck of a receiver. But they didn't have their other receiver, Speights, to go to. The main thing is I'm proud of our secondary. We played well as a defensive unit." (Courier Times, October 22, 1995)

A 13-28 loss to Lower Moreland the following week, set up two final chances at salvaging what had initially seemed such a promising campaign. The Courier's Steve Cornell highlighted the Cougar's entire season. "When it rains, as it has most weekends during the 1995 football season, the Cougars pass-reliant offense cannot move the ball consistently. Under dry conditions, however, George School quarterback Chuck Draper can throw the ball, end Rashon Thorne can catch it, and the offense can score like it did in a 29-6 win over the Rams (Wardlaw Hartridge)." (Courier Times, November 5, 1995)

In the 29-6 victory, Draper completed 14 of 23 passes for 123 yards. Thorne gobbled up 9 of the aerials for 92 yards and a touchdown. Rob Early picked up 82 yards and three scores on the ground.

Confidence renewed, the Cougars faced one more shot at redemption, the showdown with arch-rival ANC. Chuck Draper well-remembers his final GS football encounter. "Playing football for GS allowed me an opportunity to develop both my football skills and leadership skills within a positive environment. The coaches and older teammates showed me how determination and working relentlessly as a team would always pay off in the long run. During my freshman year I had the opportunity to watch the varsity team go 6-2 and beat Academy of the New Church. I remember the coaches pushing us hard from the preseason three- practices-a-day to the final practices in the dark preparing for ANC. "

Twenty years later, Jeff Haines remembers the emphasis put on winning the ANC game and how important it was for the 1995 squad. "Not only is that day, a 26-0 win at ANC, the most recent and vivid memory in my mind, but the importance of the game itself makes our final result that much sweeter. Coach Gleeson always said that we might only win one game, but if it was against ANC then it was a successful season. Damn it was awesome burying them as a final act."

The task became easier when we learned that Antoine Speights could play in his final game. As he said in a postgame interview, "Four weeks ago I made up my mind I was going to play in this game. The doctors didn't give me the okay until Wednesday, but I wasn't going to let them stop me. I've been playing football since seventh grade. It's hard to get me off the field." (Courier Times, November 12, 1995)

Speights had 4 catches for 59 yards, 15 of which came on a leaping touchdown in the fourth quarter that gave the Cougars a 19-0 lead. Thorne caught 2 passes for 19 yards and a TD. Rashawn Woodley racked up 74 rushing yards and a tally. Jeff Haines also experienced a defensive lineman's dream scenario when he intercepted an ANC pass. "That was a fun and unexpected achievement (and I still give Chuck Draper schtick for after he called an audible on the next play and threw a pick) I remember several yarns that you (Gleeson) and ESPECIALLY Tom English would spin throughout my three varsity years of prior players, their personalities, quirks, and accomplishments. To think that perhaps my interception became an anecdote for future players is surreal to me because those players I had heard about so often but never met are absolute legends in my mind."

After the game I was quoted as saying, "This has been a long season for these guys. Losing Antoine was a big blow. It was a real lift when he was cleared to play on Wednesday. You could just see it the last three days. Football was fun again. It wasn't so much fun after those tough losses in the middle of the season." (Courier Times, November 12, 1995)

Reflective of David Gonzales's letter, the 1995 Cougars had gone through some tough times. They pushed themselves hard and the effort finally paid off.

Entering the 1996 season the coaching staff underwent a dramatic change. My trusted companion of eight years, Tom English, undoubtedly inspired by his new marital status, decided that remaining in the recently revamped McFeeley Library was less stressful than journeys to Maryland, Delaware and New Jersey. Kassem Lucas, who I had already deemed a true leader, took full control as the defensive coordinator. I noticed that when I called time out when the offense was on the field I would rush out onto the field and impart whatever wisdom I had to the team. When defense called time, all the players would rush over to Kassem for advice. I sensed I still had a lot to learn about leadership. George Long, who had played for Bucknell, joined the squad as line coach and overall adviser. I came to see George as not only a close friend but also a true educator who not only knew football but really cared about the kids.

By then, preseason was a fully ingrained part for most of the fall athletic teams. The two-week period served as a boon to coaches who could condition players, work on skills and install offensive and defensive schemes. To the players it became both a necessary torture and also a time for team bonding. The football team no longer had to sleep on the wrestling mats in the gym or on the top floor of the student health center. They even got to live in Drayton and get hot meals in the dining room.

Jevon Thoresen, quarterback and team captain, valued the experience. "The most lasting memory for me is the comradery of the team. Beginning with pre-season and going through to the last game in November. Pre-season presented the most grueling of challenges but also presented the most rewards. Sitting around in the afternoons in the Drayton dorm lobby after two practices, the majority of the team could find solidarity in talking with teammates. The heat of August made each pre-season that much more difficult but provided all the more growth. Such a grueling process made each individual look within and grow all the more. I found such challenges made me question why I played and every time that question was answered with a resounding love for the game, my teammates and my coach."

Jevon's questioning took on other forms his sophomore year. "One of my most vivid memories was after the spring intrasquad game my sophomore year. In competition for the QB job I played terribly and threw a number of interceptions. I returned to my room dejected and with thoughts of quitting. However, after a teammate of mine came to my room to console me, I understood what I had to do. Rather than quit I redirected myself and got in shape for the following season where I earned a starting spot as a defensive back."

For Jevon, football opened a new way of thinking. "George School football taught me to attack challenges as well as the importance of being on a team. As a senior captain and starting QB I learned to lead in the face of adversity. With an undersized team, a young team as well as one that lacked dedication, I learned patience, communication and strong motivational skills."

All the traits paid off in our opening game against Saint Andrews. Jevon helped guide a relative group of neophytes to a 20-6 win though he admits he himself suffered some pregame jitters. "The first game of my senior year against Saint Andrews I was so nervous and wanted to win so badly I got less than three hours of sleep the night before."

On one of the earlier offensive plays we were bottled up deep in our own territory. I decided to play it safe and called a fullback dive. Jevon, who had worked out over the summer with his friend and fellow co-captain Kevin Edwards, checked off and called an audible, a pass to Kevin. The play went the distance and sparked our big, opening victory.

Having lost our next game 6-47 to Wilmington Friends, we were ready to take on our cross-river rival, Princeton Day School. The 20-7 win showcased a balanced offensive attack. Rashawn Woodley rushed for 136 yards, including a 71- yard touchdown jaunt. Jevon passed for 113 yards and two touchdowns. Kevin was on the receiving end of most of the passes, adding 111 yards to the Cougar's offense. The following week against Wardlaw Hartridge we showed a similar dual attack. Woodley ran for 142 yards, Thoresen passed for 104 yards. Edwards caught 9 passes, good for 99 yards. Unfortunately, the output was not enough as Wardlaw captured a 32-14 victory.

Win or lose, Kevin showed real leadership potential. "As a captain my senior year, I learned the meaning of leadership. First it meant knowing yourself before you could help anyone else. It was an amazing experience to be able to give someone encouraging words and then watch it transfer into a good play on the field."

Kevin utilized these lessons, both at Duke University and later in his job as a financial adviser. "The other major benefit was discipline. College has been easy because football at GS forced me to learn time management skills. There were many other benefits and rewards. Next year when I graduate from Duke, I will be working for Goldman Sachs. In my interview 75% was spent talking about my experiences as a high school football player. My ability to articulate these experiences and relate them to real life was key in landing my first job out of college."

Unfortunately for the 1996 Cougars not all of Kevin's experiences were positive. In the Faith Christian Academy game Kevin suffered a severe bruised nerve in his shoulder. This setback really crippled a team that had already lost tightend Scot Justice to mono and Icky Mount to a broken wrist. The depleted Cougars lost our last four ball games to Faith Christian, Bristol, Lower Moreland, and ANC.

Kevin somehow courageously managed to return to action against ANC, a memory he will long keep. "One of my lasting memories was coming back to play against ANC and making a 50-yard reception. I played my heart out but had a severely pinched nerve against Faith Christian. Injuries to key players was a recurring theme at GS."

Despite the physical upsets both Jevon and Kevin valued the appeal of football. Kevin liked, "The team aspect of the sport and the ability to let aggressions out in a controlled manner." Jevon reiterated these sentiments, "Football appealed to me as a way of letting out aggression and at the same time gave balance to my days. I had better grades during football season because it provided more structure to my life."

Jevon elaborated on his Cougar football experiences. "Looking back at my four years of playing at GS I see not only physical growth but an enormous amount of growth as a person. Football gave me an outlet from frustrations of school, home, friends, etc. I know that on the football field I had a family away from home and I miss it dearly. I often think now that I wish I could go back and do it again. My biggest reason to stop playing in college was the lack of a fraternal order on the team. There was no comradery and I did not get on well with the coach. I had gone from a father figure as a coach to a man who could not unite anyone on the team."

The bonding continued for the 1997 Cougars. Unfortunately, so did the injury streak. With only twenty-some players listed on the roster, losing one or two key performers would prove disastrous. We started the season with a loss at the hands of Saint Andrews. Senior Rashawn Woodley continued his sparkling play, rushing for 111 yards. A marked man, Rashawn also drew fire from the opposition's most aggressive defenders. The end result would be an injury sidelining him for the three ball games and sending the Cougars on a three game offensive slide. We suffered losses to Wilmington Friends 0-30, Princeton Day School 0-21 and Wardlaw 6-42. By the time Bristol came to town our offensive output was running on fumes. Woodley's return did generate some spark as he rushed 24 yards for our first touchdown and five yards for our second tally. In all, the hobbled ace runner would produce 121 yards, a solid effort but not sufficient to stop the Warriors from taking a 20-14 win. Two more losses to Lower Moreland and Pennington set up one last chance to notch a victory. To accomplish this feat would require a strong showing against a potent ANC squad. Several minutes into the contest, it became clear Woodley could not continue. His sub, Charles Johnson gave a good account of himself, picking up 55 rushing yards and two TDs. Sophomore Jamaal Mobley emerged as a real threat hauling in 8 passes for 145 yards. The offensive showing was not enough to overcome a 48-22 defeat.

Going into the 1998 season I really believed we could end our 13 game winless drought. In a preseason preview appearing in the local paper I said, "I think it is going to be a good year. Our schedule is a rough one and a strange one. We play archrival The Academy of the New Church in the second game of the season this year. I would hope we could get to .500. I think this team could very well come out with a winning season. I'm very impressed and that's not just coaching euphoria." (Courier Times, September 1, 1998)

Though only starting with 20 players on the roster, I based my optimism on the presence of several talented newcomers and a couple of savvy vets. Chris Haines appeared fully recovered from a shoulder injury that had bothered him the previous year. Seniors Eric Mount and Charles Johnson had filled in nicely for Rashawn Woodley the year before. Andrew Ambler appeared to be a tough linebacker/fullback combo who had a plethora of football skills and knowledge. Though light, Jamaal Mobley had all the requisite athleticism, height, concentration and hands to be an excellent receiver. Russ Nicolaysen, Josh Skversky, Ryan Bradley, Joe Krivda, Thomas Pittman and AQ Abdul-Karim sported the aggression and skill to anchor both our lines.

Russ Nicolaysen, in reflection, hit at the core of what George School football entailed, when he wrote that from his playing days, he "Learned how to work hard, with determination and pride. When I first came to George School, I saw that we weren't a school that had a huge population to choose from. If you think about it, the school has 550 students, half of those are girls so those are eliminated. The rest either have the excuse that their parents won't let them or they play other sports, or something else. It molds down to about 40 kids who want to play. Some of them are on JV and have never played. GS has always worked with what they get. The school was lucky to get players like Rashawn Woodley, Jamaal Mobley and others who have unbelievable talent. Knowing that we had to overcome odds like those drove me as a player."

This appeared to be the season when we had that combination of talent and determination. We only lacked game experience and the feeling that comes with ultimately winning. The switch to playing ANC second occurred for two reasons. The Academy played in the Independence league and was bound by their conference's scheduling. Also, playing them the second week in November clashed with our final exam schedule and the tryouts for winter sports. However, having ANC, Wilmington Friends and Pennington Prep all stacked at the top of the heap meant three straight very tough opponents.

Our inexperience showed as we lost to Wilmington Friends 0-28, ANC 0-48 and Pennington 24-36. The Pennington game indicated our offense did have some firepower. Charles Johnson picked up 84 yards rushing and scored a TD. We just needed to get the "losing monkey" off our backs. That moment finally came in our 30-16 win over Princeton Day School. Not dazzled by PDS's fancy bus or spiffy new uniform ensembles, we treated the home fans to a long-awaited victory. The game featured the emergence of sophomore running back Shaun Greene who rushed for 107 yards. When not toting the football, he executed a perfect halfback option pass to fellow Atlantic City mate Jamaal Mobley for a 20-yard touchdown. Fullback Andy Ambler, who spent most of the afternoon annihilating would-be-tacklers, tallied from 43 yards out. Mobley hauled in another score on a 15-yard pass from Chris Haines.

The Cougars obviously cherished the thrill of victory as they defeated West Nottingham 32-15 the following week. Eric Mount drew game MVP honors rushing 13 times for 121 yards and two touchdowns. Andy Ambler, who filled in for Chris Haines after Chris was ejected for questioning a call, completed 4 of 12 passes for 46 yards and a TD to Mobley.

The Cougars ran the winning streak to three games as we defeated Saint Andrews 32-20. Haines returned to action and passed for 166 yards including a 40-yard scoring strike to Eric "Icky" Mount. Shaun Greene once again showed real promise as a sophomore, rushing for 109 yards.

Our next two encounters against our public school foes Bristol and Lower Moreland did not go our way. We lost 12-43 to Bristol and 8-28 to Lower Moreland. Jamaal Mobley, however, certainly lived up to Russ Nicolaysen's praise catching 7 passes against Bristol for 104 yards and 6 against Lower Moreland for 80 yards. He finished the year as the second leading receiver in Lower Bucks County with 39 catches for 463 yards and 6 touchdowns.

Tim Hyland in his Courier Times column the following year noted my prediction that we would have a winning season in 1998. Tim wrote, "The Cougars almost pulled it off, they went 3-5. They went 3-5 even though at different points in the season they had lost their starting quarterback and starting tailback. They went 3-5 even though most of their players played offense and defense and even if they needed a breather they couldn't have taken one. They went 3-5 even though they only had 20 players. And this year they have 24. Who knows what they'll accomplish?" (Courier Times, August 26, 1999)

Tim Hyland's comments proved prophetic as we entered the 1999 season. More important than any stats, however, were the lessons the Cougars had learned, truths that held the key to a winning campaign. Jamaal had come to realize the need for unity on any team. As he would write 15 years after the fact. "I've spent a few days thinking about this (GS Football) and there are several angles to come at this from. I keep coming back to the concept of team and that no one team member is more important than the team as a whole. I carry that with me today."

Jamaal translated this concept to the gridiron. No one individual carries the load or receives the praise. "As you know in football in order for the WR to catch a TD pass, the offensive guard has to identify his blocking assignment, the QB has to read the defensive coverage, the RB has to carry out the fake and also pass protect. The play call from the coach has to understand the strengths and weaknesses of both his offense and the opposing team's defense. So while me, as a WR, might receive the glory from the crowd and newspaper coverage, none of that happens unless everyone on the team does their job. It doesn't matter how fast or strong or skilled in running routes or catching the ball I may be."

Jamaal has carried these truths to his later professional career. "The concepts here are also true as a professional in the workforce, being a member of teams working together to achieve success. If the TEAM doesn't achieve success, it doesn't matter what any team member achieved as individuals. My first understanding of that came from Coach Gleeson and GS Football."

Jamaal's fellow co-captain, Russ Nicolayeson, reiterated the wisdom of this all-important concept. "When we would win it showed what kind of reward we get for hard work, teamwork, determination and doing the best we can. Mentioning teamwork, there are no individual players on our team. There are players who are better, but not individuals, which is what makes us a tight team."

The team look started with individual determination. Russ readily admitted that football, "Was a way to channel aggression. Naturally I'm not a violent person, but that doesn't change the fact that during the day my tolerance is stressed. I've always liked being a part of a team. And since there's only 20-25 people on our team it was appealing. Eventually I wanted to hit someone really hard and as a pulling guard I got to do that."

Shaun Greene, who as a sophomore carried the pigskin 82 times for 393 yards, knew the 1999 Cougars were a special team. Later serving two tours of duty with the Air Corps in Afghanistan, Shaun would look back at the 1999 team's spirit. "Any time you can be a part of history is obviously a treasure for life but with GS football it's extra special because it's not a school known for its athletics. Coach brought a lot of fire, fueled with passion and desire, to each and every practice and by the time I got to my second year at the school, somehow the stars aligned and we ended up with really good athletes at every skill position on the field. I don't know if Glees quietly sent up prayers during Meeting for Worship the year before or what, but at the beginning of the season we all agreed, 'We could win every game this year!'". We were one game shy of an undefeated season and at the time of publishing this book, we hold the record for games won and points scored."

The historic season started with a 27-7 conquest of Calvary Christian, a team coached by former Philadelphia Eagle linebacker Mike Reichenbach. Little surprise we were happy when it took us less than 3 minutes to score our first touchdown of the season. In a picture that would replay over and over again all year, Andy Ambler threw a 36-yard touchdown to Jamaal Mobley who outjumped double coverage on a post route. The combo would click again on our second drive with Mobley scoring on a 14 yard slant pass. Jamaal would later tell writer Daryl Dobos, "They had an outside linebacker on me and a corner playing me deep. The middle was wide open. They kept double teaming me all game, but that's OK. We just kept running (Shaun) Greene at them. It keeps the other team guessing who to cover." (Courier Times September, 1999)

Greene would pick up 126 yards on the ground, including a 54 scamper to give the Cougars a 20-0 lead in the second quarter. He would be quick to credit his line, Russ Nicolayesen, Nick Vantresca, Tom Pittman, Ryan Bradley and Josh Skversky. The mercurial halfback summed up the Cougars' new team approach in a postgame interview, "There is a lot more emotion on this team. Last year before games everyone would just sit there. No one would say a word. I could tell the difference today. Everyone was talking and pumping each other up before the game. Nobody seems nervous. Everyone is ready to play." (Courier Times September, 1999)

Jamaal reiterated Shaun's sentiments. "We are a more experienced team this year. Also, we believe we can win as a team. Last year, some individuals felt that way, but not the whole team." (Courier Times, September, 1999)

The total team look would be necessary as the Cougars traveled to the Academy of the New Church in their next game. Intensity marked the game action that saw ANC take a 7-0 lead into halftime. The Cougars had several chances to score but just could not convert. The second half proved a different story. Shaun Greene capped a 64-yard drive by threading his way through the Lion's defense for a 24-yard touchdown run, narrowing the gap to 7-6. He would finish the game with 140 yards on 25 carries.

After ANC scored, GS battled back when Ambler hooked up with tight end Joe Krivda for a 15-yard TD. Mobley caught the two point conversion to knot the score at 14 all. I was quoted as saying, "I had to do that. I have a lot of faith in Mobley because he can catch the football. I went to him there and I went to him for a touchdown in overtime." (Courier Times, September 1999)

ANC scored first in overtime and elected to kick the extra point. After Mobley snared an 8-yard pass from Ambler we faced a big decision. I chose to go for the win. In the huddle we said our first target on a play-action pass was Jamaal. If he was double-covered the next option was Shaun on a dive. If that was covered, then go to the tight end release. Ambler read the defensive alignment perfectly and hit Joe Krivda for the winning score.

Russ Nicolayeson will long remember that game. "The biggest game was my senior season in the championship game against ANC. It was a hard game in general but when we had to go into overtime, I didn't know I would go on. They scored and converted with a kick. When we got the ball, we scored on our third try with a pass to Jamaal Mobley. We were to do a tight end release. I was so tired I decided to cut block my guy. I did and I looked around after I saw the ref's hands signal that we had converted and I just thought yes. It was an emotional win for us. We enjoyed it too long for we lost our next game to Wilmington Friends 15-7 for our only loss of the season."

Where it may not have been a championship game, it did assure that GS had a hold of the coveted shoe trophy. In reflection, Jamaal would put a different twist on the game. Twenty-two years later he would write, "As for memories I have a lot, including how we beat ANC my senior year and the sequence of plays. But what has stuck with me is the following week. We celebrated hard after the game (and rightly so. We beat ANC.) However, the following week of practice was a poor one. And specifically for me, I was overconfident. I sat out a few practices that week because of legit bumps and bruises, but only bumps and bruises; I was hurt but not injured. Coach Gleeson saw exactly what was going on, and at the beginning of one of the practices (the last one I sat out) he spoke very sternly and directly about the fact I was failing the team by sitting out. I don't remember what he said (honestly even at the time I didn't know what he was saying...sometimes he growled) but I knew exactly what he was communicating."

In retrospect Jamaal would take the blame for our losing the next game, a 15-7 loss to Wilmington Friends. "We lost our next game at home. I scored the only touchdown on a long catch and run. But I felt the loss and felt responsible for it primarily because of the conversation we had a few days prior. I will never forget that because it taught me to never let success today prevent success tomorrow, and always be there for your team."

The Cougars showed the resiliency necessary for a great season when they bounced back from the disheartening loss to Wilmington by easily thumping our next two opponents Princeton Day 34-6 and West Nottingham 49-16. Fullback James Lee provided the offensive spark against PDS. Tim Hyland of the Courier Times described Lee's exploits. "A bruising fullback with tailback speed, Lee carried the ball 11 times for 131-yards and two touchdowns. On his first score, Lee displayed his blazing speed, outrunning a host of Panther defenders on a 63-yard sprint. On the second, Lee showed off his power, breaking several tackles on a workmanlike 16 yarder." (Courier Times, October, 1999)

Against West Nottingham, we took a 42-point lead into halftime. Needless-to-say, everything was working. Greene rushed for 103 yards, Lee added 51 to the cause, and Atom Tabor contributed 61 yards on the ground. Ambler only threw 5 passes, completing 4 of them for 89 yards. Mobley caught all four aerials for 89 yards and 2 tallies.

In our next game against Saint Andrews, another Cougar emerged as the game MVP. Patrick McGrail-Peasley, a converted soccer player, provided the key blow to lead GS to a 27-14 win. With the score tied at 14-14, McGrail-Peasley kicked off to start the second half. When the Saint Andrew runner broke through our entire defense the 6' 6" 230 pounder wrestled the would-be scorer to the ground. Moments later Patrick would deflect the Saint Andrews quarterback pass, leading to an interception and a score. From this point on, the Cougars would roll to victory.

Shaun Greene, who rushed for 141 yards, told reporter Stephen Cornell, "We took the other team too lightly in the beginning of the game. We came out too soft. In the second half we came out and played like we know how to." (Courier Times, October 1999)

The Cougars did not take our next opponent, Lower Moreland, too lightly. GS came out of the gate on fire, scoring on an Ambler-to-Mobley 30-yard TD pass. A 49-yard scamper by Greene put six more first quarter points on the board. Greene would finish the game with 148 yards and two TDs. Mobley caught 4 passes for 108 yards and two more scores. The Atlantic City duo was in full swing as we captured a 41-7 victory.

After the game, Shaun would explain how he came from Atlantic City to Bucks County. "I came here because of Jamaal. We went to elementary school together and his father talked my family into sending me here because it's such a great environment. I'm really excited about our season. Every morning, I wake up and I think about how happy I am to be a part of this." (Courier Times, October 1999)

The euphoria would certainly carry over into our last game of the season, a home contest against Perkiomen Prep. The stakes were high for the Cougars. A win would make them the single season winningest team in the school's history. They could also be the highest scoring team. The team did not let the Cougar faithful down. Shaun Greene rushed for 270 yards and three TDs. In addition to throwing for 133 yards, quarterback Andy Ambler showed his versatility, returning an interception 95 yards for a score. Jamaal Mobley snagged two more aerials, adding another touchdown to his season total. Newcomer Ryan Mellon joined the hit parade with two interceptions as the Cougars walked off with a 34-6 victory.

Twenty-three years later, Shaun still remembers both the game and the student body response. "My most memorable moment has to be the Perkiomen game during the 99' season. It was the last game of the season and we mopped the floor with that team. It was an overall win where we dominated from all sides of the ball the entire game. It was probably the most perfect game we played that season and everyone watching knew it. At the end of the game, as soon as the clock hit 0:00…everyone in attendance (mostly students) rushed the field as if we had won a bowl game! It was the best possible way to end a near perfect season. And it is probably my fondest memory of GS football because it was clear that people were genuinely excited to share in the success of GS Football."

The Trenton Times reported the historic moment saying, "Arguably the area's best small school team, George School completed the best campaign in the 77-year history of its football program with a 34-6 victory over the Perkiomen School. The Cougars finished with a 7-1 record for the first time in school history. Explosive running back Shaun Greene just shy of 1000 yards in only eight games, game breaking wide receiver Jamaal Mobley, and strong armed, Andrew Ambler are the Newtown, Pa., equivalent of the once-dominant Dallas Cowboy trio of Emmitt Smith, Michael Irvin, and Troy Aikman." (Trenton Times, November 10, 1999)

For the record, Greene rushed 148 times for 1070 yards and 14 touchdowns. Ambler passed 99 times for 731 yards and 12 TDs. Mobley caught 24 passes for 536 yards and 11 touchdowns.

As impressive as these stats are, the dynamic trio would all undoubtedly agree that the great season was a total team effort!

The Twenty-first Century Starts with a Bang

The first decade of the twenty-first century proved a tumultuous and enigmatic time. The Twin Towers fell, Hurricane Katrina ravaged New Orleans, "pregnant chats" determined a presidential race, and the United States declared a war on terrorism. On a more positive note, 'The Curse of the Bambino' vanished, texting became the norm, some managed not to be ousted by the tribal council, and Mariah Carey sang about how 'We Belong Together'. Meanwhile, Cougar football remained a source of growth, development and bonding for many a young George School athlete.

After the historic 1999 season, the Cougars faced what to do for an encore in 2000. Two thirds of our offensive dragon had graduated. Only Shaun Green remained to anchor the running game as he strove for his second straight 1000 yard season. Shaun did get to operate behind several talented linemen in Ryan Bradley, Thomas Pittman, Tyler Caron, Mike Bell, Kevin Martinez and Joe Krivda. Replacing the Ambler-to-Mobley passing combo were juniors Ryan Mellon and Jon Compitello. Robbie Waters, a sophomore who won the Friends League 100-yard sprint championship as a freshman, showed real promise scampering out of the backfield.

In addition to a new batch of player recruits, the Cougars sported new uniforms. Gone was the old 'Buff and Brown' look. The cost of brown dye was both too costly and too hard to get. Also, the entire sports department grew tired of the mixed bag of colors the various teams wore, from powder blue to brown and gold. The new-look Cougars would all wear forest green uniforms.

Before the Cougars could test their worth in actual game combat, however, they had to suffer through another Gleeson imposed preseason, consisting of three-a-day sessions for two weeks. I told them that there are two seasons every year. Preseason would test their readiness and the regular season would determine their growth.

Junior Ryan Mellon, who had received ample time at linebacker his sophomore year, eloquently reflected back on the physical strain required of a football player. "The entirety of my football experience prior to George School consisted of one year in third grade. Needless to say, I was a novice upon choosing football as my fall sport in my freshman year. I could not have known then that football would become the most significant part of my high school experience. For four years George School football forged me into a young adult and taught me lessons that would remain relevant my entire life. Pain. Self-inflicted, unceasing, bone-aching pain. Pre-season football challenged my adolescent body more than anything that had come before, and frankly probably more than anything since. Preseason is one's first exposure to football: the rude awakening that this sport is not like the others that you have played before. In search of the proverbial 'best shape of your life', you realize the 'exercise' you had previously undertaken was woefully inadequate. It is a harsh introduction to the first life lesson: the beginning is always the hardest part."

Junior quarterback Jon Compitello shared Ryan's appraisal and agony. "I can confidently say that playing football at George School was one of the most influential experiences in my life. It shaped me into the man I am today and helped craft the principles of how I aspire to live my life. Trust, teamwork, accountability, balance. At that point in my life never had I been challenged as much physically, mentally, and emotionally. The 'shellshock' of my first preseason camp was sort of a slap across the face and a catalyst into the culture of being part of George School football. The intensity of that and the competition during the season brought out the best and sometimes the worst in me. It's funny/cringeworthy reflecting on some of my immaturity growing up and a lot of that was exemplified on the football field. Regardless, it helped me grow as a man and forced me to be introspective- which I think is critical for a teenage adolescent striving to come of age."

Looking back twenty-five years, Ben "Rudy" Fisher also recalls the agony of camp. "The football preseason camps bring back so many memories. Obviously, a great bonding experience where so many friendships were made while grinding/overcoming adversity. Personally, I will never forget the difference between sophomore year versus senior year. While being 7 inches taller and 60 pounds heavier certainly helped me have a better go of it, I also worked all summer to prepare so I'd be ready. Senior camp was fun while sophomore year was just trying to survive. That's something I continued not only into college athletics but I apply to my career on a daily basis."

Having survived preseason, the Cougars could now focus on trying to match the previous year's success. Shaun Greene picked up where he left off rushing for 115 yards and two touchdowns as GS defeated Calvary Christian 12-6. Greene credited his line for his game-winning, fourth quarter score. "On fourth down, all the seniors knew we had to dig down and find something inside and push it into the end zone. The line made the holes and I just walked in." (Courier Times, September, 2000)

The Cougar's six game win streak came to halt in our next outing against ANC. The Academy scored the first two touchdowns and appeared primed to avenge the previous year's loss. For the Cougars, surrender was not an option. Sophomore Rob Waters snagged a Jon Compitello pass for a 51-yard TD. Shaun Greene then raced 8 yards for a second score. Joe Krivda hooked up with Compitello for the two-point conversion, giving GS a 14-13 lead. They widened the margin to 16-13 when an errant punt by ANC sailed out of the end zone. Unfortunately for the Cougar faithful, our offense stalled on our next four possessions giving ANC the opportunity to seal a 20-16 victory with a TD pass with 3:32 left on the clock.

Undoubtedly inspired by the close loss, the Cougars went on a tear, handily defeating their next three opponents. Shaun Greene rushed for 148 yards to crush Wilmington Friends School 34-6. James Lee added 116 yards rushing. Greene's second tally came on a stunning 95-yard punt return. In a postgame interview I said, "He was credited with 95 yards but he probably ran about 125. He had to cut across the field and set up his blockers perfectly. It was a piece of work to watch. He caught it on the left side, scored on the right side and was pretty much weaving across the entire field." (Courier Times, October, 2000)

The Cougars followed up the win with a 37-7 victory over Princeton Day School. Greene once again spearheaded the attack rushing for 142 yards. James Lee contributed 42 yards to the Cougar cause and Atom Tabor added 44 more. Once again, the unsung heroes were the Cougar lineman. Senior captain Ryan Bradley told reporter Karen Sangillo, "We know what our role is and that we aren't going to get all the big headlines and that's okay. I try to be the leader out there, especially on defense, because I have experience and I feel that's my job." (Courier Times, October 2000)

Tom "Puff" Pittman echoed Ryan's sentiments, "I let the fast guys score all the touchdowns. Even though we don't have that much attention, we love it. We love playing on the line and we really like each other. I wouldn't trade that." (Courier Times, October, 2000)

The train kept rolling as we traveled to Delaware to defeat Saint Andrews 35-14. Shaun Greene once again led the hit parade rushing for 169 yards and four touchdowns. Shaun quickly credited his line. "They have improved tremendously since the first game and things have been going uphill since. I give them all the credit in the world." (Courier Times, October, 2000)

The Cougars had settled into a sound midseason run. Ryan Mellon, twenty-two years later, would encapsulate the whole feeling of going through a regular season of play. "As the school year begins, one becomes adjusted to the routine of afternoon practices, Friday walk-throughs, and Saturday games. Still now, the visceral memories of GS football are vivid in my mind. I can still feel the exhaustion associated with a session of end-of-practice backwards running twenty years later. The hot summer days where sweat pours off you. The blessed respite of the cool Drayton basement in between morning and afternoon pre-season practices. The constant distinctive smell of a locker-room full of teen sweat-drenched clothing and equipment. Days when the rain pours and yet practice isn't canceled, leaving you soaked, muddy and exhilarated. Holding push-ups low as you pray that your captains finally release their tyrannical grip on you. The transition to the late autumn chill where you put your hands in your pants for warmth and the impact of tackles stings your entire body. The pride of wearing your jersey to classes the day before game-day. These images are conjured in my mind as easily as this morning's breakfast."

That pride shone brightly as we tried to upset Bristol High School on our home field. Andy Vineburg wrote in the Courier Times that, "If yesterday's Bristol-George School football game was, indeed, the Super Bowl of area small schools, then the hype was well-deserved. The favored Warriors needed a couple of late defensive stops- and a disputed fumble recovery- to hold off the Cougars, 7-6 in an emotional hard-hitting game that was marred by three unsportsmanlike conduct penalties." Courier Times, October 22, 2000)

One of the few teams to hold Greene to under 100 yards, the Warriors battled back to take the lead after Rob Waters had put the Cougars ahead on a 66-yard run. The Cougars failed to convert on the extra point kick which would prove to be the margin of the Bristol win.

The entire Cougar team put the Bristol loss behind them as they took on Lower Moreland in what would be the seniors final home game. In a postgame interview I noted that, "For the seniors, it was their last time playing on this field. We said to them to go out and play your hardest and have fun doing it. If you play your best, you're going to do well." Courier Times, October 29, 2000)

The GS gridders certainly played well. In all, they accumulated 477 yards of offense. Shaun Greene alone ran for 214 yards and 4 touchdowns. As reporter Bill Kenny wrote, "The George School football community won't forget Shaun Greene any time soon. His name has been indelibly etched upon their collective consciousness. Parents, classmates and other fans hear his name constantly over the public address system during games and see his name regularly atop the newspaper statistical reports." (Courier Times, October 29, 2000)

Greene summed up the 35-7 win saying, "Today I just wanted to come out, do the best I could and show everybody in the crowd that we're a 'for real' team. What today was all about was coming out, having fun and putting on a show." (Courier Times, October 29, 2000)

The Cougars could not duplicate the show in our final game, losing to Perkiomen 28-14. Greene provided most of the offensive spark, rushing for 231 of 285 total yards. He would finish the season with 1,128 yards, his second straight 1000 plus campaign. Shaun also finished second in scoring in all of Lower Bucks County with 17 touchdowns and three extra point conversions for 108 points, and second in rushing with a 7.9 yards per carry average.

The eternal bane of scholastic sports, graduation, once again depleted the veteran Cougar forces in 2001. Fortunately, a new group of green clad Cougar warriors emerged. Halfback Robbie Waters showed real speed and agility coming out of the backfield. Tyler Caron switched to fullback to provide blocking and tough yardage carries. Lefty Jon Compitello had proven himself under fire as a strong-armed passer. Ryan Mellon and Ben Fisher looked like sure-handed receiving targets. Kevin Martinez seemed prepped to anchor a very young line.

As in years past, I realized we had to adjust our offensive strategy in order to fully utilize this talented group. I decided the best route to go would be a spread offense, featuring two wide receivers, two slots who could go in motion, a quarterback under center, and a blocking fullback. That would put more pressure on our youthful line but would allow us to spread defenses and play perimeter ball. The players bought into the strategy. Jon Compitello reflected on the team's willingness to change, writing, "Personally though my favorite times to look back on was my senior year. What we were lacking in size, we made up for with athleticism and speed. It was fun to see Coach Gleeson create a brand-new spread style offense which, looking back on, was ultimately the infancy stage of how we see most college and NFL teams run their offense now (2020). Selfishly, as the quarterback, I loved it because I threw the ball 20-30 times a game. I probably led the state in INTs but I had a lot of fun doing it. Also, being a veteran on the team, it was cool to serve as a mentor to the younger players, similar to what the older guys did with me when I first started."

Leadership also came from our captains Ryan Mellon and Kevin Martinez. Ryan reflected back on this responsibility, saying, "I learned leadership from the upperclassman and team captains who came before me. Their strength was my strength; their endurance was my endurance. Come senior year it was my turn to lead as captain. The ability to earn, keep, and command respect, to instill confidence, to know when to speak and when to listen, to lead by example, all came from George School football. Without hyperbole, it created me into the leader, professional and parent I am today. I can say unequivocally that I would not be who I am without that opportunity."

Ryan further offered me some possibly undue praise, "Leadership did not only come from my peers, however. Coach John Gleeson set an example that every player and student on these teams aspired to, even to this day. He, more than any other teacher at George School, taught me how to be a leader of men. "Glees" was a constant, literally. The same flaming cougar t-shirt worn every day (how is that even possible?), the same lovably gruff exterior varnishing a kind and gentle personality. Gleeson inspired fierce devotion to his players that lasts to this day. I never had a class with John Gleeson but he taught me more in his words and actions than any classroom teacher ever could."

Kevin Martinez, who bore the senior burden of anchoring our otherwise inexperienced line, also reflected upon his role as captain. "Throughout life, people go through so much. You have your highs and lows. But what makes us who we are is how we react and overcome these situations. I believe that GS football impacted me in that way during my tenure there. I played GS football from 2000-2002. I had the honor and privilege to play for not just a great coach, but a great human being. Coach John Gleeson was a man who instilled so much knowledge not just about football, but taught his players so much more about life. Being the captain on the team, I had to learn to be a leader. I wanted to be a voice for my teammates and Coach believed in me and, much as my teammates, that I could get the job done."

While totally accurate about my wardrobe, I think both Ryan and Kevin offered me too much credit. If anything, I could spot real leadership potential. These two captains certainly possessed the proper mindset and dedication to lead us in this transitional season. I always believed that molding a team comes from within and starts with the on-field presence of the captains.

After physically prepping in pre-season as well as learning the new offensive scheme, we were ready to take on our first opponent, The Academy of the New Church. The first half worked to perfection as the Cougars jumped out to a 14-0 lead. Ryan Mellon started the scoring, snagging a 15-yard pass from Jon Compitello. Rob Waters followed suit, racing 60 yards for a touchdown. Vince Murphy converted on both extra point kicks. In the second quarter, ANC scored on a 27-yard pass but the Cougars answered immediately with Compitello again hitting Mellon with a five-yard pass. Murphy converted to give GS a 21-7 halftime lead.

Looking back on the game, Ben "Rudy" Fisher said, "I will always remember the excitement before the game and walking out of the locker room and to the field. I remember getting a huge lead against ANC senior year with the spread offense catching them by surprise. We ended up blowing it in the second half, but I will never forget the look on their faces when we came out in a spread. They didn't know what to do."

After an extended halftime, the Academy came up with enough answers to capture a 23-21 win. As ANC coach Andy Davis told reporter Josh Daeche, "We knew we had to make adjustments. We had never seen an offense like this with four receivers. The only way we could stop them is by going at them, and that is what we did by blitzing them." (Courier Times, September 16, 2001)

While acknowledging the euphoria gained from wins, Ryan also recognized the value of defeats, "The pains of loss are sometimes even more memorable. I have never felt more physically drained than after a heart-breaking loss to Bristol 7-6 my junior year. My senior year, we stunned ANC in the first game of the season after installing the air-raid offense. Despite a comfortable lead at halftime, we could not hold on to win. It is a loss I can still feel all these years later. It is these football experiences, these wins and losses, these moments small and large, that resonate more than any that took place in the classroom. I could not tell you any particular grade on a test or topic of an assembly, but I could recall a catch, block or tackle as if it was yesterday."

Though disappointed over the loss, the Cougars sensed the spread would be a workable offense. Compitello completed 14 of 39 passes for 181 yards and 2 touchdowns. Mellon, who was on the receiving end of both TDs, caught 8 passes for 139 yards. Waters added 75 yards rushing to the attack.

Given a week to tweak our offensive strategy and examine what happened against ANC, we were ready for a home game against another rival,

Wilmington Friends. Rob Waters proved the star of this encounter, racing for three touchdowns. The Courier Times reporter Josh Daeche aptly summed up Robbie's value to the spread offense saying, "Waters' frame (5' 6", 155 pounds) does not allow him to get the ball 15 or 20 times a game. However, when he does get the opportunity to carry the ball, he becomes a nightmare for the opposing team." (Courier Times, September 22, 201)

The 'nightmare' carried the ball 9 times for 114 yards and three touchdowns. He scored on scampers of 46, 52 and 14 yards. Compitello balanced the attack, completing 7 of 13 passes for 95 yards. Mellon tallied on a 23-yard interception return as the Cougars sent Wilmington to a 26-14 defeat.

The Cougars' next three games saw the spread offense working to perfection. In our 35-7 conquest of Princeton Day School, it took Rob Waters just one play to dazzle the Princeton fans as he took a handoff and raced 78 up the sideline for a score. I was quick to note Rob's breakaway talent, saying, "Robbie only weighs 140 pounds. We can't give him the ball 15 or 20 times a game. But when he does get the ball, he's gone. The kid is a track star playing football, and we're lucky to have him." (Courier Times, September 30, 2001)

With all eyes on the speedster, Jon Compitello stepped into the spotlight and hooked up with his favorite target Ryan Mellon for an 80-yard tally. Compitello would finish the game with 5 completions for 131 yards. Mellon caught 3 passes for 135 yards. Waters ran for 150 yards on 4 carries.

Our next victim, Calvary Christian, undoubtedly prepped to stop both Waters and Mellon. True to form, Waters scored on a 44-yard run early in the first quarter. Then Tyler Caron took center stage. The tough linebacker and fullback scored his first three touchdowns of the season on runs of 3, 5, and 4 yards. After the game Tyler said of the 34-7 win, "We needed this to give our season some momentum. It was good for everybody. We weren't going to take them lightly. We wanted to come out and take it to them." (Courier Times, October 7, 2001)

Caron played a big role in our next game, a 38-21 win over Saint Andrews. Down 7-14 at halftime and with Rob Waters sidelined with a sprained ankle, things looked less than optimistic for the hometown Cougar fans. Late in the third quarter with Saint Andrews ahead 21-14, I sensed we needed to exploit a different area of attack. Caron took a pitch from his fullback position, rolled to his right and then fired a perfect strike to a wide-open Ben Fisher. The TD toss covered 74 yards and jump-started our 17-0 run in the last quarter.

After the 28-21 victory Tyler said, "It's just the kind of game you dream about. When you least expect it something like this happens. I was just trying to help out and take some of the pressure off Rob (Waters). He does a lot for this team. Everyone really works hard. I couldn't have done it without the offensive line." (Courier Times, October 7, 2001)

In our next two outings against Bristol and Lower Moreland we did not fare well. With Waters still hobbled with a sprained ankle, our running game bogged down against Bristol. Compitello was able to pick up some of the slack passing for 212 yards. Unfortunately, only one was good for a touchdown, an 80-yard strike to Waters in the second quarter.

As I told reporter Pete Roberts after the 7-29 loss to the 6-1 Warriors, "We knew coming into this game we were facing a real potent force. It means a lot to stay with a team of this caliber in the first half. I'm just sorry we couldn't do the same in the second." (Courier Times, October 21, 2001)

After a very disappointing 7-35 loss to Lower Moreland, the Cougars were ready for their final home game of the season against Perkiomen. Despite two more long TD runs from Rob Waters, however, the green clad warriors could not come up with a victory. Playing in his last game for George School, Jon Compitello kept the game in perspective. "I wish we could have won but what it all comes down to is the experience. It's about having fun and the brothership." (Courier Times, November 5, 2001)

Though a disappointing ending to the season, the Cougars proved they could adapt and succeed. The new spread offense worked because they made it work. Jon Compitello finished the year with 71 completions for 1,028 yards. Ryan Mellon snagged 34 passes for 694 yards. Ben Fisher caught 24 aerials for 414 yards. Robbie Waters finished second in Lower Bucks County in scoring with 13 touchdowns. He rushed 58 times for 652 yards and an incredible 11.2 yards-per-carry.

Such statistics only tell a small part of the 2001 success story. Twenty years later, Jon Compitello would echo his sentiments from his final game, "The formation of my relationships with some of my best friends was cultivated on the George School football field. We share a common bond of experiences that are exclusive to just us. Nearly 25 years later, we stay in touch on a consistent basis and regularly look back on our playing days as some of the best times of our lives."

Ryan Mellon readily concurred. "There is a certain camaraderie developed through literal and metaphorical blood, sweat and tears of shared experiences. My most meaningful high school, and indeed lifetime, friendships were made in the locker rooms and fields of George School. I still speak daily with my teammates and best friends that were made playing GS football. Often, there are references to those nostalgic days. I can say definitively that without them as teammates, our friendships would not have remained as strong."

Looking back, Kevin Martinez realizes how George School football influenced his emerging character. "GS football had a permanent influence on my life. Whether that's working with co-workers or doing something you have never done before. Once you play this game, you'll realize how many life lessons it teaches you. No matter what we do in our everyday lives, you will never get anywhere without hard work. Without hard work you won't get that sense of accomplishment when you complete something difficult. In football, when you win a rivalry game or a championship you think back to the time you gave 100 percent in the weight room or went all out during two-a-day practices in the scorching heat. That is when you know all your hard work paid off."

Kevin has applied that thinking to his professional life. "Once you get a job, you will always have to be hardworking. Always giving your all and doing your best will pay off in the end. Football creates an incredible work ethic that will be carried with you throughout your whole life. There are so many great moments during my GS football days, from preseason to actual gameday. At the end of the day, it was about having fun, and I had the most fun during that time with my teammates and coaches that I considered family. All I can say is whether we lost or won a game, we always left the field with our heads high."

Kevin's professional life led him into the difficult law enforcement arena. "After graduating from GS in 2002, I went onto college and graduated with my BA in criminal justice. I took what I learned not just from the classroom, but from the GS football field and applied it to my everyday life. I'm currently married, with 2 children. I'm also a veteran police officer with the New York City Police Department. I still applied what I learned and what Coach Gleeson instilled in me as a father, husband, and a police officer. Thanks Coach G and George School for giving me the opportunity to shine bright."

The entire 2001 Cougars all shone brightly. They had come away with the most important lessons derived from their football experiences...dedication is a reward all its own, being part of a brotherhood lasts forever, deriving a sense of pride and humility go hand and hand. These are just a few truisms defining what being a Cougar footballer really means.

Where graduation once again saw the departure of several key offensive stalwarts, the 2002 Cougars still had the services of running back Rob Waters and several experienced linemen in Anthony Negron, Edwin Martinez (Kevin's younger brother) and Joby Thomas. Junior Gordon Toggweiler and newcomer Andrew Biros would compete for the starting quarterback spot.

Though only a freshman, Andrew Biros already possessed enough football experience to grant him ample self-confidence. He announced in a letter to athletic director and defensive football coordinator George Long and myself that he wanted to report to the preseason, a pretty much unheard-of request at that time. The feeling was the camp would be a rough indoctrination into life at George School. Andrew persisted so we gave him the go ahead. He well remembers showing up for camp. "Having been dropped off in the Alumni Gym parking lot by my mom on Monday, August 5th (yep, I still remember the date), I walked down the stairs of the Alumni Gym and into the locker room. There I was met with a wry grin from Glees, who was fitting incoming players with helmets. Attempting to match the strong grip of his handshake, I thanked him for the invite to pre-season, and boldly proclaimed, 'I'm not here to sit. I'm here to play, and I'm here to win' To his credit, both as a coach and educator, his grin only grew wider. 'Ok, well that's good to hear. Let's see what you can do.'"

Where Andrew beamed a refreshing optimism, other returning Cougars were a bit more leery about the sport and the role they would play. Korean ESL student AeMin Kim confessed to having no knowledge of the sport. Twenty years later he would recount his initial responses. "The word 'Football' had nothing to do with me when I first moved to the USA to study abroad. When I first moved to the states, I was a timid foreigner unsure of his own identity. I never imagined myself participating in a team sport. However, it all changed when I came to know football because of the sports requirement I had to choose at George School. It was not an easy experience for me to play sports with new people in a new environment for the first time. I did not join the team thinking I would improve my football skills or achieve something meaningful. I joined because I had to. At the time, I couldn't know that something so remote from my reality would change my life."

The initial indoctrination for AeMin was the grueling preseason. "I learned athletic skills and life lessons that have shaped my present days. Of course, when we talk about sports, it's easier to think about the importance of the physical aspect of the game. Still, the mentality is just as valuable or even more valuable in a game. George School football taught me the value of having the right mindset. Players would start the season with a pre-season week where we would come to the school early to practice from 9 to 6, a morning session followed by two afternoon sessions. The required physical input was beyond what I had imagined. For the first time in my life, my body ached as if I would shatter at any point. Waking up hurt, moving your fingers hurt, laughing hurt. Things that weren't possible to hurt were painful. Experience taught me that much more than what I knew was possible. I started to think that anything was possible, which didn't always come true because our team lost games too. But I had so much fun with that mindset. It led me to become a better person overall."

Andrew Biros also remembers the preseason agony sessions. "Preseason football at George School consisted of four practices during the day. A couple hours in the morning, followed by an hour in the pool halfway across campus. Lunch followed the pool session, and anyone familiar with the campus knows that means a half mile walk in the muggy heat, up the South Lawn hill. After a short lunch we would hold an afternoon practice in the late summer sun, then dinner and finally an hour or so of practice into the twilight. Repeat that for eight straight days, perhaps get an afternoon off on the 9th day and then right back at it. The routine never changed over my four years."

Andrew saw this time as one of bonding and self-discovery. "And I loved preseason. The days were long, but we were all experiencing the agony together. Thirty players would join preseason each year and all who made it through wore it as a badge of honor. What made it special wasn't just the long practices. It was special having campus to ourselves (with the other fall athletes of course), eating meals in the dining hall and trying to steal quick naps in the Marshall student center. Each preseason brought a new sense of hope and imagination. We were building something, all a part of it forged through blood, sweat, and muscles we didn't even know existed, let alone could be sore. Having been the only freshman at preseason that first year in the fall of 2002, I reveled at the winces of my peers who would join me for their first preseasons in preceding Augusts. Preseason football was a gauntlet, one that I sprinted in full force towards every August."

Andrew also experienced a good batch of self-awareness at that first camp. As he recalls, "Other distinct memories stick out from that freshman year. The first is from preseason and served as my 'welcome to the big leagues' moment. After a few days in shorts and helmets, we strapped on the shoulder pads. As a caveat, I must admit here and now that as much as I loved football, I did not enjoy the hitting or being hit. For better and certainly for worse, I loved the chess match of play design and aerial attack. I wanted to get the ball, survey the field, and sling it. Lowering my head for contact, not so much. This facet of my game became well known by Glees, who I think was frustrated at times, and amused during others, by my preference to avoid the big hit."

What I called 'Bang-Bang' day happened on the fourth day of preseason. I told the players they could count on two parts to camp. The first was general conditioning and the second was hitting drills. The first contact involved two players laying on the ground with the crowns of their helmets touching. The coach stood over them with the ball and tossed it to one of the players. If you didn't get the ball, your job was to tackle the runner. If you got it, run over the defender.

Andrew shudders at his first introduction to this drill. "I watched two of my new teammates lay on the ground. Glees dropped a ball on one of them, they both got quickly to their feet, smashed helmets, and churned their legs into the ground. The defender successfully tackled the runner and the whistle blew. The defender got up, but the runner, junior Dan Milletello, laid on the ground. Dan writhed in pain. 'Ohhhhhh man,' I thought. Practice stopped, an ambulance quickly arrived, and Dan was carted off the field."

Fortunately, our trainer Juana Bivins was there to promptly tend to all injuries, great and small. Juana had earned my complete trust. Her word about a player's readiness became the gospel. If she said he was ready, he played. If she deemed him ineligible, he sat. I never questioned her judgement. (As an aside, Juana literally saved my life years later when I was struck with a line drive while pitching batting practice in baseball. My heart stopped. Juana rushed in to save me by using a defibrillator.)

From a player's perspective, Andrew aptly noted Juana's many virtues. "There was one trainer, Juana Bivins, who served all of George School's preseason sports. Juana was, and I have no doubt still is, a saint. You have to be putting up with the gripes of so many high school athletes. As a football player, you were lucky if she happened to be available after any one of those given practices to wrap ice on the many contusions one might collect over those two weeks."

Dan's problem went beyond a mere contusion. Later it was learned that he had ruptured his kidney. To Andrews' amazement, Dan returned to play the following season. But, at the moment, that was an eye opener for the freshman signal caller. "For a quarterback who preferred to keep his shirt clean, I knew this wasn't middle school anymore."

Thoroughly prepared and indoctrinated, the Cougars, both veterans and neophytes, were ready to take on the Academy of the New Church in our opening game. For two straight seasons the green clad warriors had lost heart-breakers to our rival in the final quarter. Gaining revenge filled their thinking. Rob Waters picked up where he left off the season before, racing 88 yards for a first quarter touchdown. Dan Suchenski recovered an ANC fumble on the visitors 14-yard line. Two plays later Dan Titus bulled his way into the endzone from 6-yards out to give GS a 13-0 lead. Waters' real heroics extended into the second half. He took the opening kickoff of the half on his twenty-yard line and sped up the left side of the field. Surrounded by ANC defenders, the mercurial halfback managed to reverse field and scamper the remaining yards to paydirt.

Opposing coach Andy Davis told reporter Mark Schiele after the game, "We knew coming in what Waters was capable of doing. We knew that play was coming. But give him credit. He made it work. He made big plays when he had the chance to make them." (Courier Times, September 15, 2002)

For Robbie revenge proved sweet. "I wanted this trophy so bad. This is what it's all about. This game has haunted me. I'm glad to bring the trophy back home, here, where it belongs." (Courier Times September 15, 2002)

Waters picked up 104 yards on 14 carries. Fullback Edwin Martinez added 42 yards to the Cougar cause. Dan Titus tacked on 27 more yards. Equally impressive, the GS defenders allowed only 99 total yards and surrendered no yards passing.

The Cougars did not let up in their second game against Wilmington Friends School, a 35-13 victory. Waters once again claimed game MVP honors rushing for 214 yards on 15 carries and hauling in a 55-yard TD bomb from Gordon Toggweiler to open the GS scoring. As reporter William Kenny noted, "Gleeson added a couple new wrinkles to George School's game plan in an attempt to exploit the Quakers' expected defensive focus on Waters. Besides their usual toss sweep plays for Waters and fullback dives for Edwin Martinez (71 yards, two TDs), the Cougars ran a handful of misdirection plays up the middle." (Courier Times, September 22, 2002)

Complementing Waters' sterling performance, the offensive line did a great job both pulling and executing trap blocks. Waters was quick to laud the effort of the "herd" as they liked to be called. "Both sides of our line, offense and defense, looked better than ever today. They opened up holes for my runs and I just read off my blocks. There were holes all over the defense." (Courier Times September 22, 2002)

Next team up to try and corral the elusive Rob Waters was Princeton Day School. They failed in their task. Waters left his mark early in the 48-7 rout, scoring four touchdowns in the game's first 15 minutes, and rushing for 153 yards overall. Dan Titus added 101 rushing yards to the Cougar attack. Dan, who usually took a back seat to the Waters parade, summed up his role saying, "I don't care who does what, as long as it helps the team. Games like this one give me a chance to show what I can do. Most of the time I just want

to take the heat off Rob. I just do what I can to help him get into the endzone."
(Courier Times October 29, 2002)

The Cougars managed to throw only one pass the entire day. Freshman Andrew Biros made the most of the opportunity, completing a 30-yard scoring strike to Will Foppert.

To steal from author Charles Dickens, our next two games were the best of times and the worst of times. In our 22-0 win against Calvary Christian, Waters and Titus once again dominated the offensive states. Waters rushed for 106 yards; a total Titus almost matched with 90 yards. Perhaps more impressive in the victory was the sterling play of the defense, led by our talented edge rushers AeMin Kim and Dan Suchenski. AeMin continually harassed the Calvary quarterback, finally sending him to the sidelines. Dan recovered a fumble and took it in for a 5-yard score. In all the defense gave up five yards rushing and 24 yards passing.

In our next outing we tasted defeat for the first time of the season. Saying we came out flat on our trip to Middletown, Delaware would be a classic understatement. Saint Andrews took advantage of two Cougar fumbles on their first two possessions to rush out to a 41-0 halftime lead. They would not relinquish the lead, finally capturing a lop-sided 41-6 victory.

Looking back twenty years later, AeMin Kim unduly felt responsible for the loss. "I still remember playing a few games, such as ANC, Calvary Christian and Saint Andrews. My best and worst games. We won against ANC, bringing back the trophy. I had so much fun playing against Calvary Christian. I even replaced their quarterback because I hit him too hard. Our significant loss against Saint Andrews was where I didn't do anything the whole game. I remember apologizing to the coaches for my poor performance that day; they responded with consolation saying that everyone has their days and we need to look up and never blame ourselves."

Showing real resiliency, the Cougars bounced back in their next game against Granville Charter. Senior Will Foppert told reporter Karen Sangillo after the game, "Last week we got beat up pretty bad by Saint Andrews. We were undefeated and that really hurt. There was no way we were going to let that happen again." (Courier Times, October 20, 2002)

The green clad warriors certainly proved Foppert's point as they scored 42 points in the first half on their way to a 42-6 victory. Foppert caught 3 passes from Gordon Toggweiler in that span, good for 42 yards and two touchdowns. He humbly appraised his effort. "This was a pretty good day for me. I don't usually see the ball that much. This is really kind of Rob Water's team right now. Any role I can play is fine." (Courier Times October 20, 2002)

Adding to the one-sided onslaught, Dan Titus returned a punt 24 yards for a score. Dan Suchenski ran an interception back 53 yards. Waters, who saw limited time in the second half, did manage to carry the ball 7 times for 45 yards and two TDs.

Unfortunately for the Cougar faithful, this marked their battling men in green's last victory of the season as they lost their next two outings to two powerful Independence league teams, Lower Moreland (27-7) and Chestnut Hill (34-13). The Chestnut Hill game proved a particularly hard ending to Rob Waters' brilliant high school career. Rob hurt his left foot on the Cougars' second series of the game and spent the next two quarters under an x-ray machine at St. Mary Medical Center. By the time he returned the Hillers had built up a 28-7 lead. Knowing of his collegiate track career plans and fearing risking further injury, I was reluctant to allow him to reenter what appeared to be an already lost cause. Rob fought me the entire time. After the game I told reporter David Stegson. "He has the heart of a warrior. Just him coming back says a lot about him." (Courier Times, November 10, 2002)

I decided to give him one more chance to add to his impressive career touchdown total (14 for the season). Rather than risk further injury to his foot running the ball I called for a slant pass. Andrew Biros, who had come into the game at quarterback, still remembers the moment. "For our final game that season I found myself playing the fourth quarter. With the ball on the twenty, the call was flood right. With Rob lined up on the left side. I rolled right and spotted him running a drag across the middle. I flipped my hips, as any lefty quarterback running right would do, and tossed him the ball, his route carrying him into the endzone. Feeling good about the play. I pumped a fist in the air and stood for a moment, admiring the scene of teammates down the field mobbing Rob. He emerged from the pack, and on his way back to the sideline, ran towards me.

With tears in his eyes, Rob put an arm on my shoulder. 'You threw me my last touchdown. Thank you, I'm never going to forget this.'"

Years later Andrew put the whole scene in perspective, "I certainly have not forgotten about it. I was happy for Rob and glad I could be a part of his moment. And also, I was freshman, so it was hard for me to grasp the magnitude of it for him, and the rest of his senior peers. I would learn."

Part of Andrews' appreciation stems from the intangibles, so much a part of what Cougar football brings. "As good as Rob was on the field, he was just as kind off of it. He was the hotshot senior. I was the lone freshman. He didn't need to, but he always made it a point to build me up, both on the field and around campus, and that made me feel that much a part of the team. Leadership is action."

The 2007 season left an indelible mark on another Cougar, AeMin Kim. From a kid with no knowledge of the game he had grown into a man with clear goals and purpose. As AeMin would reflect twenty years later. "George School football was nothing like I imagined and was everything I dreamed of. The most fun I had at George School was with George School football. I remember everything: coaches, teammates, preseason, daily practices, end of the season banquets, from glorious winning games to devastating losses. It meant so much to me. Making plays, making mistakes, sweating out, vomiting, and laughing our lungs out. George School football was life. Having this memory, I wanted to start a football team at the school I work at now with the help of Coach Gleeson and Coach Long, which I couldn't fully carry out due to many difficulties. However, I still hope to start and continue a football program in Korea one day. I would love to share my experiences with my students about how George School football gave me a new life."

With quality players such as Rob and AeMin no longer roaming the sidelines, the 2003 Cougars faced another potential building year. Fortunately, many of the foundation blocks were already present. Edwin Martinez manned the fullback position. In the Courier Times fall preview section I described Edwin as, "An all-time leader at George School. He's respected, intense, intelligent and talented. He's low-key before the games and psyched-up during them." (Courier Times, August 28, 2003) Dan Titus would definitely try and assuage the loss of Waters' rushing output. Two experienced quarterbacks Gordon Toggweiler and Andrew Biros would once again battle for the starting spot. Defensive end Dan Suchenski would bolster the GS defense.

The Cougars entered their opening game against Jenkintown filled with optimism. That optimism suffered a horrendous blow when Edwin Martinez went down with a serious knee injury. It required several minutes for the attending emergency staff to relocate Edwin's knee. Though he insisted he was okay and wanted to stay in the game I felt he was done for the season. Needless to say, losing a player of Edwin's caliber on the first play from scrimmage hurt the team both physically and emotionally.

Though stunned and falling behind 18-0 by the third quarter, the Cougars were not ready to quit. Dan Titus led the comeback scoring on runs of one and four yards. Dan would rack up 179 yards on 33 carries for the day.

The following week a hurricane forced the game against Wilmington Friends to be moved until Monday afternoon, a rather disadvantageous scenario. We practiced on Saturday, sat out Sunday, and then tried to transition from the classroom to the football field on Monday with only a few minutes to prepare. To the Cougars' credit we surpassed Wilmington in total yards 250-167. The big plays, however, proved our undoing. Wilmington scored on a 50-yard pass, a 53-yard interception run, and an 84 yard kickoff return. In a masterpiece of the obvious I told the sideline reporter, "It was just the three big plays that killed us. We told them before the game not to give up the big plays and that if we did that, we'd be fine. We didn't finish off our drives, and didn't get into the endzone." (Courier Times, September 23, 2003)

Dan Titus, who rushed for 194 yards summed up the Cougars' plight, "We pushed it hard, everyone was working hard, and we didn't get any points. We lost mental focus. We were inside the 5-yard line and got nothing, and we had bonehead penalties. If we just stay disciplined, we should be alright. We pressured the quarterback, we did everything that we wanted to do, but kickoffs and the big pass on the first play took us out of the game. We'll just have to chalk this one up to experience." (Courier Times, September 23, 2003)

The experience paid off as the Cougars traveled to Morris Catholic High School to take on a much bigger squad. Once again, we outgained our opponent 305 yards to 209 but still managed to lose 22-26. Dan Titus carried the pigskin 27 times for 227 yards. He scored two TDs and came close to handing us a win before stepping out of bounds in the closing moments of the game.

Our two quarterbacks continued to split the signal calling duties. Gordon Toggweiler guided the team in the first half. Andrew Biros came on in relief in the second half and completed 3 passes for 86 yards. He found junior Justin Quarles for a 72-yard scoring strike in the second quarter.

Years later, Andrew would admit that his youthful bravado found splitting the QB duties unsavory. "My freshman year, I split time with junior quarterback Gordon Toggweiler. Gordon was a good guy, even amidst our rivalry. My adolescent hubris was annoyed at Glees for not handing me the reins earlier. From his perspective, I was likely not as ready as I thought I was, and he wanted to give upperclassmen their time to shine."

Andrew's appraisal fit perfectly with my thinking. As Geis had said earlier, "I never had to explain to parents of a player who had practiced and played for two or three years why he had been benched to allow a better player who came in as a junior or senior to play in his position." I appreciated Andrew's drive and determination but valued Gordon's composure and leadership. It was not a matter of who was a better player. Thus, the two-man platoon continued.

After two more losses to Calvary Christian (8-14) and Saint Andrews (21-42), I am sure many naysayers started questioning my thinking. To the players' credit they maintained an upbeat approach. As Andrew would reflect twenty years later. "Football is fun when you're winning. When you're losing it can get less fun. But here's the thing about George School football, and really here's the thing about why Gleeson was such a great coach. Every week was fun. Every week, we thought we had a chance. We believed in ourselves, in the game plan, in our ability to persist and win."

Though our numbers were dwindling our spirit remained high as evident in our next game at Lower Moreland. This turned out to be the longest football game in the school's history, going to three overtimes before the Lions prevailed 40-39. The Courier Times described the offensive brawl, saying, "It was one of the wildest high school games this season. And when the dust settled,

Lower Moreland edged the visiting George School, 40-39, in three overtimes in a non-league encounter." (Courier Times, October 26, 2003)

Dan Titus once again powered the GS attack, carrying the ball 33 times for 155 yards and three touchdowns. Titus's three TDs all occurred in regulation time and set up a 21-21 tie. In the first overtime Justin Quarles snagged a 10-yard scoring strike from Gordon Toggweiler. Lower Moreland answered with a 2-yard run. In the second OT the Lions scored on an 8-yard run. Titus evened the score, snagging a 10-yard pass from Toggweiler. Titus scored again in the third OT on a 9-yard pass from Biros. Lower Moreland refused to fold and scored on an 8-yard run. The conversion kick sailed through the uprights to assure the Lions' win.

The dramatic shootout loss did not deter the Cougar spirit as they took the long trek to Bayonne, New Jersey to play Marist High School in a make-up game. Wardlaw-Hartridge had to cancel their season and Marist was the only school with a corresponding open date. The long bus ride paid off with a 18-13 victory. Dan Titus again provided the necessary offensive thrust, rushing 33 times for 157 yards. His final one-yard tally late in the fourth quarter sealed the win. Andrew Biros found what was becoming his favorite target, Justin Quarles, for touchdown passes of 26 and 12 yards.

In thinking back on the big win Andrew summed up the quarterback situation. "Gordon played much of the first half, and we went into halftime down 7-6. After regrouping during the break, the rest of the team hit the field for the second half, the stadium lights flickering in the fall dusk. Gleeson, Gordon and I huddled just outside the visiting team's locker room. Gordon had sustained an injury, his head or maybe his arm. 'What do you want to do?' Gleeson asked him. He looked up at me, at Gleeson, and back at me, and told us both, 'I think Biros should play.' I'll never know how hurt Gordon actually was at that moment. I'm confident he wanted to be out there playing. He slapped my shoulder pads as we walked out onto the field. 'You ready? Go get them.' Gordon's was an act of selfless leadership."

Perhaps rattled from the dramatics of the previous two weeks, the Cougars were unable to muster much offense losing to rival ANC 34-0 in their final game. Dan Titus did pick up 79 more yards to bring his total to 1,223 for the season. This ranked him second best rusher in Lower Bucks County. Edwin Martinez did get medical clearance and managed to pick up 25 yards on six carries in a heroic final game effort. Gordon Toggweiler completed 4 of 16 passes for 34 yards.

The 2003 Cougars record belies the effort and effectiveness of their play. They outgained all of their first three opponents, only to come out on the short side of the score. They battled a public league foe to three overtimes before losing by a one-point kick conversion. They featured the number two rusher in all of Lower Bucks County, a real tribute to their strong offensive line. What was a tough won/loss campaign could have easily turned into a winning season.

The 2004 Cougars boasted a veteran-laden line-up. Gus DiBacco, Rocky Taft, Matt Norcross, Justin Quarles, Andrew Biros, and Mike Murphy all saw ample playing time the previous year. They would well-remember the critical losses that could easily have fallen in the victory column.

Senior Justin Quarles, who had already proven his worth as a sure-handed receiver and tenacious defensive halfback, found motivation from several sources. He was the son of a former semi-pro great, John Quarles. In reflecting back over his love of football, Justin wrote, "Playing football meant a lot to me. I fell in love with football at an early age because of my Dad. Although I never got to see him play, I would read all his newspaper clippings and admire his giant MVP trophies from when he played semi-pro. He always taught me to play hard. I always wanted to make him proud and when I'd see him in the bleachers, I would play that much more physically. Football was a bond between my father and I. It was also a way to bond with old and new friends. Sports were a great way to cross paths with people from many different backgrounds, especially at GS which is a very diverse community."

Justin's football genes became evident his very first year. "My first big moment playing at GS came in my freshman year. I was one of the smaller players on the team and wasn't starting. Although I was undersized, I had a lot of experience and knew I was talented enough to start. After two weeks of not starting, I decided to make it so they had to start me and that week of practice I did just that. I practiced hard, hitting everyone in sight and earned a starting spot on defense."

Such determination would help motivate his fellow seniors in 2004. The Cougars vowed to get off to an early start against Jenkintown. Quarles would start the season's scoring, snagging a 57-yard pass from Andrew Biros. He would then catch Matt Norcross' halfback option pass for the two-point conversion. The first quarter heroics would not hold as two Cougar miscues gave the Drakes excellent field position. Down 8-16 entering the final quarter, the men in green knew they had to rally or experience yet another tough loss.

We opted to go to the air to combat the slippery footing caused by a steady rain. I told reporter Jason Haslam after the game. "We started mixing it up better in the second half. I think we got run-oriented and we didn't want to throw because of the rain. Win or lose we had to go out there and start throwing the ball." (Courier Times, September 19, 2004)

The strategy worked as Biros completed 11 of 24 passes for 178 yards. In the fourth quarter alone, he went 6-for-9 and 82 yards, setting up touchdown gallops of 13 yards by Kwasi Agyeman-Kagya and 7 yards by Jared Rosenberg. The Cougar comeback worked, granting them the 21-16 victory.

The Cougars started out strong in their next game against a 4-0 Calvary Christian team. After a sustained drive, Andrew Biros ran a one-yard quarterback sneak to give GS a 7-0 lead. The lead would hold up until the fourth quarter when two Calvary Christian touchdown runs gave them the 12-7 win. Jared Rosenberg provided a bright spot for the Cougars rushing for 103 yards on 14 carries.

Traveling to Wilmington, Delaware to take on the Friends, the Cougars resorted back to their old ways. We outgained Wilmington 260-204 yards but managed to fumble our way to defeat. Three turnovers allowed Wilmington to start drives at the George School 5, 11, and 30 yard line. The Cougars showed heart rallying behind a 52 TD pass from Biros to Pat Matsagas and a one yard Kwasi Agyeman-Kagya run but it was not enough to stop the 20-35 loss.

Old patterns kept emerging as we lost our next away game to Saint Andrews by a 8-14 score. Unfortunately, our already long bus ride to Delaware was made even longer when our bus got lost. Despite delaying the game 45 minutes from its original start time, we had only a few minutes to warm up prior to kickoff. Little wonder we looked a little dazed as Saint Andrews scored two early TDs on a 31-yard pass and 69-yard run.

Reporter Chay Rao summed up the game saying, "The Cougars controlled the game from its outset, but lost it on two broken plays." (Courier Times, October 17, 2004)

Saint Andrews coach Mike Hyde would concur. "We're a running team. When we got the lead, we were able to run. George School really had us on our heels. They probably won the time of possession advantage." (Courier Times, October 17, 2004)

For their next home game against Red Lion Christian Academy, the Cougars wanted to be ready from the start. It took eight plays and three Red Lion turnovers for the green clad Warriors to score three touchdowns. Kwasi Agyeman-Kagya scored twice on runs of 10 and 1 yards, Justin Quarles returned a pass interception 55 yards for another tally, and Roger Perez scored from a yard out. Zac Glaeser rounded out the 40-0 first half lead scoring on a 25-yard run and a 34-yard pass from Biros.

Quarles described his interception to reporter Wes McElroy, "We knew they were going to throw to number 80. We went over everything in practice and we got beat a couple of times. So, we knew what was going to happen when it happened, we went up for the ball and I got it." (Courier Times, October 24, 2004)

The Cougars could not carry their winning way over in the next three games, losing to Lower Moreland (7-21), Pennington (25-40) and ANC (6-15). The loss to Pennington ranked high on Justin's memory list. Having fallen behind 7-27, our halftime gathering seemed a pretty somber affair. It did provide Justin with a life lesson he still utilizes 20 years later. "My biggest moment in GS football came from the Pennington game senior year. Statwise (7 catches for 100 yards) it was probably my best game at GS and I would learn a valuable life lesson. I had a great first half racking up some tackles, a forced fumble, and a couple catches. Although I was happy with my efforts, I was still frustrated because we were still behind. At halftime a teammate spoke out some words of encouragement to the team and out of frustration I shouted at him to shut up because he didn't play. Coach Gleeson immediately pulled me to the side to set me straight. He reminded me that's not how a leader acts or talks to his fellow teammates. It didn't happen as nicely as I'm putting it, but the message was received. It took a few weeks to really set in, but I had finally realized why I wasn't a team captain. Although I was one of the top players on the team, I wasn't a leader."

Justin did lead by his play on the field but he had really seized upon an important truth. A successful professional twenty years later, he would realize the true impact of his football career. "Football at GS was a great opportunity to play a sport that I was very passionate about with my friends. A lot of great memories, laughing on bus rides, watching American Gladiators in the basement of Drayton in between two-a-days, and even listening to Motown in the locker room. Even bigger than football, I was taught lessons that would help me be a better person in life and in my career. Hard work and respect are something my parents taught me but sometimes you need reinforcement from your community. Coach Gleeson and Coach Long were passionate about teaching football, but they were even more passionate about teaching us how to be good people. GS football has helped show me that I am determined and hardworking enough to achieve the goals I create."

Justin transferred these concepts to his professional and family life. "As owner and operator of my own contracting business I had to work to build my reputation and prove I can do the job. I have also learned the importance of being a positive influence in someone's life. As a business owner it is important to respect, encourage and build up my employees because their success will positively impact my business. Beyond being a business owner, it is important to be respectful and uplifting to all those in my community as well. As a husband and a father, I am also a teammate and a leader. Respect, hard work and kindness are the cornerstones my wife and I use to build our family."

Justin's words hit at the heart of what being a member of the George School football family really entails. Truths that go way beyond wins and losses.

Senior Mike Murphy in a Courier Times preview to the 2005 season echoed Justin Quarles' thoughts. "Last year we had a lot of heart, more than any team I played for. Our record may not have shown it, but we did. That's something we hope to carry over to this year." (Courier Times, September 1, 2005)

Being rather slight in frame, Mike hardly met the dimensions of your typical offensive guard and defensive tackle. He quickly learned that a strong cardiac system and proper technique would provide the necessary balance to succeed. Looking back twenty years on his gridiron career Mike would note, "I remember fondly the training under Coach Long, or "Coach" as we called him. He was coaching at GS my freshman and sophomore year but not my junior and senior year. He taught me a lot about the technical side of playing defense, and, perhaps more importantly for me, how to stack the deck in my favor on the offensive line. Being that I weighed 167 pounds, I was very undersized for my position at offensive tackle and offensive guard my senior year. Wrestling prohibited me from bulking up as a lot of other football players would do in serious programs. Instead I went up against guys who were literally twice my size in some instances. But it's not the biggest dog in the fight that wins and there are always little ways around beating a Goliath. I remember a kid stomping on my back every time I chop blocked him. He was huge, easily 50 pounds heavier than me. But I remember even then thinking that he's doing this because I keep catching him using the same trap and I'm outplaying him. He's frustrated because I'm making him a nonfactor on defense. And I owe a lot of that to "Coach" for the technical side but also Gleeson on the smash-mouth side."

For Mike, who also excelled at wrestling, the team concept counted most. "Wrestling is probably my best sport, but it's not my passion. I love football and I love lacrosse. A lot of it comes from the team concept. It's a team event in wrestling and I love the competition, but you get that feeling of brotherhood in football. It's the type of feeling where you would do anything to help your teammates win." (Courier Times September 1, 2005)

In reflection Mike felt a good deal of the fraternal feeling started in the rigorous preseason camp. "I think the collective memory that keeps coming up for me is preseason. I'm sure that's true of a lot of us players because it is so memorable. It was a lot like bootcamp in the USMC. Maybe not quite as tough as that but similar in a lot of ways; 'Three a Day' practices and swimming with Barbie (Gale), three actual meals where you are consuming calories because you need them, and at the end of the day you go to bed early because your body is exhausted. OMG, and how that locker room would stink after a week. But That's just the surface of preseason. There is a sense of collective suffering that brings the players together quickly. You form extraordinarily tight bonds with the men you suffer through the two weeks with. I think that is the factor that is most like the military, and it is also what sets the fall sports apart from the other two seasons, winter and spring. We grow a kinship with the players during the preseason that is tighter and more memorable. Make no mistake though, the physical and mental beating you take is essential to bringing the players together as a unit."

Similar to Andrew Biros' appraisal of preseason, Mike saw these agonizing moments in a positive light. "I always loved those two weeks despite the heat and bruising, but I know it probably kept a lot of guys away too. Not everybody is cut out for the two weeks of torture by Gleeson, because Glees will make you tough. And the preseason heat is a real thing when you're wearing pads and helmets. You were thankful to have them though come "Bang Bang Day" as Gleeson called it. This is what I was referring to earlier when I mentioned the smashmouth side of football. You spend a lot of time in preseason just growing accustomed to getting pummeled and dealing out pain, back and forth, as simple as that. Complaining about the bruises and the aches was how we coped with them but there was no getting around it even if you were 6'6" and 250 lbs. Everyone suffered and everyone made it through together."

Kwasi Agyeme-Kagya, stellar linebacker and fullback, shared Mike's appraisal of the preseason bonding effect. Twenty years later he still remembers these moments. "Playing football at GS was probably one of the best experiences of my life. To this day I can still remember the smell of the grass, the feeling of putting on the pads, and being yelled at by Glees for missing a block or tackle. I remember each year when summer vacation was almost over, even though I was looking forward to playing football, dreading preseason and the long grueling practices. Though it was very tough and very challenging I loved being there. This is where I made some of the best friends of my life that I still have to this day. The camaraderie that we formed through the grueling three-a-day practices, watching tapes, learning new plays all in an effort of becoming the best football players we could be was priceless. This taught me about discipline and how to persevere through any challenge no matter how tough it is and this was only through preseason. The season was where all that pain and sweat was put to use."

Joining the Cougar brotherhood was a new coach, Ben Croucher. Ben, who played college ball for Division One Siena college, showed up at George School to teach history and serve as an assistant coach. When our former defensive coordinator, Tom Waters, decided to move on a week before preseason, we found a big gap in the coaching ranks. We were down to one coach. When Ben showed up the first day of camp, I sensed he knew both football and young athletes. I asked him if he wanted to be the defensive coordinator and line coach. Not sure what he had gotten himself into, he consented.

As always, graduation claimed several of the previous season's veterans but this year's crop of seniors seemed both capable and determined. Andrew Biros returned at quarterback. Jared Rosenberg and Kwasi Agyeme-Kagya would provide a solid inside and outside running tandem. The line showed promise with Mike Chen, Mark Hugick, Stanley Aladi and Mike Murphy shouldering the load.

Andrew, in reflection, valued the efforts of the unsung heroes in the line. "Each year they were out here with us, grinding away, learning the game, getting their butts kicked. Each year, coming out for preseason, learning technique, watching film and getting their butts kicked by upperclassmen. By the fall of 2005, Mark, Ed (Wong), Stanley and Mike were football players."

In his new leadership role, Mike Murphy shared the seniors' projected goals. "There are really some games we really want to win, games against rivals Calvary Christian, ANC and Jenkintown. But I'm ready to step up and be the role model to the kids coming up. That's probably more important than winning." (Courier Times, September 1, 2005)

Part of being a role model included helping others while keeping an even keel yourself. Andrew valued both qualities in Mike. "Murphy was the best natural athlete amongst all of us. He went on to serve as an Officer in the Marines. But also, he was a silly son of a bitch too. Mike had a ritual of watching Teenage Mutant Ninja Turtles Saturday morning before games, and would prowl around practice pretending to be a wild beast from the inner reaches of

THE QUAKERLY GRIDIRON BROTHERS

his mind when things got slow. I don't think I ever heard him say a bad thing about someone else either."

The wild beast persona failed to produce a win in our first three defeats to ANC (6-42), Jenkintown (13-41) and Calvary Christian (13-42). Entering our fourth game against Maryland Christian we faced not only a three-game losing streak but rainy weather and morning SAT exams. To say the least, the trio bode poorly for any kind of post-game victory celebration.

This time, however, the GS gridders were not going to be denied. The Courier Times summed up the contest, writing, "The Cougars used the legs of Jared Rosenberg and the muddy conditions to post a 32-0 win over the Maryland Christian Saints Saturday in a non league contest."

Jared picked up 136 yards on seven carries. He sprinted to four touchdowns of 5, 4, 45 and 48 yards. Rosenberg was supported by Jose D'Oleo (44 yards), Kwasi Agyeman-Kaga (36 yards) and Matt Bitzer (34 yards). The dominant running game necessitated only one pass the entire rain drenched afternoon. I summed up the winning affair saying, "The conditions really did dictate the flow of the game. We normally run a spread offensive set. This week, with the weather, we went back to the straight-I formation." (Courier Times, October 9, 2005)

In our next outing against Saint Andrews the spread formation was back in vogue. It worked as Biros passed 31 times for 248 yards. He hit senior Alex Desantis 6 times for 105 yards and senior Femi Ogundadegbe 3 times for 23 yards. Both senior receivers had come out for football for the first time. Unfortunately, the Cougar offensive showing could not match Saint Andrews' big play attack as they converted a 75-yard kickoff return and 75-yard interception run into a 28-14 win.

Two consecutive losses to Princeton Day (18-26) and Lower Moreland (14-42) put the Cougars in what we considered a must-win situation. Andrew Biros will long remember both the preparation and the outcome of this all-important showdown with a very potent Tower Hill team. "Heading into that final game, another losing season already confirmed, it was paramount we got that win."

Practice before the 'big game' became intense. In Andrew's recollection, "Practicing up on the field that Thursday before the last Saturday football of the year, our team was flat. It was just a bad practice. Chalk it up to a long season, the cold weather, guys just being done. Gleeson read us the riot act. The team's captains, myself included, kept everyone behind when Gleeson and the coaches were finished. I got it in my mind that what we needed was to wake up, and knock some of the rust off each other. 'Line up, goal line drills,' I instructed our team. We placed the ball on the 2-yard line. An offense and defense assembled, I hiked the ball and handed it off to a plunging Kwasi through the goal line. 'Again!' I yelled. We lined up again but before I could get the snap off, a yell pierced the air. 'Hey. What the **** are you doing!?' It was Gleeson, who had emerged from the stairway that led onto the field. It was the angriest I had ever seen him- and remember we lost a lot of games. He screamed at all of us to get off the field. As an adolescent I saw an angry coach. As an adult and an educator what I came to realize is that Gleeson's anger was also punctuated by fear, fear that one of us would have gotten hurt in that moment and he would have been burdened by the fact he wasn't there."

The aftermath brought one of those learning moments shared by a coach and a dedicated player. "Feeling dejected, we sunk off into the locker room. 'Drew' he bellowed to me, calling me out into the hallway of the alumni gym, away from the team, the two of us sitting on a bench. 'What were you thinking?' he snarled. And that's when I began to weep."

"Even writing this now, my eyes tear up some. Through sobs, I apolo-gized to my coach, and sought to convey everything that I had inside, much of which had been building since my first preseason practice my freshman year. I was there to win and had failed to accomplish that. But it wasn't about me. I felt responsible for our team, for losing. I felt like I had let my teammates and friends down. I had cajoled guys to come out and play on our team, try football. It's fun. I watched my peers put in years of work to become bona fide football players, especially my offensive line, who protected me week in and out, and afforded me a chance to play a game I loved. I had teammates who suffered through bone breaks and tears, and kept coming back week after week to try just as hard to get a win. As the quarterback, the kid who didn't come to sit and was there to win, I had let them down. And I didn't know what else to do. I'm not sure if I even knew all of this while we were up on the field minutes prior to this. But it all came out of me, sitting on that bench with Gleeson."

Andrew's frustration was understandable, perhaps even inevitable, but the key is what it meant to his growth and development. "I don't know what Gleeson said at that moment, as my sobs turned to sniffles. He sat there and listened. I think he understood and maybe even felt the same way. We both loved football, and both had committed so much of ourselves to George School football. And George School football, at least during this time period in history, was an experience for many young men to learn about the limits they're able to push themselves, and the extent to which you'll push yourself for your teammates. It wasn't about trophies or championships. But when you put in so much hard work, you deserve to experience winning, because winning football is the culmination of a team's collective effort. And our team deserved to win. We had one more shot."

The Cougars, emotionally and physically, played with conviction in defeating Tower Hill 40-24 in this last hurrah. After the Hillers drew first blood, the Cougars put on a total display of football mastery. Isaac Yang reeled off a 58-yard scoring run. Jared Rosenberg hit pay dirt from 8 yards out. Alex Desantis hauled in a 35-yard scoring strike from Biros. Jose D'Oleo tallied on a 65-yard punt return. Mike Murphy capped off the first half explosives with a 66-yard pass interception score. Kwasi Agyeman-Kaga would finish off the Cougar scoring with an 8-yard TD in the fourth quarter to seal the 40-24 win.

In his final post-game interview, Andrew told reporter Karen Sangillo, "I'm sad because this is my last game. But I'm happy that we played so well in it and I'm so excited to have this win for Glees. We had some rough times this year but I'm so glad those guys know how it is to win. Everyone's been telling me that I'll always remember my last game, and I know it's true. I'll remember this." (Courier Times November 5, 2005)

Seventeen years later, Andrew still remembers this post-game response. "When the final whistle blew, I hugged Gleeson and started to cry again. For a different reason this time, of course. Our team celebrated around us, friends and family coming onto the field to join in. I was joyful for my teammates. I was proud we could do it for Gleeson. And I knew like Rob (Waters) had known (four years earlier), that my football career was over."

Andrew carried away the most important message taught by his football commitment. "George School football taught me the power of persistence. It's easy to win and keep the good times going. It's much harder to learn to face defeat, and not just come back from it yourself, but set an example for others that the pursuit is worth it, and together success is in reach. That's leadership. I learned that from Gleeson, and I learned it from my teammates. And I'd never trade gaining that formative understanding as a 17-year-old, for a silly trophy or a few more W's. It's carried me through life, and made me the man I am today."

Seventeen years later, Mike Murphy also reflected on the impact GS football had on his life. As he wrote, "I think the last thing worth mentioning for me is mentioning the impact that GS football had on my life. And I really hate phrasing it like that because it sounds so hackneyed but it's true. As I sit here and write this, I know the bonds formed through the crucible of preseason played a small part in me wanting to join the military. I knew that I would be much stronger and have extraordinary ties with the men with whom I underwent the process. It harks back to what our ancestors must have felt in the shield wall or the closeness I associate with the word "Tribe". Yes, GS was a community of Friends… but give me "the Tribe" any day of the week."

Kwasi Agyeman-Kayga, also reflected on the value of GS football seventeen years after suiting up for his final game. "I remember sitting in class and looking forward to getting out on the football field. I even looked forward to Tuesday practices and watching tapes to learn how I could better my skill. Then there was game day. There is nothing in this world that could ever compare to the experience of football game day. The feeling of running out on the field and the crowd cheering. The adrenaline that is running through your body as you are doing pregame drills and trying to focus on the mission ahead of us. Finally, you and your brothers get out on that field and give everything you have to get that win. I never left a game without feeling drained because I left everything out on that field. And this was all behind our leader John Gleeson who never gave up on us and brought the best out in us whether it was on or off the field. Overall playing football at George School is one of my greatest memories. It taught me about hard work, leadership, and teamwork, all traits that I still have to this day. Honestly, playing football at GS formed me into the person I am today. Thank you George School Football."

The 2006 Cougars faced a big challenge in what ranked as a classic building year. The Courier Times fall preview summed up the plight of the men in green, saying, "The Cougars lost nearly all of their offensive statistical leaders from last season and are going to have to replace a ton of production." (Courier Times, August 31, 2006) In fact, we had only two returning starters on both offense and defense.

I recognized the fate that awaited us, saying in the Courier's fall preview, "Several of our young guys are good athletes, but they're going to have to learn football and learn the intricacies of the game. These young guys are going to take some lickings and make some mistakes." (Courier Times, August 31, 2006)

The two proven veterans, Jose D'Oleo and Isaac Yang, knew they would need to carry the load as several promising but inexperienced sophomores and freshman developed. The previous year Jose had caught 9 passes for 110 yards. He also returned a punt 65-yards in our final victory. Isaac had raced 58 yards for a score to ignite the offense in that big win over Tower Hill.

Isaac represented another growing twist in Cougar football that paralleled the experience of AeMin Kim. The new administration wanted George School to have a more global look. Where that opened the doors to a refreshing exchange of international ideas, it meant fewer athletes with any real knowledge of gridiron wars. Coming from Seoul, Korea, Isaac readily admitted to being a football neophyte. "When I came from Korea, I wanted to try something new. I didn't think I'd play football in college, so I wanted to do it when I had a chance." (Courier Times, August 31, 2006)

I saw him as a real offensive threat. "He's a very fast kid. He has exceptional speed. We played him at outside linebacker last year when we realized his coverage potential." (Courier Times, August 31, 2006)

Another upcoming gridder, freshman Matt Brown, showed up at our first preseason practice session. As always, leery about such an abrupt and rough introduction to George School, I told him to wait two weeks until the other freshmen arrived on campus and then join the team. Matt not only refused my advice but rapidly became the leader throughout most of our drills. A soccer convert, he only needed to add some football knowledge to his 5' 6", 160 pound frame to become a starter.

Though raw, the new men in green played surprisingly well in our opening game. Reporter Jean-Paul Lautenschlager wrote, "George School proved that heart and effort are a substitute for experience. With only six seniors on the roster and 18 lost to graduation, coach John Gleeson thought this fall would be about developing his underclassmen. A mix of seniors, juniors and sophomores set the tone Saturday afternoon, lifting George School to a 16-6 win over Maryland Christian." (Courier Times, September 10, 2006)

Junior Jose D'Oleo spent little time making his mark on the game. On the opening kickoff, he weaved his way 59 yards to set up a six play, 21 -yard scoring drive. Sky Jaffe plunged in from 1 yard out for the Cougars' initial score of the year. Jose would add the two-point conversion to give GS an early 8-point lead. He would later score a third quarter touchdown and intercept two passes. D'Oleo knew he needed to emerge as a team leader. In his post-game interview he said, "My main focus is to try and help the team the best way I can on both offense and defense. I try to let people feed off my energy." (Courier Times, September 10, 2006)

Jaffe, also showing real senior savvy, relied on his legs to keep the chains moving. Five of his seven carries came on third or fourth down. Jaffe would sum up the game's importance, saying, "We needed to start the season off on the right foot. I can't even tell you how essential this win is." (Courier Times, September 10, 2006)

Unfortunately, the combination of inexperience and untimely injuries doomed the Cougars the rest of the season. Jaffe hurt his shoulder early in the campaign and was replaced by sophomore Justin Cancellieri. With little experience at the position but plenty of athletic talent, Justin faced real on-the-job training. Justin was a stellar athlete in football, basketball and baseball but he knew nothing about the art of signal calling. Later on, Jose D'Oleo would sustain a season ending knee injury and Matt Brown would suffer a concussion.

That proved too big a depletion to our offensive attack as we scored under 10 points in our next six games. Our only chance at salvaging the season would be upsetting a strong ANC team in our final game. ANC tallied first and took a 7-0 lead early in the first quarter. For one shining moment, the Cougars retaliated. Back from his injury, Jaffe took a handoff from Cancellieri, faked an end sweep, and fired a perfect strike to a wide-open Isaac Yang who raced 64 yards for a touchdown. Cancellieri then hooked up with his big tight end Tom Wayda for the two-point conversion.

ANC quickly dispelled any hopes of an upset, scoring on their next four possessions before the half. With the Cougars down 14-41 in the final frame, Isaac Yang got one last taste of gridiron glory, shaking off several would-be ANC tacklers en route to a 38-yard touchdown. For Isaac, his final taste of scholastic football was a most pleasant and memorable one.

The 2007 season marked a new era in Cougar football. The team had played an independent schedule for the last 39 years, a fact denying the GS gridders a shot at all-league honors or team championships. The old Penn-Jersey League saw its last heyday in the early eighties when schools such as Germantown Friends, Friends Central, Pennsylvania School for the Deaf and Mitchell Prep abandoned their football programs. For a few years the Cougars tried competing in the Independence League, a mixture of local public and private schools. As this league expanded, many parents felt the competition was unequal and wanted GS to play only prep school rivals.

Several athletic directors and coaches gathered at George School in the spring of 2007 to discuss the formation of a new Tri-State Prep League. The teams comprising the new league were George School, Princeton Day School, Perkiomen, Saint Andrews and Tower Hill. All these schools adhered to similar policies about recruiting and all faced small squad turnouts. Understandably, one issue faced by everyone was the distance that had to be traveled. That was compounded by the fact that three of the teams had previous commitments to other leagues. They would have to adjust their schedules accordingly. All drawbacks were duly considered; the new league was set to begin in the fall of 2007.

Senior Ben Durey, a transfer from Central Bucks West his junior year, relished the new opportunity. "It's exciting. It's been 21 or 22 years since the George School has been in a league. Everyone is excited because we have a chance to win a championship. Last, we were a young team, with only five seniors, plus we had players who never played before. And it was just a sched-ule…we played with nothing to go for. Once we lost some key players to injuries it was tough to win games." (Courier Times August 31, 2007)

Ben's football background made him a likely candidate to assume leadership responsibilities. "Oh, that's how I see myself. For me it is a second nature thing. As a senior, I want to make sure the younger players are not walking around with their heads down during a water break. The seniors have to make sure all of us are putting 100 percent into every drill." (Courier Times, August 31, 2007)

The effort certainly manifested itself in our opening game against West Nottingham. Jose D'Oleo, who missed a good portion of the 2006 season with injuries, spearheaded the Cougar attack. The offense opened the game with an 18-play, 77-yard scoring drive that chewed up 10 minutes of the first quarter. Justin Cancelliere capped off the march with a 1-yard quarterback sneak. Jose knew the importance of starting well. "We came out hungry trying to make a statement. We wanted to play hard and see what we could do. We can do it this year." (Courier Times, September 9, 2007)

The Cougars did not let up, tacking on four more touchdowns before halftime. Jarron Speller scored on a 44-yard run. D'Oleo caught two TD aerials from Cancelliere good for 27 yards apiece. He also finished off a scoring drive with a 1-yard plunge into the endzone. Cancelliere, who went to a quarterback camp over the summer, showed far greater calm under center. Justin com-pleted 5 passes for 91 yards and two touchdowns. Describing the 44-6 win in his post-game interview, Justin said, "We just have to come out and play strong and prove everyone wrong. They all think we're weak but we are not a weak team. We're a little team but we have a lot of heart." (Courier Times, September 9, 2007)

The Cardiac Cougars, however, could not keep pace the rest of the season. A sound thumping at the hands of Calvary Christian (0-35) brought up our first league game against Perkiomen Prep. A close 6-18 loss put us in a tough bind in terms of the new league. With only 5 teams represented, a single defeat could prove devastating. We viewed our next opponent,

Princeton Day School, as a must win. Hopes dimmed on the first play when Princeton Day returned the opening kickoff 80 yards for a score. Not despairing, the green clad warriors rallied back and knotted the score at 6 all by halftime. PDs, however, rallied in the fourth quarter to seize a 17-6 victory. Senior Jose D'Oleo explained the game's impact, "Coming into the season, we were really excited to be part of a league. But we never had to play with the pressure of being in a league before, and that's an adjustment. Now we'll have to work harder to win our next three games. We need to have a whole team effort the whole game. We've got to get it together and step it up, and it has to be all eleven people. That's what football is all about. We beat ourselves. We had the momentum and lost it on penalties at the end of the first half. That hurt because it messed up our flow." (Courier Times, September 29, 2007)

Our next outing added another historic note to Cougar football history. We were scheduled to play league leader, Tower Hill at home. For the first time in the 84-year history of the program, the Cougars would do battle under the lights. We rented several auxiliary lights and placed them on the track and above the stands. Unfortunately, two sets of lights malfunctioned and two never reached their full height, casting a somewhat eerie glow on the field. This prompted the Tower Hill coach to ask me prior to the game, "Please say you have done this before!"

Technical difficulties aside, the game was highly anticipated. As D'Oleo had said after the Princeton game, "We're definitely looking forward to that (game). Everyone is going to come out; it's like homecoming. Hopefully, we'll step it up and get excited. I saw the excitement in everyone's eyes in this game. Early in the season it seemed like we weren't ready to play but I saw in this game we were. That's a big difference because I think we can pick it up." (Courier Times, September 29, 2007)

Friday Night Lights had finally come to George School. Almost twenty years later, Tom Wayda, stellar defensive and offensive lineman, remembers the entire atmosphere. "The most memorable moment of George School football was the school's first home night game. If memory serves me right, it was my junior year and we played Tower Hill. There was a ton of buzz because the school had rented lights, so for the first time we were no longer waking up at the crack of dawn to play our typical Saturday afternoon home games. They wanted to give us an opportunity to have that 'Friday Night Lights' experience; however, those were the same lights that are used on construction sites along the highway, so it wasn't exactly the same but close enough for a 17-year-old high school kid. I remember there being a good crowd, and it had seemed the whole school had come out to support us. Teachers, students who definitely had never been to a game before, and even people I was sure had no connection to George School whatsoever. It was a real spectacle for a Quaker school."

Though Tom's actual recollection of the game itself proved a little rusty, he will never forget the contest's aura. "The day heading up to that night seemed to have dragged forever. The excitement amongst myself and team members was palpable. Coach Gleeson gave a particularly inspiring speech that night and I remember everyone coming out of the Alumni Gym fired up. I'm not 100% sure if this is selective memory or if it actually happened, but I'm pretty sure one of our first plays was a touchdown pass. We put up a good fight, but ultimately lost that night. I don't even remember the score, only three things; coach's speech. That first play. And the lights."

Actually, Tower Hill jumped out to a 24-0 halftime lead. Perhaps initially stunned by the lights, the Cougars did not fold in the second half. The men in green opened the fourth quarter with an eight play, 75-yard drive. Jose D'Oleo capped off the march with a 19-yard dash to paydirt. Jose would finish the night with 97 yards rushing and 51-yards on two pass completions. His heroics fell short as Tower Hill won the game 37-20.

The Cougars still had one more shot at some Tri-State League success when they took on Saint Andrews in their final home game. Though falling behind early, GS rallied back to put up some pretty impressive second half statistics. Quarterback Justin Cancelliere threw 3 touchdown passes in the second half: a 15-yard pass to sophomore Ian Wiggins, and a 50-yarder and 83-yarder to Jose D'Oleo. Cancelliere finished the day with 205 yards passing. D'Oleo had 145 receiving yards and 45 yards rushing.

After the game Justin expressed both his disappointment over the 34-20 loss and his future hopes. "We wanted to win for the seniors because it's their last time playing on this field. That didn't work out for us but we played better in the second half. I think we're really getting confidence in ourselves. We thought we could win the league at the beginning of the year. That didn't work out, so now we have to adjust our goals. Now we want to try hard and win our next two games." (Courier Times, October 13, 2007)

A heartbreaking last-minute defeat to Maryland Christian (10-13) and a loss to ANC (12-38) left the Cougars in a wait-until-next-year frame of mind. Against rival ANC sophomores Lamar Milton and Franklin Cueves grabbed some of the spotlight. Milton hauled in a 6 -yard pass to tie the game 6-6. Cueves caught a 38-touchdown pass to round out the scoring in the last quarter. Cancelliere completed 8 of 20 passes for 162 yards and two TDs. That upped his total for the season to 44 completions for 736 yards and 10 touchdowns. Dave Foppert picked up 38 tough yards on 10 carries. All of that offensive punch would be returning the following season!

Impressive stats alone, however, belie the true nature of being on a football team. It goes beyond games won or individual achievements. The bonding and support that takes place in victory or defeat ranks as the greatest benefit afforded a football player. Fourteen years after playing his final scholastic football game, Justin Cancelliere wrote, "It was such a great experience to have the opportunity to play for George School. Even though we may not have won many games my teammates became lifelong friends."

Entering the 2008 season Justin had matured greatly as the starting quarterback, a journey that included dealing with a good deal of personal hardship. Four years earlier he experienced a tragedy no youngster on the verge of his high school career should face. His mother, step-father, and three sisters all perished in a plane crash. Justin found support in the George School community and the Cougar football team. As he told Rick Woelfel in the Courier Times 2008 fall preview, "Coach Gleeson has been my number one supporter. He's always been there, but my friends and my teammates have all been there. It feels good to know that you have that support system within the team. We're a close community. Everybody's there for you." (Courier Times, August 29, 2008)

That is the true essence of team camaraderie. With the team's backing, Justin developed a sound and heartfelt response to his situation. "You have to keep your head up. A lot of times it's, 'Ah, I feel like quitting. Why am I here?' You ask why, but you need to look past that and think, 'You're still alive. You need to make your family proud. You're living their Legacy.' You're the only one left to represent your family and you've got to represent them well and stay positive." (Courier Times, August 29, 2008)

By his senior year, Justin had certainly earned the respect of his Cougar teammates. He became a multiple offensive weapon. He could throw a pass 60 yards. He learned to read defenses. His elusive scrambling gave opposing defenders fits. His kickoff returns always threatened to go all the way. You could not ask more of a player.

Justin readily awaited the 2008 season. "We had a lot of young receivers last year but pretty much our starting running backs and receivers are all juniors and seniors now. I'm starting to throw a lot farther and my passes are more accurate." (Courier Times, August 29, 2008)

The Cougars took two heartbreaking games to finally get focused. A loss to Maryland Christian (20-23) and Perkiomen (14-24) set up another "Friday Night Lights' home contest with Princeton Day School. The game bore double significance. It was a home night game which always brought out an enthusiastic crowd and it was a Tri-State Prep League affair. The men in green did not disappoint the Cougar faithful, scoring a touchdown and two-point conversion in every quarter en route to a 32-18 win.

Senior Dave Foppert, who gained 67 rushing yards, was understandably elated. "It was our first-ever win under the lights. It's a great feeling. This was a lot of fun." (Courier Times, September 27, 2008)

Foppert lauded the efforts of Franklin Cueves and Justin Cancelliere. Cueves had 111 yards rushing and Cancellieri checked in with a six-yard tally. "Cueves was just blowing it up, and he's a junior, and Cancelliere was running all over the place. They couldn't touch him on kick returns. It was definitely a team effort. Everyone worked really hard to make this happen." (Courier Times, September 27, 2008)

The GS gridders did not fare as well in their next two away games against league opponents Tower Hill and Saint Andrews. Big plays dimmed the Cougar cause as they sustained a 14-35 loss. George School had several long drives but could not find the endzone Justin Cancelliere once again drew raves from the local reporter. "Cancellieri was a human highlight reel as he scrambled around the field on virtually every offensive play. He was often able to find open receivers but a lack of pass protection caused three interceptions." (Courier Times October 4, 2008)

Mistakes and penalties haunted us again in our 24-38 loss to Saint Andrews. Fumbles and interceptions found the Cougars down 8-38 in the fourth quarter. Cancelliere provided the offensive spark in the final frame, passing for two touchdowns and returning a kickoff 73 yards for a touchdown.

With hopes of a league title shattered, the Cougars took on Elkton Christian Academy in a home contest. Once again, having fallen behind 19-0 we had to play catch-up ball. Franklin Cueves got the team rolling, scoring on a 5-yard touchdown run with 10:55 left in the game. Christain Prajzner then pounced on an Elkton fumble. Cancelliere immediately capitalized on the miscue and tossed a 23-yard screenplay to Dave Foppert.

After Elkton scored again, Cancelliere lit up the home crowd with a sensational kickoff return to the Elkton 33-yard line. He then fired another screen pass to Foppert for the final tally.

In my post-game interview, I praised the team's unwillingness to fold. "These players have shown me a lot. We have a small team, and most of our players play both sides of the ball. It would have been easy for them to have given up; we were tired and down a lot but they kept fighting." (Courier Times, October 19, 2008)

The Cougars decided to switch strategies in our next game against Saint Joseph of the Palisades. This was a make-up game that we scrambled to find when another opponent canceled their season at the last minute. Against Palisades we opted to start strong and not wait for a last-ditch rally. The Cougars jumped out to a 22-0 score on runs by Cancelliere, Cuevas and Foppert

Cueves, who lived only minutes from the Palisades stadium, ran for 149 yards on 20 carries. He was quick to credit his blockers for the 28-21 victory. "The left side of the line was unusually strong today. And Foppert helped open some holes today. "(Courier Times October 26, 2008)

The big win bode well for our upcoming game against a very strong ANC team that sported a 7-2 record. We decided to come out firing against our confident archrival. On the first play of our initial possession, Justin Cancelliere wound up and fired a bomb to junior Jake Skolnick. Jake to this day remembers the play. "Probably my most memorable moment that some guys still bring up to this day was against ANC during my junior year. We were heavy underdogs (as usual) and all week at practice we had planned to open up the game with Justin throwing a deep fade to me. ANC I believe turned the ball over to begin the game and our first play from their 30 we ran a fade and Justin threw a perfect pass in the back corner of the endzone where I fully flat out dove to catch it. The crowd went crazy. I believe we went up by two touchdowns to begin that game and it was very exciting to have the momentum against them. We ended up losing and it wasn't much of a game at the end, as ANC had a far superior team, but the memory of starting the game with that catch was something I'll always remember."

Jake's recollection of the contest proved most accurate. After the big pass, we scored on a Dave Foppert 4-yard run after an ANC fumble. Unfortunately, the Cougars could not keep the momentum. ANC quarterback and Drexel basketball recruit Shannon Givens showed his athleticism, passing for two scores and running in a third to give the Academy a 22-12 halftime lead. The green clad warriors did not fold. They capped off their first drive of the second half with Cuevas plunging in from 1-yard out to make the score 22-20.

ANC coach Andy Davis summed up the final score saying, "In the future, people will see 36-20 and think that wasn't much of a game. George School took us to the limit today. It was a hard-fought win for us today." (Courier Times, November 2, 2008)

As evident in a postgame interview, I was euphoric over George School's showing. "I have been coaching at George School for 40 years now and I have never been as proud of a team as I am these guys. They defied the predictions (a 42-0 loss) and played them tough all game. It came down to the fourth quarter. They never quit." (Courier Times, November 2, 2008)

For the season, Justin Cancelliere completed 41 of 90 passes for 566 yards. Jake Skolnick caught 14 passes for 225 yards and a 16-1 yards per catch average. Franklin Cueves rushed 70 times for 457 yards and Dave

188

Foppert followed close behind with 294 yards on 46 carries. Their 2-6 record certainly did not do justice to the caliber of their play.

The 2009 season showcased the talents of the unsung heroes. The offensive lineman, who toiled every day in practice and games, would finally get their due recognition. Leading the pack, Matt Brown and Christian Prajzner formed an impressive pulling guard combo. Nick Simone, a tight end convert, manned the right tackle spot. Ishmael Ba, Kevin Simone, Nick Gonzales and Tyler Campellone would alternate at the other line positions.

This impressive group would offer protection for rookie quarterback Rex Roskos. They would open holes for all-purpose back Franklin Cueves. And they would ward off opposing defensive pass rushers while receivers Jake Skolnick, Ian Wiggins, Dylan Gleeson, and Lamar Milton would find gaps in the opposition's secondary.

Matt Brown was the leader of this band of stalwarts. Matt, who had walked into preseason camp four years earlier and proceeded to impress both the coaches and upperclassmen, won a starting job as a guard and linebacker as a freshman. Already displaying both athleticism and determination, Matt perfected his skill set and learned the intricacies of the game. His junior year he would never leave the field of play, a situation Matt loved. "Iron-man football. It was a fun thing to do. But in pretty much every game by the two-minute warning I was (running out of breath) on the field." (Courier Times September 4, 2009)

A little windedness did not phase Matt. He had already met and overcome his share of serious life challenges. His mother passed away from a heart attack when he was eight years old. The summer before entering George School his father, a colon cancer survivor underwent surgery to replace a heart valve. Through it all, Matt showed the heart of a warrior, a non-too-surprising fact considering all three of his brothers served in the military. Matt was paving his way for a military career when he took part in the United States Naval Sea Cadets program in the summer of 2008 and went through The Special Operations (SEAL) training in Norfolk, Virginia.

Defending his views about the military at a school with a Quaker and pacifist background presented some challenges for Matt. He quickly adapted. "Freshman year, I did have quite a few heated arguments with people but I learned to keep my mouth shut. I'm not afraid to say what's on my mind, but I don't feel like fighting with people about it. I find people are pro-soldier. They just happen to be against the war." (Courier Times, September 4, 2009)

After graduating from George School, Matt did a tour of duty in the Marines and then returned to graduate from West Point Academy. Thirteen years later, he would describe the role Cougar football played in his life journey. "Playing football at GS was a fundamental part of becoming the man I am today. Not only did it help me develop a core of friends throughout my time at high school, many of whom are still my best friends today, but it allowed me to continue to be a part of a team and develop a set of skills that has greatly aided my Army career. I was fortunate enough to be able to play all four years on the varsity team, and as a freshman at a brand-new school, knowing no one from grade school, the team became my first home away from home. I loved learning about the game and simply gave it my best shot in every drill or play we ran that preseason. This earned me a starting spot on the team and from that first year on, I played because I absolutely loved the game and being able to throw all of my body and energy onto the field."

With the future Lieutenant Matt Brown in command, the Cougars were ready for a strong 2009 campaign. In their first game against Maryland Christian Saints, a school made up of kids who are home schooled or who attend schools that do not have football, the Cougars took a half to get untracked. Spotting the Saints a 25-0 lead, the GS gridders battled back in the second half with Jake Skolnick scampering for a 18-yard TD and Ian Wiggins hauling in a 13 yard scoring strike from Rex Roskos. Roskos finished the night completing 11 of 26 passes for 119 yards. Franklin Cueves carried the bulk of the rushing, going 119 yards on 20 carries. The comeback fell short leaving the Cougars on the losing end of a 25-16 score.

In our next contest, the Cougars once again faced a two-and-a-half-hour road trip to take on the New York Military Academy. The game was a last-minute addition after another team canceled its season. This time the Cougar offense did not wait for the second half to get rolling. Jake Skolnick jump-started the Cougar attack by returning the opening kickoff 83 yards to paydirt. Skolnick added another 43-yard run in the first quarter. Franklin Cueves added to the Cougar offensive output, catching a 25-yard TD from Roskos and scoring on three two-point conversions. Lamar Milton would ice the 30-8 win with a 3-yard run. I summed up the game in a post-game interview. "We made a point of getting out early, and getting there early, so we could get the rust off and be stretched and ready to go. I think Jake's kick return showed us that we would be fine." (Courier Times, September 20, 2009)

Returning to the comfort of our Bucks County surroundings, we took on league rival Perkiomen Prep. The offense looked sharp in the beginning, going on a 13-play opening drive that ate up 8 minutes and ended with Franklin Cueves scoring from 3 yards out. The momentum, however, switched back immediately when Perkiomen returned the ensuing kickoff to the Cougar 4-yard line. They scored on the next play and went up 8-6. Two more Indian tallies led to a 23-point halftime lead. Perkiomen then returned the opening kickoff all the way back for an 81-yard TD.

Franklin Cueves, who scored another touchdown to slightly pad the 14-35 defeat, summed up the Cougar's plight. "We have to tighten those aspects (kickoff coverage) of the game up. I think that once we get the special teams together, we're going to be a good football team." (Courier Times, September 27, 2009)

Cueves made sure that specialty team miscues did not haunt the GS gridders in our next game against Princeton Day School. He rushed for 304 yards on 39 carries for two touchdowns. He was quick to credit our offensive line. "The blocking was great, the whole line was opening holes and I just took them. The first drive was a normal drive, but I just kept running. I felt strong and we were pushing the defense back, so, after we scored the first time, I knew we had this game." (Courier Times, October 4, 2009)

Coming away with a 28-12 win, we also introduced a big boy package to our offensive scheme. Christian Prajzner switched from guard to fullback for a few plays, just long enough to score a touchdown and two extra point conversions.

The GS ground attack once again took center stage in our next 35-14 win over Tower Hill. This time, the total team racked up 265 yards rushing. Cueves ran for 133 yards and two TDs. Skolnick added 88 yards and a touchdown. Prajzner tacked on 44 more yards.

The Courier Times reporter was quick to spot the real contributors. "While the George School backfield is talented, the offensive line is a major factor in the backfield's success. The front five, including Matt Brown and Christian Prajzner, helped the ball carriers gain 670 yards the past two weeks." Courier Times, October 11, 2009)

Christian Prajzner offered a more simplified explanation. "I'm just trying to get down the field, find the first person I see and knock them down, and the next person I see and knock them down and make a hole for my runner. I have to protect my runner." (Courier Times, October 11, 2009)

The Cougars next outing proved to be a real shootout with league rival Saint Andrews. Once again Franklin Cueves led the rushing brigade chalking up 128 yards on 27 carries good for 2 touchdowns. Balancing our attack more than the previous two games, Rex Roskos passed for 146 yards and two tallies. Jake Skolnick caught 5 passes for 97 yards and two TDs.

Jake explained the Cougar strategy, saying, "I'm usually a running back along with Franklin, but today, they used me out at wide receiver a lot. On my first touchdown I got past the linebacker easily, but they had a safety deep. He was even with me but, when the ball came out, I just ran past the safety. It was a real good pass from Rex." (Courier Times, October 18, 2009)

Any chance we had of claiming the Tri-State prep League championship, however, went away with the 30-36 defeat. Facing a bye weekend, the Cougars had plenty of time to ponder the loss and prepare for our last home game against New Hope-Solebury. Both states of mind seem to work as the Cougars set off an offensive explosion.

Cueves once again led the rushing attack with 64 yards and two TDs. Skolnick added 36 yards to the Cougar cause. Despite the rain, Roskos completed 6 passes for 100 yards. Senior Ian Wiggins caught 2 of the scoring strikes.

For Wiggins the 42-20 victory carried special meaning. "This was my last home game. We were in the mindset that we know we're a good football team, and we practiced like we had a challenge ahead. For two weeks, we worked hard to keep everyone motivated." (Courier Times, November 1, 2009)

In our final game against ANC, both Franklin Cueves and Matt Brown wanted to end their senior year on a positive note. Even though losing 18-35, both players reached their personal goal. Against ANC, Cueves rushed for 234 yards and 3 touchdowns. He would finish the year with 1170 yards on 159 carries. He scored 94 points.

A true leader, Brown relished every one of Franklin's scores, "I like it when he scores, because I think it reflects a little bit on me." (Courier Times, November 8, 2009)

Matt would add, "It was so much fun playing. I'm glad I gave up soccer. All four years we always got beat on big plays, but at George School we never quit." (Courier Times, November 8, 2009)

Thirteen years later Matt would still relish every moment spent on the GS gridiron. "Although our program was not overly successful, I feel like we never had a defeatist attitude and went into every game knowing we had a chance to win. As the years went on, playing football was the highlight and backbone of my high school experience. The friends I gained on the team were those who I spent the vast majority of my time with. My best friend today is still my teammate Tom Wayda and this is now 13 years removed from our time on the team together. Additionally, continuing to build my discipline, physical fitness, leadership skills (junior and senior years), and most importantly willpower enabled me to feel very comfortable in the Army environment. Rigorous team sports, which are mentally and physically demanding, are a great developer for a future soldier. I am immensely grateful that I was given the chance to play and look back with fond memories of my time on the team."

Jake Skolnick completed his senior year with 41 catches for 540 yards and 8 touchdowns. He too looks back with fondness at his scholastic playing days. "From a nonplaying standpoint, the biggest takeaway was that as a result of the football environment at GS many of my teammates became lifelong friends. I still talk to a bunch of the guys regularly. I still remember competing in August at preseason and "Bang-Bang" as Glees called the first day of hitting."

Later next spring a father, who chose to remain anonymous, generously set up what was called the John Gleeson III '65 Football Scholarship. It was awarded to a junior who has been a committed participant in the Varsity

Football program for at least two years. The recipient will have demonstrated a commitment to hard work, good sportsmanship, leadership, ideals, and character both on and off the field. In my estimation, every Cougar was deserving of such an award.

Going into the 2010 season we boasted only two returning starters on the squad and 24 players on the roster. That ominous combination was somewhat balanced by the presence of several talented but inexperienced younger players. Rex Roskos and my son Dylan Gleeson claimed veteran status and were named, along with Kyle Conklin, captains of the team. In the Courier Times fall preview Rex summed up the Cougars plight saying, "We have a young team with a lot of raw talent so it's going to be interesting to see how it pans out for us this year. We lost some good people from last year and they're going to be hard to replace but we still have a core group of strong players from last year. Our bread and butter is to get the ball to the outside. If we can do that, we'll be alright." (Courier Times, September 3, 2010)

Rex had established some personal goals for his final season of football. "I know because of my size (6-0, 160) there's no way I'll play in college so this is it for me. I've come to grips with it and realize that's all the more reason to lay it all on the line this year and play with intensity. I want to leave it all on the field." (Courier Times, September 3, 2010)

Reflecting back on his playing days, Dylan Gleeson also noted the size factor and how it would influence the Cougars. "My senior year of George School football cannot be described as successful from a win-loss perspective. We went 1-7 in my senior year largely due to the graduation of a number of key figures from the prior year. For a team that can be charitably compared to the island of misfit toys, we found ourselves competitive in a surprising number of games."

Dylan continued to add specifics to his size theory. "Robbie Van Pelt, also affectionately known as Ricky Bobbie, and Kevin Simone were mainstays along both lines throughout the year. Kevin Huang, commonly known as Shadowfax due to his majestic speed rivaling that of the mythological horse, started opposite me at receiver and played in the secondary. Rex Roskos manned the quarterback spot and Kyle Conklin played both fullback and linebacker. All of us could best be described as too small to play football. However, this contingent did not waver despite our size limitations and mounting injuries."

The "misfit toys" started the season with a rough away contest against New Hope Solebury, a team aspiring to join the larger public school league. The Lions built a commanding 35-0 halftime lead and went on to take a 42-0 victory. The Cougars showed some offensive spark with Rex Roskos completing five passes for 48 yards. Four of those aerials ended up in Dylan Gleeson's hands. Jeremy Tyson added 38 yards of rushing to the attack. It all could not offset Division one recruit Ted Kaminoff, who scored all 6 of New Hope's touchdowns.

A bit dazed from the slow start, the Cougar warriors sought to put on a better display when they returned home to take on Riverdale Country Day School. Falling behind 0-20 at half the Cougars managed a strong comeback in the second half that would lead Rex to say, "Our team has the potential to do well; we just need to execute. It's a young team, but we have to go out and do our jobs. We didn't do what we had to do in the first half. After that we started to play some football, but it wasn't enough." (Courier Times, September 12, 2010)

Though falling on the short side of a 32-12 final score, the offense started to show life. Roskos completed 9 passes for 153 yards and 2 TDs. Dylan Gleeson hauled in 5 of those passes for 101 yards and one touchdown. Jeremy Tyson rushed for 79 yards on 15 carries. We just needed to learn to stop playing catch-up ball.

The Cougars next challenge was a home night game against Perkiomen where we once again brought out the construction crew flood lights. Perhaps blinded by the glare, the Cougars handed Perkiomen an early score on a 45-yard fumble return. Sophomore Asa Brooker evened the score with a 45-yard run, but Perkiomen immediately answered with a 31-yard scoring strike. Once again, GS came out to play in the second half. Jeremy Tyson scored on runs of 10 and 6 yards. Brooker added another 45-yard scoring gallop to put GS on top 26-13. Kyle Conklin iced the game, diving in for a 3-yard tally. The Cougars had finally prevailed by a 33-13 score.

The following week, the injury bug started to plague the Cougars. In Friday's "check" practice Tyler Campellone, linebacker and center, severely sprained his ankle and was sidelined for Friday's away night game with Tower Hill. The loss hurt. Campellone led most of our end sweeps and anchored the middle of our defense. After the game Roskos would say, "I did what I could but losing Tyler Campellone hurt. We usually do a lot of running on sweeps and he is a key blocker on them." (Courier Times, October 8, 2010)

Roskos had another good showing, completing 10 passes for 135 yards. His favorite target Dylan Gleeson caught six of those aerials for 101 yards. Jeremy Tyson rushed for one touchdown and caught a 18-yard pass for a second tally. It, however, was not enough as Tower Hill hung on to capture a 22-14 game.

After a 6-42 thumping at the hands of Saint Andrews, the Cougars remained battered but determined. Dylan Gleeson would later recall. "By the end of the season both my hands were in protective wraps, a precarious predicament for a wide receiver and defensive secondary player, positions where players are notoriously reliant on being able-limbed. Kevin Huang likewise was casted on one hand for much of the season. I can't recall facing an opposing team which featured two receivers without the full use of their hands as we had, an unconventional stratagem to say the least."

The Cougars' woes continued when, at the last minute, our next opponent had to drop football due to insufficient players. We scrambled around but the only available team would be an away rematch with Riverdale Country Day. The game started well. After a Riverdale touchdown, Asa Brooker reeled off a 55-yard touchdown tie the game at halftime.

GS regained the lead in the second half when Roskos scored on a 1-yard sneak. Unfortunately, our already depleted forces suffered yet another blow. Rex Roskos broke his hand and would be sidelined for the rest of the season. Riverdale immediately took advantage, scoring four straight times. A late 55-yard passing touchdown from backup Evan Clinton to Dylan Gleeson offered some solace as the Cougars suffered a 21-35 defeat.

Though limited in numbers, the men in green refused to succumb. The Cougars went out to a 14-0 lead in their next outing against Emily Fisher Charter School. Jeremy Tyson scored on a 9-yard run and Kyle Conklin tallied on a 1-yard fullback plunge. Julien Strachen kicked both extra points to give

GS a 14-8 lead at the half. The GS gridders extended their lead to 28-14 on runs by Clinton and Brooker but could not seal the deal. Two questionable pass interference calls allowed Emily Fisher to tie the game at 28-28. They would win in overtime 34-28.

Jeremy Tyson, who ran for 126 yards on 25 carries against Emily Fisher, knew that the last game against ANC would be a tough closer. "That's our last chance. That's going to be a tough one because ANC is really good. We have to regroup and try to get something going. We just haven't been playing well, and it's frustrating, and we've had some injuries that have really hurt us." (Courier Times, October 31, 2010)

Tyson's evaluation proved most accurate as ANC scored five straight times before Jeremy returned a kickoff 90 yards for a touchdown. He would later say "They were bigger than us, but our hearts were in there. We were in there just as much as they were. (Courier Times, November 7, 2010)

The Courier Times reporter described the 21-49 defeat saying, "But it was two completely different skill levels out there, especially in the first half. Most of the Academy of the New Church's defensive backfield, if not all of it, was bigger than George School's offensive line." (Courier Times November 7, 2010)

Dylan Gleeson well-remembers going into his last scholastic football game. "Despite our size limitations and mounting injuries, this core contingent played the whole year without substantial time lost due to injury. In our final game of the season against ANC, with both my hands wrapped heavily due to injury, Vince Campellone (Head of grounds at GS) fortunately knew how to make my protective mitts functional: tree sap. Prior to the game and very much outside the rules of the sport, Vince was kind enough to lather both my hands and protective mitts in tree sap from the trees around George School. I would be hard pressed to find a more direct connection between the logo of the school itself, the George School tree, and the George School football program."

Dylan Gleeson finished the season with 24 catches, 375 yards and a 15.6 yards per catch average and earned Courier Times Golden Team second team honors. More importantly he hit upon the true meaning of George School football saying, "While I can't claim to have gained a competitive advantage from my tree sap covered hands, I do believe that this ad hoc solution is something of a microcosm for the team as a whole. Just as my hands were held together with wrappings and sap, the team, we misfit toys, were held together with a more intangible resin. This adhesive is more difficult to describe than the physical thing, an unspoken but felt bond between these oddly shaped sizes and pieces. Indeed, I am not sure that one can fully identify or describe what it is that holds a motley crew, such as we were, together. Language frequently fails to adequately convey our lived experiences and felt emotions and language fails me here when attempting to describe what precisely it was that held us together."

"As I mentioned, we never tried to press the spoken word into service to describe what it was that kept these toys ticking. But when the season was over, the indescribable ties were no longer necessary and we were acutely aware of this fact. I recall myself and a few others, Kyle and Rex included, were brought to tears following the game as we were aware of this lost element even if none of us could identify precisely what it was or what we lost. What we knew, however, was that all the misfit toys on this peculiar island of George School football had been bandaging ourselves and each other all year and we held together; we made this island our own and, win or lose, the oddly shaped pieces fit together into a strange, eclectic and unforgettable mosaic. You always had confidence not that this ragtag outfit would win, but rather that the mismatched outfit would stay welded together. With this confidence, and with both tangible bonds and very tangible tree sap, we did. While our record will display us as an unsuccessful team, the players themselves know that simply by holding together, we would end our careers victorious."

Another band of brothers had learned the most important George School gridiron lesson!

A New Decade of Hopes and Promises

The second decade of the new century brought with it many promises of desired changes. Barack Obama vowed to make health care affordable. The Paris Accords sought to ease global warming. The "Me Too" movement aimed at eliminating sexual harassment. Even the Green Hornet sought to reduce criminal activity. Of a far less global nature, the George School footballers hoped their proposed new turf field would prove cathartic.

In the spring of 2011, the George School committee voted to construct a new all-purpose athletic field and track that would serve football, soccer, field hockey, lacrosse and track. The new turf arena was dedicated "To Coaches who Made a Difference" including Bob Geissinger, Anne Leduc, Dave Sattherwaite, and John Gleeson.

For the gridiron Cougars that meant they no longer needed to play in a corn field or a mud bowl traversed by night crawlers. The new all-weather stadium included a seating area for fans, a new scoreboard, and a permanently lined playing area. Unfortunately for the 2011 gridders, construction delays turned them into a band of nomadic wanderers. Home games became traveling affairs, leaving the athletic director, George Long, desperately searching for available playing fields.

Our 'home' opener against New Hope Solebury was played at Council Rock North. The disadvantage of playing in foreign confines was compounded when our starting quarterback Evan Clinton dislocated his shoulder in practice the week before. Jeremy Tyson, our feature running back, volunteered to take on the duties of signal caller. The gridiron gods did not shine favorably on the Cougars when Jeremy also dislocated his shoulder midway through the first quarter of the New Hope battle. Our third option at QB, Asa Brooker, had already been sidelined with a pulled thigh muscle. Jesse Lax, normally a wide receiver, took control but knowing few of the plays confined his efforts to sweeps to either side. His woes became compounded when little black pebbles from the turf field gathered on his sweat-stained forehead. Unable to generate any offensive thrust, we succumbed by a 0-38 score.

After another 0-21 loss to Jenkintown, the Cougars regained some offensive firepower in their game against Perkiomen with the return of Evan Clinton. A capable signal caller with a particularly sharp eye for reading defenses, Clinton managed to complete 14 of 35 passes for 193 yards. He connected with six different receivers along the way. Jake Kaplan caught four passes for 66 yards and Trevor Stone hauled in three passes for 70 yards. The aerial attack kept the Cougars in a close affair until the fourth quarter when the Panthers scored two rushing touchdowns to take a 34-17 victory. The game bore no league implications as the Tri-State League had folded the year before when Princeton Day School dropped football.

Two more away losses to Delaware County Christian (21-50) and Tower Hill (20-42) left the GS gridders with only three more shots at redemption. They finally got the opportunity to play on their new turf field. It was an historical moment. Asa Brooker, who logged the Cougars lone touchdown told reporter Bill Kenny, "I keyed in and went right into the hole with fullback Chris Helmuth and cut back outside. This is beautiful (the turf field), it doesn't hurt to fall on it and you're never going to get dirty. We were so excited when we came out here on Tuesday for our first time up here. We had hitting drills and we were destroying each other, the hardest we've been hit all year, including myself." (Courier Times, October 16, 2011)

Jeremy Tyson, who picked up 56 yards rushing, noted that, "We saw a couple of things they were doing and we adapted to that. This game, the first home game of the season on our new turf field, we came out to play and we were ready." (Courier Times, October 16, 2011)

For Jeremy, getting ready included strapping on a cumbersome shoulder brace that greatly restricted his mobility. Eleven years later he would reflect upon the increased national awareness of the long-term injuries sustained on the gridiron. "In a day and age where the research around CTE and repeated concussions stemming from American football has become more and more conclusive, I often ask myself the same questions. (Why did I play?) For someone who was unable to sit still in academic settings, sports provided another outlet to develop the muscle memory behind tolerance and discipline. I wouldn't say this makes me any better than non-athletes, just that it was a more natural way for someone like me to get accustomed to being uncomfortable, more specifically the type of uncomfortable needed to be good at anything. Now the answer to what I got from football in particular usually involves some sort of hyper-masculine virtue surrounding the difference in violence between this sport and others. It takes guts to go to practice and work your body in any sport, but any football player will try to convince you of the unique courage it takes to literally ram your body into brick walls for three hours at a time at full speed. As the measure of negative consequences surrounding long term health effects becomes more objective, the subjectivity behind this felt courage remains the same, dependent on how much you internalize it."

Jeremy would have to drag his battered parts through two more contests, an away game in Bronx, New York against Riverdale County and hopefully a home game with Emily Fisher Charter. The long trip to Riverdale ended with another defeat (13-35). Later Jeremy would remember the GS gridders approach to what proved to be the most difficult 2011 campaign. "My experience playing the game at GS gave me the unique experience of being captain of a team that did not win all that often. That translated into a meaningful leadership trial of finding a way to continue to motivate a group in scenarios where the chance of success was low. The thing I loved about George School was that us football players did not take ourselves very seriously. At other schools, where high school games sell out large areas of bleachers, football players take themselves extremely seriously, which always ends up being funny when everybody grows up and learns life meant very little back then, as compared to what comes after it. We joked that the soccer team was more popular than us, sometimes laughed quietly about how we had trouble winning games, and played the Lord of the Rings soundtrack in the locker room to get hyped up before practices in a true outlandish GS fashion."

All the reflections aside, Jeremy still valued his GS gridiron days. "I had fun. I am reluctant to put my kid into football, sure, but I had fun."

The fun took on a tangible result in the Cougars' final game against Emily Fisher. The morning of the contest a nor'easter roared through Bucks County, threatening to cancel any sporting events. Luckily, the referees looked at our new turf field and, despite mounting snow, deemed it playable. The men in green were ready, piling up 24 points in the opening quarter. Junior As Brooker started the scoring for GS with a 35-yard touchdown run.

After Emily Fisher scored to make it 8-6 George School, the Cougars caught fire. Jeremy Tyson returned the ensuing kickoff 87 yards for a TD, and defensive tackle Andy Young picked off a pass and returned it 24 yards for the Cougars' third tally. Tyson would then add a 23-yard scamper into the end zone in the second quarter that made it 30-6 at halftime.

In my postgame interview I said, "Jeremy had a great game and played really well. Our game plan even before the snow was to run the ball because of what we had seen (scouting Emily Fisher). We thought they would be more vulnerable to the run." (Courier Times, October 30, 2011)

In the second half, Chris Helmuth tallied on a two-yard plunge after he had blocked a punt from his linebacker spot a few minutes earlier. Tyson closed out the Cougar scoring on an 18-yard run. The 42-12 win gave all the Cougars a chance to play the Lord of the Rings soundtrack in their postgame celebration.

James Langeler, stellar offensive lineman and linebacker, would later reflect on his last year of GS football. "George School football wasn't so much an extracurricular activity as it was a state of mind. I had spent my first semester at GS on the JV team, which was detached from the tradition that made the varsity squad so special. My grade had the opportunity to join the varsity team (the 2000 squad) for the last week of the season leading up to the final game against ANC. I only knew the upperclassmen on the team from off the field, and by and large they were a rather farcical bunch of teenagers. When we got to the practice field all that changed, and the same group of guys I saw pranking one another on the academic quad became a determined unit of young men."

James would further note the real importance of GS football. "There were no stakes at face value. The season and the semester were winding down, and the Friends School League didn't even have a playoff for football. Not to mention ANC was always the favored team. That wasn't the point, I came to realize during the week of practice. Other teams' aspirations at the start of their respective seasons were tied to wins and playoff titles. GS football's ultimate objective was a more lofty one: take a group of high school boys, and for 10-12 hours of the week, unite them to pour their hearts into a cause that promises no sure returns other than making them into better men. I was hooked!"

Little wonder that at the end of the Emily Fisher game I would be quoted as saying, "Today we played a complete football game and it was a nice way for our kids to end their season. I was very proud of the way they finished things up." (Courier Times, October 30, 2011) Another group of proud combatants had carried away the more important values from their GS gridiron experience.

The 2012 campaign started on a rather ominous note. Only eighteen players showed up for preseason camp. In addition to the normal graduation depletion, two key starters decided to opt out of their senior year. Having their sights aimed at collegiate careers in sports other than football, they had been advised not to risk injury. Universally, football itself had undergone intense medical scrutiny. The concussive effects of constant hitting drew the biggest concerns. The new concussion protocol called for players experiencing any concussion symptoms to be removed from the field of play. They then had to wait two weeks for symptom-free activity before returning to the active roster. This seemed like the wisest precaution. Parents appeared increasingly uneasy about the long-term effects of such a constant physical pounding and would not sign the agreement allowing their sons to play.

The problems of Cougar football were heightened by the new academic demands, agreed to by all the faculty. The academic day became extended, reducing the time for sport's practices. Considering taping and getting in pads, we could realistically get about an hour of practice a day. The big fear among gridiron faithful was that we would go the way of schools such as Princeton Day and Wardlaw-Hartridge and abandon the football program.

In an effort to ease the pressure on our quarterback Evan Clinton's injured shoulder, I decided to alternate him with a new junior transfer student Christian Sparacio who along with his senior brother, Joe, had transferred from Peddie. Unfortunately, Evan's shoulder problems continued to be a source of concern even when he moved out to wide receiver.

Our first two losses, 314-34 to Morrisville and 15-34 to Lower Moreland, showed that the Cougars were struggling to come up with a winning combination. We seemed to rectify the situation in our home contest with Jenkintown but a few plays spelled defeat. We fumbled early in the game, setting up a Jenkintown score. Unfazed, the Cougars roared back. A Joe Sparacio interception in the second quarter gave the men in green the ball at their own 40 yard line. Driving to the Drakes' 15 yard line, the GS gridders looked ready to put some points on the board.

Then the unspeakable happened. The Courier Times reporter described the ensuing play, "As (Desi) Smith received a draw and ran right off tackle, he was hit as he crossed the goal line and the ball came loose. The officials ruled that the ball was knocked loose before it broke the plane, and Jenkintown received possession on its own 20-yard line." (Courier Times, September 16, 2012)

The Cougars did not let the official's call upset them. Joe Sparacio returned another intercepted pass to the Jenkintown 9-yard line. Desi Smith then swept left end to score, this time with no controversy. Trailing 6-7 going into halftime, the Cougars appeared ready to explode. Unfortunately, a shanked Cougar punt on their own 23 yard line gave Jenkintown excellent field position. Two plays later the Drakes scored to take a 13-6 lead. They would tack on an insurance tally with seven minutes left in the game to ice their 21-6 victory.

Perhaps stunned by the twist of fate in the Jenkintown game, the Cougars lost their next encounter 8-36 to Perkiomen. The following week, the GS gridders traveled to Wilmington, Delaware to take on Conrad Science. For Christian Sparacio, it proved a breakout game and one the Cougars sorely needed.

Ten years later, Christian would reflect on his GS career and the role the Christian Science game would play in solidifying his play at quarterback.

"George School football changed my life. As a transfer from an elitist, toxic, kill or be killed program near Princeton, NJ, I lacked confidence. I didn't feel as though I was the guy, the one that could alter a game in a moment's notice. That all changed when we played Conrad Science my Junior season and Coach Gleeson put the ball in my hands and said 'Win it!'"

Chrisian will long remember the game scenario. "We were down by 6 and we had just had a game tying touchdown called back because of an illegal man downfield. I was switched to quarterback and my co-starter to wide receiver. We alternated depending on the situation and scheme."

One certainty for Christian was knowing precisely where brother Joe would be on the field. "Coach Gleeson didn't waste any time and called a deep fade pattern to my brother who was split out wide to my left. I dropped back and was patient with my progression, knowing the exact tempo at which he ran and the moment, to the very second, when he would break open and I could deliver the football. I didn't blink, and fired a 30-yard strike to my brother to tie it up."

Christian's heroics did not stop here. He was a dual performer who not only excelled at quarterback but was also a mainstay at linebacker. In his words, "Our successful extra point put victory in sight, but we had two minutes left and had to stop the Conrad Science offense. I soon realized our best tackler (Chris Helmuth) had just gotten injured, which placed me, a much underwhelming linebacker, with the responsibility to stop the offense in its tracks to win this game. Saying I was scared shitless is an understatement. It was at this moment, when I could not rely on the freakish tackling of my injured teammate to bail us out that I thought 'if not me then who?' and it has driven me for the past 10 years. We went on to win that game, and I must have had every tackle on that final drive, terrified we were going to lose."

The loss of Chris Helmuth, our tough and dependable linebacker and fullback, adversely affected the Cougars as we lost our last three games. The season finale with Morristown Beard the GS gridders battled for three quarters before succumbing 6-33. Down 0-13 halfway through the third quarter, Christain Sparacio hooked up his brother Joe on a 30 yard touchdown pass. He would complete 4 passes for 53 yards, giving him 538 passing yards and six TDs for the season. Chris Helmuth, in his return to action, ran for 70 yards on 13 carries. Desi Smith added 21 rushing yards to the Cougar attack.

Senior defensive lineman Jake Kaplan summed up the season in a postgame interview with Joe Jones, "It hurts. Every day, you come out and hit someone and it hurts. We started out with 18 (players) this season. We had some players go down, we lost a captain, and you can't really practice (with such few players). You're hurting every day." (Courier Times, October 21, 2012)

Despite the loss Jake felt the experience was a valuable one. "It was worth it. It's the camaraderie. You really get to love these guys." (Courier Times, October 21, 2012)

I completely agreed with Jake. Despite being 65 and having undergone open-heart surgery three years earlier, I did not want to retire. As I told Joe Jones, "At the end of the last few seasons, I thought that was it. But then I start thinking about it and I want to be around these guys and continue coaching them." (Courier Times, October 21, 2012)

For the 2013 season the Cougars, though short on quantity, certainly had the quality. Christian Sparacio returned at quarterback. At 6' 2" and 215 pounds Christian not only manned the helm but also played linebacker and punted. Chris Helmuth, fully recovered from his arm injury, was back at full-back and linebacker. Christian had several receivers to throw to with Jesse Lax and Chris Beverly providing veteran savvy and newcomers Harrison Fritz, Max Klaver and Cody Haney ready to lend support. The line was relatively inexperienced but would progress rapidly under the guidance of coaches Terry Christianson and Nick Nastasi. Ian Hodgins, Ben Haferl, Evan Ortega, Charles Tongluo awaited the wisdom their line coaches would impart. As always, our biggest nemesis was 'numbers'. Should injury plague any starters we would struggle to find backups.

The season started with a long trip to Bergen Tech High School in Hackensack, New Jersey. Undoubtedly weary from the long bus ride, the Cougars could not get unwound, losing 12-42. More tellingly, we also lost one of our captains, Jesse Lax. Jesse was a dedicated, versatile and team-oriented player who during his GS career had played wide receiver, running back, quarterback, linebacker and offensive tackle. In our next game against Jenkintown, junior Max Klaver, who had sat out his sophomore year to explore an acting career, took over for Jesse at wide receiver.

Max readily recalls his first varsity start. "My breakout game, and one of my most memorable during my time at GS, was against Jenkintown. Most unfortunately one our best players and our captain was unable to play the 2013 season. I, a bench-warming wide receiver who didn't scratch the team's public depth chart, had just resumed my football "career" after taking the previous season off to explore life as a thespian. Having come off the bench for one admirable catch, a thirty yard post route, during our season opener against Bergen Tech and with our receiving corps now down its star, I was given the chance to start against Jenkintown. The game, and my play in it, started innocuously enough. Then, sometime in the middle of the first half, Glees called a fade. As our quarterback Christian Sparacio took the snap, I tore down the field. Christian, a known cannon, waited until I was about twenty yards from the line before lofting the ball, which came sailing over my outside shoulder. Both the Jenkintown CB and I went up for it. I felt the ball hit my hands, and I held on with everything I had. Coming down, I managed to land on my feet, throwing the defender in the process and running easily."

In Max's eyes his glory was short lived. As he wrote, "Fast forward to the start of the second half and repeat, exactly the same play, exactly the same outcome, minus the touchdown. Down 6-10 in the final seconds of the game, Glees called for a fade. I knew the pass was coming to me. Christian took the snap, dropped three steps, and fired. I turned too late. The ball passed right over my head. The loss was sealed. Though I finished the game with (what might have been my career high) impressive stats - four catches, 127 yards, and a touchdown - that game still leaves a sour taste in my mouth. Needless to say, in the weeks that followed, perfecting my route became a near obsession."

Max was far too hard on himself. Without his early heroics we never would have found the end zone. In our next contest against Perkiomen he showed what a dangerous deep threat he had already become. With seconds left on the clock and GS down 0-20 Max hauled in a 34-yard Sparacio aerial that ended on Perkiomen's one yard line as time expired. In this game our young defensive line sacked the quarterback 5 times. Chris Helmuth also picked up 54 rushing yards.

Having shown steady improvement in their first three loses, the Cougars appeared ready to break into the win column. That victory came in our first home game of the season against Conrad Science. Reporter Joe Jones summed up the game, crediting Christian Sparacio with most valuable player honors. "Sparacio passed for 124 yards and two scores and threw a two point conversion pass that put George School up 22-21 with 6:58 to play in the fourth quarter. He also ran for 79 yards, a touchdown and a two-point conversion, averaged 41.5 yards on six punts - including 61 and 56 yarders - and made a number of tackles." (Courier Times September 29, 2013)

On the game-winning drive, Chris Beverly came up with two big receptions. His 25-yard catch on fourth-and-13 put the ball on the Conrad Science 12. He then hauled in another Sparacio pass for the score. Max Klaver caught the two point extra point conversion pass to give GS a much needed 22-21 victory. In a postgame interview, Christian Sparacio would describe Klaver's effort, saying, "Max Klaver has great hands and is an awesome receiver. They had coverage on Chris Beverly, who is also an awesome receiver and had the touchdown catch. They had a weaker corner (on Klaver) and we ran a slant pass." (Courier Times, September 29, 2013)

The only downside to the big win was losing our captain Chris Helmuth with an elbow injury that would hamper him the rest of the season. The green clad warriors could not repeat their triumphant ways losing their next two games to Tower Hill (8-35) and Saint Andrews (0-38).

With Chris Helmuth back in action the Cougars showed great resilience, bouncing back to beat Calvary Christian 22-13 on Parents' Day at George School. In his postgame interview, Chris, who rushed for 91 yards, would summarize the teams' spirit. "We emphasized all week to work hard and play hard and that we could win. We came out playing hard. It was 6-7 at the half and we were down by one point. We said that we need to play hard and stay in this game and win this game." (Courier Times, October 19, 2013)

Christian Sparacio figured on all three of the GS scores. He had a pair of touchdown runs and connected with Harrison Fritz for a 39-yard score. He also led the team with 105 rushing yards.

In many ways, the Cougars saved the best for last. Facing Newark Collegiate Academy on their home field, the GS gridders pulled off a convincing 36-18 win. Christian Sparacio and Chris Helmuth each finished off their scholastic careers in fine style. Christian passed for 162 yards and ran for another 20 yards. Chris had 66 rushing yards and a pair of scores. Max Klaver caught 4 passes for 80 yards and a pair of touchdowns.

In his postgame interview, Christian praised his teammates. "This is a great thing to remember. We had a great game - me and Chris Helmuth and the rest of the team. I came here as a junior, looking to find guys I could appreciate playing football with. I found these guys and they will be my friends for life." (Courier Times, November 2, 2013)

Nine years later, Christian would fully realize the impact GS football had on him. "Some things will sit with you forever. Coach Gleeson, and the soul of George School football as a whole, motivated me to pursue all my dreams, and to bet on myself. When I felt the urge to sing in front of my school with the risk of being made fun of, I did it, (and appreciate Coach Gleeson's kind praise for doing so). When I graduated from an elite New England college and thought about bypassing full time work to pursue a music career, I did it. I attribute much of my boldness to George School and the football program especially. I am forever grateful for Coach Gleeson's belief in me and his trust that I was indeed the guy that could flip the script and win us a game when we needed a spark."

With only two senior starters listed on the roster the 2014 season looked like a classic time for learning. Max Klaver and Ben Haferl provided the veteran leadership that would aid a talented group of young gridders including Cody Haney, Evan Ortega, Shadimere Coles, Kaelan Frederic, Brian Vearling, Kiany Probherbs, Chet Kogut, Luke Haug, Cleo Chowaiki and Matt Wisniewski. Haug would assume the main quarterbacking duties. Though lacking any football experience, Luke was a talented athlete who had led GS to championships in soccer and baseball. The center, Brian Vearling also played a key role, having to snap the ball in one of two different directions depending upon the play call.

In addition to learning the fundamental skills, the players also had to adjust to a totally new offensive system. In keeping with my philosophy of adapting the system to the athlete's abilities, I had devised a rather unique scheme. In essence it called for an unbalanced line with a tight end and two wide slots on one side, a wide out opposite them, and two quarterbacks lined up four yards deep and behind the guards. Key to the success of the new look was the center. He had to snap the ball sideways to one of the quarterbacks for the play to begin. We used motion with one of our slots and ran a lot of counter plays. The new scheme presented an entirely different look than any of our opponents had faced.

That year we had four coaches on our staff, George Long, Nick Nastasi, Terry Christianson, and myself. All had played football in college. All but me had coached in other programs. Most importantly, all were educators who cared for the total well-being and growth of each player. When I introduced my new concept, however, they all looked a little befuddled. This was not a plan you could find anywhere on the internet or in any other coaching playbooks. It did, however, suit the various talents of the available personnel.

The new concept got a rather rude introduction when a loaded Academy of the New Church ran all over us in our opening game. We understandably needed a lot more polish to eliminate the fumbles and mistakes our offense showed. In our next game against Jenkintown we came close, losing a heart-breaker 9-14. The offense could only manage to get a total of 93 yards for the game. In our following contest, a 20-41 loss to Perkiomen, we began to show some offensive spark. Luke Haug emerged as a real triple threat. He had 24 of the Cougars' 26 rushing attempts, amassing 212 yards and punching in three touchdowns. He kicked all three extra points. He also completed six of his 13 passing attempts for 62 yards.

Luke would tell the Courier Times reporter. "It's definitely what I signed up to do. Having to do everything shows leadership. It's something new." (Courier Times, September 20, 2014)

On our first tally against Perkiomen, Max Klaver returned a kickoff 40 yards to the 50-yard line. On the next play Haug ran for 25 yards. Then, on fourth down, he escaped for an 18-yard gain to give the Cougars first-and-goal on the 1-yard line. He then plunged in for the score and booted the extra point.

Luke's effort proved an omen for good things to come. Even though we lost the next two games, 17-48 against Conrad Science and 35-49 against

Tower Hill, the offense was starting to really solidify. Traveling to Saint Andrews, the Cougars finally hit the win column. Once again, Luke led the attack, scoring four touchdowns and kicking five extra points. Cody Haney contributed a 9-yard tally to the Cougar offensive thrust and Kiany Probherbs caught a 12-yard pass from Haug for the final score.

George School wasted little time in unveiling its explosive offense in our next outing against Newark Collegiate Academy, a team ranked No.9 in New Jersey in the prep/independents division. Haug rushed for the first two scores of the game and then completed passes to Cody Haney and Kiany Probherbs to build a 28-12 lead at the end of the first quarter. He then broke off a 26 yard run to give the Cougars a 35-12 halftime lead. A 9-yard Haug to Klaver scoring strike and a 21-yard Chet Kogut run gave the green clad warriors a 49-12 lead with 4 minutes, 52 seconds left in the third period, invoking the mercy rule and bringing out the Cougar's substitutes.

Luke Haug rushed for 113 yards and three scores in the game. Chet Kogut added 35 rushing yards to the Cougar cause. Max Klaver caught 3 passes for 48 yards. Max was quick to praise the fledgling quarterback. "It's amazing he is in his first year playing football. He has gotten a lot better. He is an amazing athlete. We've been working on offense, and it's really gotten amped up." (Courier Times, October 19, 2014)

After the game Luke would credit the improved play of his offensive line for the 49-36 win. "The past few games our offensive line has really played well, and that has helped us score so much. We've had some tough losses. We could have won against Tower Hill. The Jenkintown game, too." (Courier Times, October 19, 2014)

The final game of the season against Calvary Christian would provide a real test for the improving Cougars. Calvary, who was coached by former Philadelphia Eagle Mike Reichenbach, sported a 6-1 record. The game proved every bit as challenging as promised. Calvary broke out to a 14-0 lead in the second quarter. Haug then scored on a 35 yard run. After another Calvary tally Haug hooked up with tight end Kiany Probherbs for a 7-yard touchdown to narrow the margin to 14-21 at halftime.

Haug then tied the score with a 1-yard run and extra point kick in the third quarter. That did not end the offensive fireworks as Luke found his favorite target, Max Klaver, for touchdown passes of 30 and 32 yards. The game sealing second touchdown did not quite go as planned. As reporter Bill Keen noted, "Clinging to a one-touchdown lead over Calvary Christian on Friday, George School had the ball on Calvary's 32-yard line just 90 seconds away from its third straight win to close out the season. That's when the center snapped the ball about ten feet over the head of quarterback Luke Haug, who runs the Cougar offense out of the shotgun. A lot of high school players might have panicked; Haug calmly turned it into an unbelievable touchdown to a wide-open Max Klaver that sealed the 35-21 win." (Courier Times 26, 2014)

Today Max still remembers the play but puts a slightly different twist on it. "The final minutes of my time on George School football were among the wildest of my 'career'. Playing away against Calvary Christain, we were up by a slim margin in the twilight of the fourth quarter. On (I believe) third down and many to go, with the ball around the Calvary 30-yard line, our quarterback, Luke Haug, lined up in the gun. The route was one I had adopted as my (relatively successful) signature as a wide receiver over the previous two years - a deep fade down the right side of the field. Our center snapped the ball, which must have sailed 10 feet over Luke's head. Lost in the tunnel vision of my route, I turned to call for the pass, only to see Luke scrambling wildly out of the pocket, roughly twenty yards behind the line of scrimmage. Luke was fast and made impressive runs over the course of the season, but we needed more than his legs could give us if we were to convert this third down and wrap things up. I broke my route, beelining back towards Luke. Nearly hit as he threw, Luke got the pass off, a brilliant twenty-yard bullet, which I caught in the clear; the cornerback tasked with guarding me broke coverage in an effort to record a sack. I turned upfield and was off to the races. As I crossed into the red zone, I felt a tug on my left shoulder. Calvary's safety closed an impressive gap and was nearing to knock me out of bounds. I hit the brakes, sending him flying past into the sidelines. Savoring the moment, I strolled cheekily into the end zone, scoring the last touchdown of my football career. Before I could fully process the moment, I was descended on by my teammates, in jubilatory endzone celebration."

Always a reflective being, Max remembers the lesson to be learned as well as the dramatic reception. "Trotting off to the sideline, Glees met me with a smile. 'That was a helluva play, which is why I hate to tell you that you should have taken a knee.' I didn't understand. Glees gestured to the scoreboard. We were up but there was at least a minute left on the clock. As quickly as it had soared, my heart sank like a rock. Had I taken the knee, we could have run down the clock and clinched the win. Now, I had to take the field again, cursing myself relentlessly for potentially costing us the game. Calvary Christian worked their way up the field into our territory somewhere within the forty-yard line, burning their timeouts in the process. With 20 seconds on the board, they went for a hail Mary. My myopia was redeemed by some stealthy coverage on the part of a cornerback, Ty Graves, who picked them off to seal the game, giving me the gift of going out a champion, despite my efforts to the contrary."

Max, in his striving for perfection, was way too hard on himself. He definitely went out a champion. As I said in a postgame interview. "I don't know how Luke saw Max open! Max has great hands, he runs great patterns. I can't say enough about him, plus he's a leader." (Courier Times, October 26, 2014)

In our last four games of the season Max had 12 catches for 260 yards and five touchdowns. Cody Haney caught 13 passes for 239 yards and 2 TDs. Kiany Probherbs made 12 catches and 5 tallies. Our 'rookie' quarterback, Luke Haug, during that span, ran for 522 yards and 10 touchdowns. He passed for 776 yards and 11 scores. Our new offense was really starting to work.

As impressive as the stats are, it is football's intangible lessons and challenges Max remembers most. "All-in-all, playing football was one of the most meaningful experiences I had at GS. Football taught me how to find the strength within myself to overcome any obstacle in the way. Hammered into me by Glees during too many 'down at halftime' speeches was the mantra, 'always keep fighting.' No matter the score, no matter how down and out you are, the only way out is through caring, so kit up and 'give em hell'."

That mantra seemed to loom large in the upcoming 2015 season. The Cougars had lost only two starters to graduation and were fresh off a three game win streak to close out the 2014 season. Success often breeds further success. Knowing how to finish off a game, how to keep control even when down, and how to battle in the face of adversity usually shows up in the win/loss column.

The sophomores and juniors from the year before had not only mastered the unique playbook but had also proven themselves both talented and dedicated. Spearheading the charge, Luke Haug established himself a true multiple threat athlete. The receiving corps lead by Cody Haney, Kiany Probherbs, Kaelan Frederic, and Shadimere Coles added additional strength when Chris Beverly and Chris Gilbert decided to return to the gridiron wars. Evan Ortega and Brian Verling anchored a line that also boasted such proven vets as Matt Wisniewski,Rex Trice, Cleo Chowaiki and Alex Hodgin. Barring any injuries, this group promised to add to their winning ways.

Senior Luke Haug,after his inaugural campaign, admitted his junior year was a time of football education for him. In the Courier Times 2015 fall preview he said, "I learned a lot last year. I had never played before but I watched a lot of football on TV and that was helpful and I think it made it easier for me to pick things up. It did take time to learn some of the more tedious things. We finished strong and I think we can pick up where we left off. We have a lot of starters back from last year. Last year we started a new offense so this year we're a lot more familiar with it. I am playing with a lot more confidence this year and I think everyone else is as well." (Courier Times, September 3, 2015)

The confidence factor certainly loomed large in our opening game against Calvary Christian. Playing under the lights at our home stadium, the Cougars got off to a questionable start, being flagged for two penalties before its first offensive snap. Calvary capitalized off an early interception to take a 7-0 lead with 6:35 remaining in the first quarter. The seasoned Cougars answered immediately when Haug swept end and raced 47 yards to paydirt. Two defensive gems, a Chris Gilbert fumble recovery and a Cody Haney interception, led to two more touchdown runs by Haug.

Leading 21-7 at the half, the Cougars showed they had the killer instinct. Two more second half TD runs by Haug iced the 38-12 victory. All told, the triple threat Haug rushed 25 times for 306 yards and five touchdowns. He also converted every extra point and booted a 40-yard field goal.

Luke, who sat out most of the fourth quarter, showed he had learned the importance of knowing when to pass and when to tuck the ball and run. As he said in a postgame interview, "We always say the broken plays are good plays. Let me run. They are not always designed runs, but we'll take what we can get." (Courier Times, September 4, 2015)

Morrisville was the next team to taste the wrath of Haug. Not wasting any time, on our first play from scrimmage Luke swept right end on a 52 yard scoring jaunt. Later in the quarter he hit Kiany Probherbs with an 8-yard scoring strike to put the Cougars ahead 14-6 at the half.

Not willing to sit on a narrow lead, Luke ran an end sweep to the left side on the first play from scrimmage in the second half. The 55-yard TD burst seemed to dim any Morrisville comeback hopes. Luke would score two more touchdowns to assure a 35-6 victory. He summed up the game saying, "We started off strong. That first play was big. We knew Morrisville was going to put up a fight, and I thought their defense was strong, so I was happy we got one right away. We just had to keep it up and, to give them credit, they got one right at the half, and we had to regroup, but obviously scoring right away in the second half got us back on the right track." (September 12, 2015)

The next away game with Jenkintown High School showed just how far the 2015 Cougars had progressed. Haug displayed his total versatility throwing for 297-yards and 5 touchdown passes. Kiany Probherbs, who was on the receiving end of 174 of those yards and three TDs praised his senior quarterback. "It's great to have him at quarterback. If you are open, you know he will get you the ball." (Courier Times, September 20, 2015)

Haug also accumulated 210 yards rushing and two tallies, several of the runs coming on QB scrambles. Tri-captain Evan Ortega explained how life with Luke at the helm can be an interesting experience. "We just try to push the defenders to the second level. That's what we were able to do. We just create gaps if he runs. It's real tough not knowing what he will do, but we just look back and see what he is doing. It certainly works." (Courier Times, September 20, 2015)

Haug finished the 49-14 victory by amassing 507 total yards. He accounted in some way for all the Cougar points. He passed for five touchdowns, rushed for two more, and converted on 5 extra-point kicks. He even caught a pass from Chet Kogut for a 2-point conversion following a bad snap.

The next game featured the battle of the unbeatens as the Cougars took on Perkiomen Prep in an away game. The Panthers jumped out to an early 16-3 lead behind a rugged running attack. The Cougars', however, were not about to fade and roared back to take a 17-16 lead in the third quarter. Perkiomen went up 24-17 early in the final frame but once again Luke Haug engineered a long drive that climaxed with him plunging in from a yard out. The attempted game-tying extra-point kick led to yet another Haug game film highlight. When the snap from center ended up rolling on the ground, Luke picked up the errant pigskin, scrambled to his right, then threw the ball to wide out Chris Gilbert who hauled in the pass for a 25-24 lead.

Perkiomen then used its tough running attack to march the length of the field. With the ball on the Cougar 5-yard line, however, the Panthers opted to put the ball in the air. Reporter Joe Jones described the play, saying, "Chris Beverly was smack in the middle of players all going for a pass that probably had too much air underneath it. He jumped up for the ball and fell backward. And, as he started to head to the ground, Beverly was able to snatch the ball out of the air and come up with a highlight-reel type interception in the end zone." (Courier times, September 27, 2015)

From that point on, we relied on Luke Haug's running talents to seal the deal. He had seven carries for 65 yards, recording three first downs, including a fourth-and-1 by less than an inch. For the game, Luke had 197 yards rushing and 122 yards passing.

The post game euphoria received a huge dampening blow early the following week when we learned that Luke had injured his shoulder and would be out for the season. The key play occurred late in the first half when he tackled a Perkiomen wide receiver. Having been cleared by the field doctor, Luke returned to play and heroically spearheaded the final drive. Later on Monday he complained about a soreness in his throwing arm which was then diagnosed as a broken collarbone.

Losing a talent such as Luke really hurt. In only his second season of football, Haug had already rushed for 899 yards with a 9.8 rushing average. He was the leading rusher in Lower Bucks County. He scored 14 touchdowns. He also had the second highest passer rating (155.2) in Lower Bucks. Luke summarized the team's plight, "It was obviously a heartbreaker, for me and the team - very disappointing. For all the yards we had gained early in the season.

The players had to pick up a big workload, distributing them among everyone else." (October 29, 2015)

The Cougars rallied to take our fifth straight win with a 13-2 victory over Saint Andrews. Obviously reeling from the loss of our stellar quarterback, the offense sputtered in the first half, not only being shut out but also failing to move the ball beyond midfield. Late in the third quarter the defense managed to turn the game's flow. Defensive end Kiany Probherbs swatted the ball out of the hands of the Saint Andrew's quarterback. The Cougars recovered on the opposition's 19 yard line. Three plays later Chet Kogut connected with Chris Gilbert on a fade pass in the corner of the end zone. Kogut would ice the 13-2 victory hitting Shadimere Coles with a 31-yard scoring pass.

The following week proved disastrous on many levels. Traveling all the way to Newark, New Jersey to take on Newark Collegiate Academy, we found ourselves locked out of the field until right before gametime. Despite my every protest, we had only 20 minutes to warm-up, not nearly enough time to get prepped. Understandably the GS gridders once again struggled in the first half. Down 0-16 late in the third quarter the Cougar offense finally came to life. Cody Haney caught a 57-yard touchdown pass from Chet Kogut. Chris Gilbert caught a 2-point conversion pass from Kogut to narrow the margin to 8-16.

Kogut would run 7-yards to score early in the fourth quarter to bring the Cougars to within two points of tying the game. By then, however, our forces had been depleted. Evan Ortega suffered a badly sprained right ankle. Cleo Chowaiki broke his collarbone. Jeremy Haug, Luke's younger brother and key linebacker, had a concussion. Shadimere Coles and Kiany Probherbs tried to rally the wounded warriors. Coles rushed for 101 yards on seven carries and caught a pass for our final touchdown. Probherbs caught six passes. The efforts were not enough as we suffered our first defeat by a 22-32 score.

Minus five starters, the Cougars, who only had 27 players on their roster at the beginning of the season, strove valiantly in their next encounter against Tower Hill. The scenario, however, got even worse when back-up quarterback Chet Kogut injured his arm with 4:04 left in the first quarter. Two minutes later Chris Gilbert suffered a concussion. Both players were done for the season.

Kaelan Frederic, who I labeled Mr. Dependable, moved from wide receiver to quarterback. He completed seven of 13 second-half passes, four of them to Kiany Probherbs. Kaelan described the Cougar's plight saying, "All week, we've been practicing even with key guys out, getting prepared for anything that happens. I wasn't really too nervous going into the game. I just wanted to put out my best effort and to be the greatest teammate I can be." (Courier Times, October 18, 2015)

The Cougars knew the challenge entering our final game against an undefeated New Hope Solebury squad would be intense. The seniors, despite the dwindling numbers, still looked forward to one last game. Chris Beverly, who had an earlier scare when he experienced breathing issues, received an EKG and was cleared to play. He said in a pregame interview, "I'm grateful to have an opportunity to play this game, especially at the George School, and it helped me to look at life a little bit differently. I'm young, and obviously this was a little bit scary, and it changed my perspective." (Courier Times, October 29, 2015)

Tri-captain Evan Ortega, though still hobbled from his ankle injury, saw the New Hope game as a matter of pride. "We have depth on this team, and the players know that, so we've had a next-man-up mentality; we won the next game after Luke Haug was injured. It would show a lot of character, if we can win this game, especially with two captains being down during the season. It would show a lot of maturity for a very young team, because we know this is a very tough game against a very tough opponent." (Courier Times, October 29, 2015)

The other tri-captain, Cody Haney, shared Evan's views. "I know we are facing a very good team. Even though we have so many players hurt, I know we're still a great team, and we hope to push through and to win this game." (Courier Times, October 29, 2015)

The win never materialized. New Hope, on the verge of joining the larger Suburban One League, had too many guns in their arsenal and won the game easily, 48-14. Shadimere Coles provided a lone spark for the Cougars rushing 22 times for 107 yards and 2 touchdowns. He kept the game in perspective, "In the beginning of the season, we really had a good team. We knew we were really going to have a good season, but then we had so many injuries. We fought through and, unfortunately, we lost those games at the end, but I still think we kept our heads up and I'm proud of that. George hasn't been 5-3 in many years and we take pride in that. It's been a really good season, and I'm grateful that I had that experience. We knew they were a really good team, and we practiced hard all week. We've played good teams before and, just like any other game, we went out there and played hard. That's all I could ask for." (Courier Times, November 1, 2015)

Seven years later Kiany Probherbs, who emerged as a real leader his junior year, would reflect on his total GS gridiron experience. "George School football meant opportunity and perseverance. I started playing my sophomore year and I remember feeling proud to be around 20 other guys who were willing to throw their bodies around for each other. It was an opportunity to be aggressive in a school that emphasized peace and I think it was a valuable lesson for me looking back. It's about knowing when to be assertive and when to go with the flow. When to cut block someone or use a swim move. We were constantly doubted by the whole campus and that never changed how we practiced or played. Once we started winning, it's not like much changed, because we had built a culture that fostered brotherhood, accountability and a hunger for success."

Win or lose those three qualities became the more meaningful goals for Kiany. "We played through injuries, had preseason in the scorching heat and then would finish the season in 10 degree weather. To me that epitomizes perseverance, the ability to go against all odds and succeed. And not only did we persevere but we ended up having an 8 game winning streak and fought through all the blood, sweat and tears ultimately changing the way the campus looked at George School football. Football was an opportunity to go to college and do what I wanted to do but the lessons instilled in me about pushing through adversity, running through the line not to it, and an ability to recognize when to just have fun remained. George School football showed me that not everything is easy but when you consciously dedicate your time and effort into something you will reap the rewards."

Kiany's words speak the thoughts of so many former players who number themselves among the George School football family. The lessons learned resounded down through the years.

A Final Reflection

George School football represents a rich and varied history. From the personal interviews and press clippings, it can be seen just how much being a part of the GS football tradition meant to all the players. Some spoke of big games, especially against The Academy of the New Church. Many remembered the grueling preseason practices, a time of agony and self-discovery. A few expressed the disappointment of being injured and missing the opportunity to join their teammates. Almost all, however, recalled the lasting bonds they developed and the fraternal feeling that pervaded every practice and every game. My only regret is that I could not include everyone who donned the GS uniform. That would have been beyond the scope of this project. As for me, I finally retired at age 69 in the summer of 2016. Paraphrasing a former North Carolina basketball coach, I realized that it was time to go when I could no longer ask of myself what I asked of my players. I will always remember the players I coached, the one's I played with, and the one's I watched in admiration before entering George School. They are all part of what I consider the George School football family...a band of gridiron brothers.

Appendix

The following appendix offers a list of many of the players from the various George School teams. It is compiled from past documents, old programs and newspaper accounts.

1923 Season

J Dutton

W Willis

S Kirk

E Potts

M Collins

R Palmer

A Johnson

R Fletcher

D Amelia

R Sebring

R Fletcher

R Rogers

E Landon

1924 Season

R Rogers

W Coles

W Brice

H Cleaver

F Swain

A Lockhart

W Leighton

A Skidmore

H Townesand

M Collins

L Paschall

T Jackson

D Amelia

1925 Season

D Amelia

W Russ

C Malloy

L Paschall

R Temple

H Mann

A Cocks

L Frescoln

A Lockhart

H Green

W Sickler

M Hires

R Booth

K Davies

1926 Season

A Lockhart

M Hires

C Biddle

R Turner

H Sipler

J Frescoln

W Mitchell

B Jones

D Detwiler

F Christian

J Evans

R Woodsman

1927 Season

M Hires

H Sipler

J Bond

R Willis

C Garrett

C Wildeman

E Walker

M Williams

H Miller

R MacPherson

A Brosius

P Bond

E Stevens

W Hecks

E Leher

L Heacock

K Yeatman

R Woodman

W Borden

J Evans

G Locke

A Brosius

H Miller

1928 Season

H Sipler

J Long

J Bond

J Crockett

W Holbrook

M Dresden

R MacPherson

J Wilson

L Davis

W Cope

R Bond

1929 Season

J Wilson

S Cavin

W Holbrook

H Roberts

D Patterson

A Palmenberg

E Singmatter

T Atkinson

R Cunningham

M Cooper

T Taylor

H Evans

J Thomas

S Ashelman

H Starks

R Hardy

G Forney

1930 Season

G Forney

J Thomas

H Davis

C Major

C Van Wickl

R Griffith

J Fletcher

S Ashelman

C McKillips

R Small

J Engle

R Frishmuth

E Tyson

E Van Schloick

H Rockwell

R Post

H Starks

B Jackson

1931 Season

H Davis

R Lewis

W Worall

R Post

G Borden

H Wardell

C McKillips

B Jackson

A Walton

B Lackey

A Turner

W Marris

1932 Season

C McKillips

B Farquhar

J Haines

J Hancock

M Clement

W Deitcher

H Rockwell

B Lackey

W Cadwallader

A Turner

A Jamieson

W Smith

B Carvin

L Meredith

E Clarke

B Sherwood

R Baer

1933 Season

B Laskey

R Stabler

W Ash

R Wilson

H Waddington

H Walters

R Trocger

M Dunn

R Acuff

C Huey

E Clarke

A Jameison

F McGuigan

W Cadwallader

J Hancock

B Farquhar

1934 Season

R Wilson

C Eves

N Davis

C McCall

J Esser

H Miller

G Martindale

J Roberts

W Cooper

R Acuff

R Farquhar

C Baldwin

1935 Season

W Cooper

C Eves

R Farquhar

M Thomas

R Williams

C McCall

W Ayars

G Farrier

S Asmusen

N Booth

G Foster

C Baldwin

R Adams

H Miller

T Winner

J Huhn

W Kuhn

B Heisler

1936 Season

C Eves

J Adams

W Ayars

C Brooks

H Cupitt

J Gerner

R Haberman

S Hicks

L Hines

S Howard

C McCall

L Mercer

J Miller

J Musser

W Plummer

E Waddington

E Wagg

R Wilson

T Wessner

D Woodward

1937 Season

W Plummer

M Ayars

D Ballinger

M Brown

A Cadwallader

A Collins

R Conroy

J Cox

W Howard

T Kirk

W Satterthwaite

E Waddington

R Wilson

1938 Season

E Waddington

A Cadwallader

C Harry

D Sutton

W Gramley

W Ashton

R Conroy

W Satterthwaite

L Walton

D Woodward

F Wildman

G Saxton

D Mercer

J Campbell

S Willets

1939 Season

A Cadwallader
M Crooks
J Bartram
J Campbell
W Gee
W Gilland
W Gramley
S Green
E Heinlich
G Hobbs
H Hummal
D Mercer
G Saxton
J Taggart
E Waddington
R Waddington
W Wade
P Weiss
D Wilson
K Swayne

1940 Season

S Green
F Dudley
E Heimlich
A Bluethenthal
D Helms
G Hobbs
W Kemp
P Klaphaak
W Marble
J Park

J Taggart
R Waddington
R Wise
P Bullock
T Lott
F Bradley
B Snipes

1941 Season

F Dudley
J Sinclaire
R Johnson
S Harris
D Bernard
D Boring
J Park
B Gannett
M Swayne
D Wilson
S Hunter
M Leicher
J Paxon
T Dawson
S Kraus
N Perry
E Jenkins
R Bansen
D Goodman
V Ohlsen
R Curtis

1942 Season

J Paxan

A Porter
M Swayne
R Baker
D Goodman
D Boring
R Curtin
S Hunter
R Johnson
E Kline
M Leicher
D Wilson
J Sinclare
R Vernon
J Reese
V Ohlsen
T Baldwin
S Haines

1943 Season

R Baker
T Bartlett
H Bond
C Gilbert
C Ewing
R Harris
M Leicher
M Swayne
J Mason
V Ohlsen
T Wright
J Livingstone
J Reese
R Miller

N Chance

F Wiedeke

L Kenderdine

1944 Season

J Armstrong

C Beck

H Bond

J Bradley

N Chance

W Cromwell

W Dunn

G Ewing

F Fowles

C Gilbert

B Hollinshead

G Hossfeld

L Kenderdine

M Lash

C Marshall

R Miller

J Saurman

W Swayne

T Wright

1945 Season

P Anderson

C Beck

T Bushman

G Conover

W Cromwell

F Fowles

P Frederick

T Guglielmo

C Lightfoot

C Marshall

J Saurman

C Schultz

G Shannon

J Smith

B White

1946 Season

J Baker

G Bikler

T Bushman

D Campbell

G Conover

P Frederick

T Guglielmo

A Henrie

R Krichown

C Lightfoot

A Lincoln

J Saurman

C Schultz

G Shanno

S Shoemaker

F Wiedke

J Witherington

1947 Season

A Greist

E Boyer

R Abbott

S Shoemaker

A Colson

P Muhlenberg

R Killhom

H Dunn

D Eldridge

H Pettit

F Grupp

W Stinnson

J Sailor

J Witherington

H Ridgeway

W Finney

P Anderson

1948 Season

T Burr

J Carpenter

H Dunn

D Elderidge

W Finney

F Grupp

W McKee

P Muhlenberg

H Ridgway

J Sailer

C Scudder

J Seabrook

C Stewartt

F Thomsen

D Thomson

J Van Hart

J Witherington

1949 Season

H Arnold

R Bullock

T Burr

W Calvert

E Frances-Fenisha

W Hipple

W Loucke

R Maust

R McFeely

W McKee

D Peterston

A Phillips

P Righter

J Rogers

W Rusch

C Scudder

J Seabrook

R Temple

D Thomson

R Townesand

J Williams

1950 Season

J Alden

T Ragland

H Arnold

J Rogers

B Campbell

W Scheffer

J Ekingo

C Scudder

H Haines

J Seabrook

W Hipple

L Thomsen

C Weir

W Marshall

H White

R Maust

J Williams

M Muskat

A Phillips

R McFeely

W Loucks

1951 Season

J Alden

A Berman

B Campbell

L Eisele

J Hanic

G Kummer

W Marshall

R Maust

J Powell

T Ragland

W Scheffer

R Seitzer

L Thomsen

J Townsend

C Herman

C Wain

H White

D Woodall

1952 Season

E Bachman

J Battin

C Bidder

J Briscoe

W Clark

E Dawes

L Eisele

H Hoyt

R Jafchen

F Jobes

F McFaden

C Miller

P New

W Pickering

J Raushenbush

W Scheffer

J Townsend

H Wambaugh

P Zavitz

C Willis

1953 Season

J Brewar

J Briscoe

H Colson

E Dawes

T Ghebeles

P Gum

H Hoyt

R Japchen

D Kinsey

J Lippencott

C Miller

W Mould

J Penrose

W Pickering

B Powell

J Purdy

E Walsh

N Winde

1954 Season

J Briscoe

W Cadwallader

M Capecchi

C Cook

H Colson

W Eveland

R Hahn

J Hancock

H Hoyt

C Mansbach

K Miller

J Penrose

W Pickering

J Thompson

M Kosoff

1955 Season

D Booth

W Cadwallader

H Colson

C Cook

K Eveland

J Haines

J Hancock

J Hirsch

W Houghton

M Hoyt

M Kosoff

J McAllister

G McCammon

E Noyes

C Palmer

W Strandwitz

J Templeton

J Thompson

J Watson

D Willison

1956 Season

C Bromberg

J Allen

A Cadwallader

S Gowdy

J Haines

D Hancock

W Houghton

M Hoyt

T Huf

J Johnson

G Pickering

J Pusey

P Ross

J Templeton

C Tyson

M Westcott

W Wilson

1957 Season

H Andrews

C Bromberg

A Brosius

A Cadwallader

B Gowdy

D McGourty

G Pickering

F Spruance

C Tyson

M Westcott

W Wilson

G Wyler

T Worth

J Templeton

D Haines

E Vehliy

1958 Season

H Andrew

W Bernard

A Brosius

M Brown

E Clarke

J Corts

A Fleschner

W Fry

D Haines

F Hardy

R Hardy

D Johnson

H Kay

J McDaniel

F Spruance

R Warner

W Wilson

G Wyler

T Worth

1959 Season

H Andrews

T Aston

H Bernard

C Betts

A Brosius

M Brown

E Clarke

T Colman

J Corts

A Fleschner

R Fry

R Hunt

J McDaniel

T Palley

J Syrett

R Warner

R Woll

N Ziegler

1960 Season

W Andrews

T Aston

C Bernard

L Betts

E Blumberg

P Brick

N Brosius

M Brown

C Evans

K Fox

D Griscom

C Guild

R Noyes

T Palley

J Strong

S Utton

J Syrett

W Tait

H Townsend

N Ziegler

1961 Season

M Acuff

W Andrews

E Blumberg

G Corts

C Evans

S Gessner

K Hopkins

H Norris

P Plunkett

V Rothschild

L Russell

S Sullivan

W Tait

H Townsend

R Williams

1962 Season

M Acuff

D Adkins

J Ambler

W Aufderheyde

T Cooch

R Griscom

S Hancock

N Jaffe

H Marshall

J Pratt

D Pusey

L Rembar

G Scarlett

S Sullivan

T Turner

W Wright

1963 Season

D Adkins

W Aufderheyde

T Davidson

A Foster

J Gleeson

R Griscom

S Hancock

S Griscom

G Hobbs

R Lyons

H Marshall

D Pusey

T Turner

C Walton

C Willson

W Wright

I Vickery

1964 Season

C Croft

N Degraff

J Gleeson

S Griscom

S Hancock

T Huseby

R Lyons

B Musser

R Nichols

J Perlman

D Pratt

M Smith

I Vickery

C Willson

R Swayne

1965 Season

B Aaron

E Altman

N Degraff

J Heisler

M Heverin

S Holden

J King

J Monego

D Miller

B Musser

D Pratt

C Stark

S Steelman

W Stone

K Strehle

T Thomas

C Willson

1966 Season

E Altman

G Betts

R Eareckson

S Esser

S Holden

J King

M Landis

J Madden

D Miller

J Monego

S Steelman

K Strehle

D Stevans

S Sweitzer

T Thomas

J Waddington

S Warner

D Williams

1967 Season

D Allison

M Battersby

G Betts

K Cleaver

P Fegelsen

E Foster

R Hackett

M Hallowell

S Hersloff

S Holden

T Monego

K Park

T Simmons

S Steelman

D Stevens

S Warner

D Williams

1968 Season

P Bowers

J Caulkins

K Cleaver

N Custer

N Emlen

E Foster

D Hancox

R Hancox

M Jupiter

T Monego

P Moyes

J Runge

T Simmons

T Trowbridge

S Waddington

D Williams

1969 Season

J Baker

M Battersby

G Blackshaw

P Bowers

P Cox

N Custer

G Fischer

J Griscom

R Hancox

A Jackson

J Meredith

P Moyes

H Oldach

L Potter

T Raynolds

T Trowbridge

1970 Season

D Bakkila

J Clark

J Cox

S Drorbaugh

G fisher

D Hancox

R Hancox

J Mason

J Meredith

M Newbold

H Oldach

F Paine

J Plaisted

L Potter

T Raynolds

J Stein

D McKamey

1971 Season

J Clark

M Colcord

J Cox

G Fisher

W Forest

W Hancock

W Hudson

C Johnson

D McKamey

J Oldach

J Plaisted

T Raynolds

J Stein

D Comley

D Maloney

1972 Season

J Clark

M Colcord

R Downs

W Forest

P Freeman

W Hancock

W Hudson

C Johnson

J Mason

W Matthews

D McKamey

D McDaniel

T O'Connell

J Oldach

J Powell

T Raynolds

C Sotres

S Stein

1973 Season

J Brenner

R Downs

S Ehret

F Harris

D Lehner

J Lewis

W Matthews

E Mazer

T O'Connell

J Peacock

J Powell

W Rowe

M Sander

J Seabrook

L Smith

C Sotres

Scott Stein

J Turner

T Walker

1974 Season

S Allison

K Bergland

R Downs

S Ehret

E Gibbs

G Goodman

F Harris

E Mazer

T O'Connell

J Powell

W Rowe

J Seabrook

J Shove

J Turner

R Waddington

H Seigel

1975 Season

S Alexander

K Bergland

P Carpenter

L Chambers

J Collier

N DeLaPena

G Frew

D Gittelman

D Greenstein

D Koffman

J Levin

D Lipshultz

R Randelman

D Rice

J Seabrook

W Seabrook

J Shore

H Siegel

D Stoudt

W Twyman

1976 Season

P Carpenter

G Schwartz

W Twyman

W Seabrook

B Bald

J Boccardo

R Haines

G Frew

S Austin

D Rice

R Hunter

C Heyer

R Marshall

T Spare

R Randelman

1977 Season

J Aisenstein

S Austin

B Bald

J Boccardo

T Bingham

W Farley

G Frew

D Hostetter

T Hiatt

R Hunter

R Keever

A Kardish

J Marshall

R Marshall

L Martini

S Miller

N McCollum

W Seabrook

S St. Clair

M Taylor

L Whitmore

1978 Season

W Bald

J Boccardo

S Boccardo

S Cordell

M Etzrodt

L Favata

G Frew

T Hiatt

D Hostetter

R Hunter

A Kardish

H Kimoto

L Martini

N McCollum

N McKee

P Mowry

A Paschall

H Ripley

T Sekiya

C Stancil

M Taylor

D Wertz

L Whitmore

J Zinsser

1979 Season

K Abbott

S Boccardo

D Broad

A Cadwallader

S Cordell

M Etzrodt

J Haun

H Kimoto

R Kissinger

S Kramer

W Moyer

J Marshall

A Paschall

H Ripley

C Stancil

M Taylor

R Thomas

D Wertz

A Yablin

1980 Season

S Boccardo

M Etzrodt

A Yablin

A Cadwallader

E Padilla

R Lowers

A Popkin

S Graciosa

D Wertz

S Bald

J Fox

D Cadwallader

S Kramer

J Marshall

D Broad

J Haun

L Aizen

R Kissinger

S Kittner

B Moyer

J Makita

E Levengood

J Kim

1981 Season

A Cadwallader

E Padilla

R Lowers

S Bald

V Wiley

M Fine

E Levengood

T Pesce

J Kim

M Etzrodt

W Hoffman

J Jorgenson

A Popkin

1982 Season

J Hancock

J Uyeki

J Padilla

R Wiley

M Jones

S Buki

A Popkin

A Sexton

S Malasky

J Soli

D Cadwallader

Jeff Freedman

N Messina

M Tulp

B Shoemaker

R Rose

R Wiley

K Waldman

R Ray

F Haun

1983 Season

A Sexton

R Ray

K Waldman

F Haun

J Hancock

D Itzhovitz

D Rabinowitz

J Uyeki

J Padilla

K Waldman

A Cramer

S Malosky

S Buki

M Etzrodt

H Preece

R Wiley

M Jones

A Merritt

J Schwartz

K Fredendal

P Atherton

J Soli

W Hoffman

1984 Season

R Pino

W Fabian

S Buki

C Minter

R Wiley

P Caputo

J Uyeki

L Jenkins

B Preston

T Hjelt

R Eveleth

C Jasper

M Jones

D Meranze

H Preece

D Belt

A Merritt

A Sexton

1985 Season

T Hjelt

C Kelly

M Hutchinson

M Laviera

P Hardy

C Jasper

S Rangel

C Minter

M Carluccio

P Caputo

M Esser

K Fredendall

W Fabian

P Renninger

N Cheskis

D Brumfield

T Hackman

D Frame

M Wilson

D Brown

E Cosby

J Schwartz

B Preston

1986 Season

E Albee

D Brumfield

A Burke

P Caputo

M Carluccio

N Cheskis

E Cosby

C Dixon

G Dixon

M Esser

C Everett

A Farmer

T Hackman

P Hardy

T Horne

C Jasper

J Jones

C Kelly

L Kennedy

C Minter

D Minter

D Peters-Burton

K Tate

N Waits

1987 Season

T Hackman

C Dixon

M Carluccio

C Everett

D Farmer

C Kelly

N Waits

L Lewis

R Stafford

D Peters-Burton

D Brumfield

T Horne

D Minter

N Smith

K Lucas

B Lowe

E Papatestas

E Brown

1988 Season

N Smith

D Brumfield

D Minter

K Lucas

R Stafford

K Wildmann

B Miller

D Peters-Burton

L Green

M Radi

D Mittleman

J Johan

L Hulack

J Wennick

J Cain

F Kolp

O Carrero

T Waters

J Parker

1989 Season

K Lucas

D Mittleman

S Goldberg

B Miller

R Trumbette

O Carrero

L Hulack

C Tabor

D Buhler

E Papatestas

L Green

J Cain

K Bangura

J Wennick

R Piechoto

K Stamper

T Draper

J Crosby

K Jones

J Allen

E Witzman

S Cummings

1990 Season

K Bangura

J Cain

R Piechota

J Wennick

K Stamper

N Haverkorn

A Barea

B Gavin

B Wells

R Hardy

J Allen

T Draper

E Witzman

S Cummings

J Crosby

K Jones

K Anderson

G Fischer

I Clark

G Davis

J Ford

M Ozols

J James

1991 Season

J Allen

K Jones

T Draper

I Clark

B Walmer

J Dildy

S Woodley

A Rogers-Wright

J Crosby

J Dudnyk

S Laybourne

K Anderson

M Crocker

K Stamper

S Cummings

J Ford

G Fischer

G Davis

M Ozols

J Zlock

E Witzman

J James

D McCoy

M Nadler

I Fletcher

1992 Season

I Clark

S Woodley

J Dudnyk

A Rogers-Wright

P Zuber

S Laybourne

S Weigl

M Crocker

S Cummings

J Ford

G Fischer

G Davis

B Forstein

L Onori

M Nadler

T Binslev

J James

K Anderson

I Fletcher

D McCoy

1993 Season

B Walmer

C Draper

S Woodley

I Fletcher

A Speights

A Rogers-Wright

E Miles

W Lenzner

P Zuber

J Harvey

C O'Neill

D Gonzales

M Crocker

L Onori

R Thorne

J Haines

J James

D McCoy

1994 Season

J Brown

C Draper

D Gonzales

J Haines

A Speights

R Thorne

W Lenzner

W Adams

F Afzal

H Capellon

D Chiocchi

R Earle

K Edwards

J Harvey

E Miles

J Thoreson

A Wade

A Walter

J Wilson

1995 Season

C Draper

R Thorne

A Speights

J Haines

R Earle

W Adams

R Woodley

K Edwards

J Thoreson

H Capellon

A Wade

S Justice

B Ochoa

F Afzal

S Staton

R Boynton

1996 Season

J Thoreson

K Edwards

R Boynton

H Capellon

R Woodley

B Dinola

S Justice

E Mount

C Haines

J Shipp

B Halloway

E Gist

D Kingham

C Waghorne

C Johnson

J Schroeder

R Davilla

1997 Season

R Woodley

J Shipp

E Mount

C Haines

B Dinola

T Pittman

J Seltzer

R Nicolaysen

J Schroeder

B Flaccus

C Sharkey

B Adams

D Justice

L Russell

C Johnson

M Jaffe

J Skversky

R Bradley

1998 Season

E Mount

C Haines

J Mobley

R Nicolaysen

A Ambler

S Greene

J Skversky

N Vantresca

J Lee

J Krivda

R Bradley

T Pittman

J Seltzer

J Belding

D Justice

A Tabor

A Q Abdul- Karim

1999 Season

S Mahoney

A Ambler

J Mobley

J Smith

R Nicolaysen

N Vantresca

J Skversky

P McGrail-Peasley

D Wright

J Lee

S Greene

A Tabor

AQ Abdul-Karim

J Krivda

T Caron

R Bradley

T Pittman

M Bell

G Best

K Lee

S Lunger

J Compitello

R Mellon

B Fisher

Y Choi

2000 Season

J Compitello

R Waters

M Fernandez

R Mellon

A Tabor

J Lee

S Lunger

M Gray

AQ Abdul-Karim

S Greene

J Krivda

A Kim

T Caron

R Bradley

T Pittman

K Martinez

M Bell

M Gretz

C Conklin

P Sandhu

K Lee

G Best

2001 Season

J Compitello

T Caron

R Mellon

K Martinez

B Fisher

J Beloux

C Lapphen

R Waters

D Titus

V Murphy

A Negron

J Day

D Suchenski

A Kim

D Renzulli

D Sellinger

A Kelleher

M Gretz

M Fernandez

J Ding

2002 Season

R Waters

A Kelleher

A Kim

D Renzulli

V Murphy

B Wayda

W Foppert

M Lichtenstein

D Titus

B Lee

M Leigh

E Martinez

G Toggeweiler

T Thomas

J Day

P Cassidy

A Negron

D Suchenski

J Viernez

2003 Season

P Cassidy

J Day

B Lee

E Martinez

D Millitelo

A Negron

D Suchenski

J Thomas

D Titus

G Toggweiler

G DiBacco

Z Glaeser

P Matsagas

M Norcross

R Perez

J Quarles

J Rosenberg

C Straube

R Taft

J Viernes

R Arhun

A Biros

M Murphy

K Agyeman- Kagya

2004 Season

G DiBacco

Z Glaesar

P Matsagas

M Norcross

J Quarles

J Rosenberg

C Straube

R Taft

J Viernes

K Agyeman-Kagya

R Arhun

A Biros

M Murphy

J Turner

M Chen

M Bitzer

P Harkins

M Hugick

S Aladi

I Yang

2005 Season

K Agyeman-Kaga

S Aladi

A Biros

M Bitzer

M Chen

A Desantis

P Harkins

M Hugick

C Koslo

M Murphy

F Ogundadegbe

J Rosenberg

J Stevens

E Wong

D Cisse

S Jaffee

I Yang

J D'Oleo

S Kim

T Wayda

2006 Season

D Cisse
B Finkel
S Jaffe
D Moffitt
I Yang
J D'Oleo
C Jorgensen
S Kim
K MacWhorter
C Newby
E Steel
J Cancelliere
D Foppert
B Olayinka
T Wayda
M Brown
T Darby
B Durey
A Wang
G Centis
M Oppong

2007 Season

J D'Oleo
C Jorgensen
S Kim
K MacWhorter
C Newby
E Steel
J Cancelliere
D Foppert
T Wayda

M Brown
G Centis
B Durey
T Gitlin
A Wang
R Crompton
E Engelhardt
J Speller
F Cueves
R Kerr
L Milton
J Skolnick
I Wiggins

2008 Season

J Cancelliere
E Engelhardt
D Foppert
J Speller
T Wayda
M Brown
F Cueves
R Kerr
L Milton
J Skolnick
J Vinglass
I Wiggins
N Simone
K Lee
C Prajzner
T Darby

2009 Season

T Ellis

D Gleeson
L Milton
R Roskos
M Cho
J Skolnick
F Cueves
K Conklin
T Stone
H Rosenthal
R Kerr
C Palmiotti
I Ba
M Brown
C Prajzner
N Simone
S Rubin
T Campellone
N Gonzales
K Simone
J Langeler
I Wiggins
C Prasad

2010 Season

J Strachan
D Gleeson
R Roskos
E Clinton
L Storey
J Tyson
D Smith
K Conklin
M Maloberti

A Brooker

H Rosenthal

C Hellmuth

J Gonzalez

T Campellone

S Popkin

P George

K Chen

K Erskine

N Gonzales

G Long

L Sanchez

D Kim

R Van Pelt

R Cox

K Simone

J Langeler

J Kaplan

A Young

C Prasad

Z Huang

2011 Season

E Clinton

L Storey

J Tyson

D Smith

J Strachan

A Brooker

H Rosenthal

C Hellmuth

T Campellone

K Chen

K Erskine

N Gonzales

G Long

L Sanchez

D Kim

J Langeler

J Kaplan

A Young

C Prasad

J Lax

T Stone

2012 Season

E Clinton

D Smith

C Hellmuth

K Chen

K Erskine

D Kim

N Gonzales

G Long

J Kaplan

J Sparacio

C Sparacio

J Lax

2013 Season

C Sparacio

C Hellmuth

J Lax

C Haney

C Beverly

H Fritz

I Hodgins

K Kong

E Ortega

B Haferl

C Tongluo

M Klaver

T Graves

2014 Season

L Haug

K Frederic

S Coles

C Haney

T Graves

Z Caplan

D Paek

A Hodgin

S Shao

E Ortega

I Hodgin

M Wisniewski

C Kogut

C Rodgers

B Haferl

B Vearling

M Klaver

K Proherbs

C Chowaiki

O Williams

2015 Season

L Haug

C Beverly

M Gilbert

C Chowaiki

C Kogut

K Frederic

S Coles

J Haug

C Haney

R Trice

M Wisniewski

E Ortega

K Probherbs

A Hodgin

T Graves

B Vearling

D Paek

D Freckleton

O Williams

C Rodgers

About the Author

John Gleeson played three varsity sports when a student at George School. He was co-captain of the 1964 George School football team. He went on to earn a BA degree from Haverford College and a MALS degree from Dartmouth College. He taught English at George School from 1969 t0 2016, serving as English department chairman, dorm head, advisor, and coach. He spent the last 30 years as head coach of the football team. John also wrote a weekly sports column for a local Bucks County newspaper from 1977 to 2020 that earned several Keystone Press Awards. His other book is *Sportscape,* a gathering of some of his more successful articles.